Successful Management of Juvenile Residential Facilities:
A Performance-Based Approach

Joseph Heinz, L.I.C.S.W.,
Former Corrections Administrator, Hennepin County Corrections
and Rehabilitation Department,
Minnetonka, Minnesota

Theresa Wise, M. Ed.
Former Superintendent, Hennepin County Adult Corrections Facility,
Plymouth, Minnesota

Clemens Bartollas, Ph.D.,
Professor of Sociology, University of Northern Iowa,
Cedar Falls, Iowa

Mission of the American Correctional Association

The American Correctional Association provides a professional organization for all individuals and groups, both public and private, that share a common goal of improving the justice system.

ISBN 978-1-56991-313-0

This publication may be ordered from:
American Correctional Association
206 N. Washington St., Suite 200
Alexandria, Virginia 22314
800-222-5646 ext. 0129
For information on publications and videos available from ACA, contact our worldwide web home page at: www.aca.org

Library of Congress Cataloging in Publication Data

Heinz, Joseph W.
Successful management of juvenile residential facilities / Joseph Heinz, Theresa Wise, Clemens Bartollas.
    p. cm.
Includes index.
ISBN 978-1-56991-313-0
1. Juvenile detention homes—United States—Management. 2. Correctional institutions--United States—Management. 3. Juvenile corrections—United States. I. Wise, Theresa. II. Bartollas, Clemens. III. American Correctional Association. IV. Title.
  HV9104.H39 2009
  365'.42068--dc22
                2009035248

TABLE OF CONTENTS

DEDICATION

To Our Spouses,
Margaret, John, and Linda, with our love

ACKNOWLEDGEMENTS

This book could not have been completed without the special support of Hennepin County and the University of Northern Iowa. A special thank you is necessary to the staff at Hennepin County Home School and support staff of Community Corrections, especially Laurel Johnson, Lee Ann Hicks, and Fay Williams. We are grateful to Kristin Bartollas Polatty for editing our manuscript and for bringing lucidity to our ideas.

A number of individuals, including Edward Latessa, Gerald Schields, Jerry Rodeman, Vickie Brownsmith, Jay G. Lindgren, Jr., Richard Kelly, Carl Wicklund, Brian Griffiths, Betty Fox, and Paul Eastwold, were willing to discuss their beliefs with us about good juvenile facility operations and care.

Finally, we would like to thank Alice Heiserman, manager of publications and research for ACA, for her support of this project. It was her idea that we do this book, and she has continued her encouragement through the years it took to write and revise the manuscript.

FOREWORD

This innovative text breaks down all the elements that are necessary for a successful, well-managed and mission-focused juvenile program. It begins with a brief history of juvenile corrections and institutional care, and then provides a profile of youth currently committed to residential detention. From there, the authors who all have practical experience working with juveniles move into a lengthy discussion of leadership, mission and the administrator's duties and responsibilities. Models of residential care are examined and information on everything from staff training to transitional programming is covered.

This book will give new and veteran administrators a fresh view of what it takes to manage an effective and efficient residential facility, and students will benefit from the thorough coverage of the topic as a whole.

ACA has published numerous titles focusing on juvenile corrections and programs and we are pleased to add Successful Management of Juvenile Residential Facilities to this collection. You can view all of our publications on our Web site, www.aca.org.

James A. Gondles, Jr., CAE
Executive Director
American Correctional Association

INTRODUCTION

This book is for administrators of a juvenile facility, especially new administrators. We intend to walk them through all phases of administration and supervision and help these individuals either open a new facility or turn around one that needs reform. Two of the co-authors have spent their careers working in administrative aspects of institutional care, and they guide the new administrators and students through these processes. We focus on practices that are exemplary and offer models for emulation.

One of the reasons this book is important is that it fills the gap found in the literature on juvenile residential institutions. In the 1960s and early 1970s, many studies, as Chapter 1 notes, evaluated juvenile institutionalization in the United States. Then, between 1975 and the mid-2000's, relatively few studies were done that examined the quality of juvenile institutions. What this means is that following a number of critical studies in the 1960s and early 1970s, during the past three decades relatively few studies have evaluated the quality of juvenile institutional life.

However, in the mid-2000s, two evaluations of juvenile institutions in California and Texas were completed. These evaluations, like earlier ones, have been critical. Christopher Murray and colleagues illustrate in their report why they believe institutions for youthful offenders in California are broken (Murray, Baird, Loughran, Mills, and Platt 2006: 1). The institutions have:

- High levels of violence and fear

- Unsafe conditions for both residents and staff

- Antiquated facilities unsuited for any mission

- An adult corrections mentality with an adult/juvenile mix

- Management by crisis with little time to make changes

- Frequent lockdowns to manage violence with subsequent program reductions

- Time add-ons for infractions adding more than eight months to average lengths of stay

- Lengths of stay almost triple the average for the nation

- Hours when many youths have nothing to do

- Vocational classrooms that are idle or running half speed

- Capitulation to gang culture with youths housed by gang affiliation

- Low levels of staffing and huge living units

- Low achievement despite enormous outlays for education

- Information systems incapable of supporting management

- Few partnerships with counties and a fragmented system

- Poor reentry planning and too few services on parole

- Enormous costs with little to show for it

The report concludes—"it is not reform that is needed. Everything needs to be fixed." Then, it questions: "Can it be fixed?" It answers this question by saying, "Yes. But it will take great effort, money, and lots of time" (Murray, Baird, Loughran, Mills, and Platt 2006: 1).

The report notes:

> that reform is needed because the state of California is failing its children. Youth, who often have been abused and neglected and many of whom have failed in multiple domains, arrive at California's institutions with little chance of leaving with their lives turned around. Indeed, some leave worse off than when they arrived. California is failing its taxpayers. This is a very expensive system with little to show for it (Murray, Baird, Loughran, Mills, and Platt 2006: 6).

In 2009, California chose to close its larger youth facility, the Herman G. Stark Youth Correctional Facility in Chino, which will be converted into an adult prison. With this closure, the state will have five youth prisons, down from eleven in 2003. From a peak of nearly 10,000, the population of youths in state custody has declined to 1,700. The Division of Juvenile Justice is further reducing its workforce by 400 employees to save the state up to 40 million dollars. The plan is further geared toward reducing the annual cost of caring for and incarcerating each youth from $252,000 to $175,000 (Rothfield 2009).

> California needs to reform its institutions for juveniles because it's the right thing to do for California's children, and second because it is the right thing to do for everyone. It is argued that successful reform will make safer communities, stronger families, and less crowded prisons (Murray, Baird, Loughran, Mills, and Platt, 2006:6-7).

In another state, in March 2007, responding to the reports of sexual abuse of youth at the Texas Youth Commission institutions, Texas Governor Rick Perry placed the Texas Youth Commission under conservatorship to guide reform of the agency. In April of 2007, Ed Owens, then Interim Executive Director of the Texas Youth Commission, asked Dr. David W. Springer to form a Blue Ribbon Task Force defining a new rehabilitation system, and developing evidence-based practices in the treatment and case management of delinquents committed to the Texas Youth Commission. The Blue Ribbon Task Force Report, *Transforming Juvenile Justice in Texas: A Framework for Action*, was published in September 2007.

The report noted that some of the challenges of working with adjudicated delinquents in Texas include:

> too great an emphasis on punishment, with insufficient resources for education and treatment; a fragmented healthcare delivery system; non-violent offenders being housed at Texas Youth Commission facilities; high caseload and high turnover rates among staff; a shortage of correctional officers; too many incidents of violence at Texas Youth Commission facilities; youth being sentenced to Texas Youth Commission facilities that are too large and too far away from their home communities; dorm designs that make it difficult to monitor youth; and lack of accountability and transparency, including facility staff with too much control over the complaint process (Springer 2007).

The report defined a number of principles, proposing that

1. The Texas Youth Commission should have a safe environment that promotes health and facilitates appropriate educational and moral development of youth

2. Youths should spend as little time as absolutely necessary within the Texas Youth Commission system

3. The Texas Youth Commission system should be as least restrictive as possible, in placements ranging from the most integrated to the most segregated

4. Staffing capacity needs to be commensurate with the size and needs of the population

5. Evidence-based policies and programs need to be implemented

6. Facilities of the Texas Youth Commission should be child-focused, family-focused, and nonviolent

7. Communication should be effective

8. The Texas Youth Commission facilities should be grounded in positive youth development where education and treatment, rather than punishment, is its primary work

9. Youth with disabilities need to be identified and accommodated

10. Youth, as well as their families, should have easy access to attorneys and advocacy groups (Springer 2007: 21).

If California and Texas were the only states dissatisfied with the performance of juvenile facilities, then the issue of juvenile institutionalization would not be considered such a serious matter. However, the mounting evidence from other states indicates that dissatisfaction with juvenile institutionalization is a mounting national concern. A report by the U.S. Department of Justice found a number of abuses at four juvenile residential centers in New York. This excessive physical force resulted in broken bones, shattered teeth, concussions, and other serious injuries over a period of less than two years. This report raised the possibility of a federal takeover of all New York's youth prisons if the problems are not addressed quickly (Confessore 2009).

The federal courts and the U.S. Department of Justice Civil Rights Division have also voiced concern about the quality of life within juvenile residential facilities. The U.S. Department of Justice Civil Rights Division authorized the Attorney General to conduct investigations and litigation relating to conditions of confinement in state or locally operated institutions (the statute does not cover private facilities). Under the statute, the Special Litigation Section investigates covered facilities to determine whether there is a pattern or practice of violations of residents' federal rights. The section is not authorized to represent individuals nor to address specific individual cases (The Civil Rights of Institutionalized Persons Act [CRIPA] 1977).

As of July 6, 2007, sixty-five residential juvenile facilities were being monitored and operated under settlement agreements. This report primarily focused on youth's constitutional rights to reasonable safety, adequate medical and mental healthcare, rehabilitative treatment, education, and healthcare. As was stated in the report:

> Moreover, once a mental health need has been identified, it is not enough simply to have a psychiatrist who rarely visits the facility prescribe psychotropic medications. Professionals must be involved in providing individualized treatment and in considering what reasonable accommodations are necessary to permit the juveniles to benefit from the services offered at the facility. Juvenile with learning disabilities must be provided special education services to enable them to benefit from educational services, juveniles with cognitive disabilities may require special assistance to benefit from substance abuse programming, youths with severe attention deficit disorder may require accommodations in facility rules to prevent their disability from resulting in disciplinary sanctions.[1]

For Bartollas, these findings are not surprising. In the 1970s and 1980s, he and his colleagues had found similar negative evaluations of correctional institutions in Ohio, North Carolina, South Carolina, Iowa, and California.[2] He can still vividly remember the four years he worked in a maximum-security juvenile facility for older males in Ohio, where violence and exploitation was a part of everyday life.

Another way to improve conditions is to prevent youth from reaching detention and correctional confinement. Efforts underway under the Juvenile Detention Alternative Initiative (JDAI) are proving successful (Annie E. Casey Foundation 2009 a and b).

When Alice Heiserman, manager of publications and research at the American Correctional Association (ACA), asked Bartollas to write a book about operating an effective and rehabilitative juvenile facility, he found this to be an exciting possibility. He had long thought that juvenile institutions—with good leadership, committed staff, and community and organizational support—had the possibility of creating humane care for juveniles. However, he needed co-authors who knew the "nuts and bolts" of daily operations of a juvenile residential institution. Fortunately, Joseph Heinz and Theresa Wise, both of whom had been administrators of innovative facilities, were willing to participate.

All three authors believe that the vision contained in the nine chapters of this book promise the direction and possibility for creating a new day in juvenile institutionalization. Chapter 1 provides a quick sweep through the history of juvenile institutions. Chapter 2 portrays a national profile of youths committed to residential facilities, including developmental and chronological age, gender, race/ethnicity, family, education, community, mental health, chemical use/abuse, and capacity for violence. Chapter 3 is based on the premise that the quality of what takes place in juvenile institutions will depend to a large degree on administrators' management styles. Beginning by examining previous managerial styles used in juvenile institutions, this chapter also includes important broad considerations for administrators of these facilities.

Chapters 4 and 5 present the important consideration of mission. Mission, the foundation of juvenile residential facilities, is important because it guides the short- and long-term planning, operating and capital budget development, and the overall priority setting of the facility. Chapter 6 discusses the administrator's role as leader in support of treatment to achieve positive outcomes.

Chapter 7 examines the manager's role in building positive culture. This chapter articulates the important truth that effective treatment of youth will not take place unless the facility has developed and maintained a positive, prosocial culture, a culture that is safe, supportive, and nurturing. Chapter 8 considers training, and Chapter 9, the final chapter, examines model institutions and considers the process of replicating their programs and philosophy in other places. The book concludes with an appendix containing programs and ideas that have been successfully used in other juvenile correctional settings.

ENDNOTES

[1] http://www.usdoj.gov/crt/split/documents/juvspeech.htm

[2] See Chapter 1 for a description of these studies.

REFERENCES

Annie E. Casey Foundation offers a variety of publications on the Juvenile Detention Alternatives Initiative. http://www.aecf.org/knowledgecenter/publicationsseries/JDAIResources.aspx

Civil Rights of Institutionalized Persons Act, 42 U.S.C. 1997.

Confessore, Nicholas. 2009. *4 Youth Prisons in New York Used Excessive Force*. New York Times. August 25.

Murray, Christopher, Chris Baird, Ned Loughran, Fred Mills, and John Platt. 2006. *Safety and Welfare Plan: Implementing Reform in California*. Sacramento, California: California Department of Corrections and Rehabilitation; Division of Juvenile Justice.

Rothfield, Richard. 2009. *California to Close Its Largest Juvenile Prison*. New York Times. August 28.

Springer, David W. 2007. *Transforming Juvenile Justice in Texas: A Framework for Action*. Austin: Blue Ribbon Task Force Report.

CHAPTER 1

A BRIEF HISTORY OF INSTITUTIONAL CARE FOR JUVENILES

Juveniles need to become computer literate to function well in the society to which they will be released.

This book is designed for administrators of juvenile residential facilities and those who aspire to be. However, before we get to the present, it is necessary to understand the past. Knowing the history and context of any social phenomenon helps us because the past will inevitably tell us much about the present. Residential facilities for juveniles have changed in many ways in recent decades, but in other respects, they remain much the same as when they were first founded. Certainly, those who founded juvenile institutions had high ideals, but the intervening 180 years have demonstrated that even good intentions may have their idealistic base destroyed by disastrous results.

THE EARLY HANDLING OF DELINQUENTS

In the 1820s, the United States established institutions for delinquents, widely hailed as the savior of this nation's wayward youth. In the 1970s, the nation considered dismantling those same institutions because they were viewed as violent, criminogenic, and inhumane settings for youth. In the 1990s and increasingly in the twenty-first century, this country depends on public and private training schools more than ever before.

In *The Discovery of the Asylum*, David Rothman graphically portrays the avenues considered by communities in the late 1770s and early 1780s when juveniles transgressed the boundaries of community propriety. Youths in those days did not know the meaning of incarceration, nor, for that matter, did anyone else. Local jails were used to hold an offender until it was decided what to do with him or her. Indeed, even punishment was not considered useful in rehabilitation, as the colonists "placed little faith in the possibility of reform. Prevailing Calvinist doctrines stressed the natural depravity of humankind, and the sinfulness of humankind, then, was what led juveniles to transgress the law" (Rothman 1971: 53).

The colonists were not totally pessimistic about controlling vice, for they believed that appropriate community reorganization would prevent deviance. The family, the church, and the network of community relations were all conceived of as important weapons in the battle against sin and crime. If these bodies functioned well, it was reasoned that towns would be spared the turbulence of crime and enjoy a high degree of order and stability. To these ends:

> Families were to raise the children to respect law and authority, the church was to oversee not only family discipline—but adult behavior, and the members of the community were to supervise one another, to correct and detect the first signs of deviancy (Rothman 1971: 16).

Between 1790 and 1830, many dramatic changes, such as the growth of towns and the settlement of new territories, made old techniques of social control ineffective. One of the problems created by the new social conditions was societal disorganization. The unsettled environment, rather than the natural depravity of man, now became the cause of delinquency.

Society sought ways to put order and predictability back into the lives of juvenile offenders. Their answer was the house of refuge, "the well-ordered asylum," an institution which used the family as its model of organization (Rothman 1971: 206-236). Of some importance was the fact that not only juveniles, but also adult criminals, the aged, the mentally ill, vagrants, orphans, unwed mothers, the lame, and the poor were put in institutions, which tried to order their lives and thereby guarantee their inhabitants successful participation in society. The principle was simple: construct the asylum, with all its variations, so that a resident could not help but be programmed into moral and right ways of living.

To accomplish this end, the house of refuge was constructed with the greatest of care. Early administrators left no part of institutional design or program open to chance; details as exact as the placement of heating and ventilating ducts, the type of furniture, and, especially, the overall design of the building were carefully calculated to provide the milieu appropriate for the inculcation of order:

> Boys and girls occupied separate buildings, each structure of bare brick and unvarying design. . . . The buildings were usually four stories high, windowless, with two long hallways running along either side of a row of cells. The rooms following one after another, were all five by eight feet wide, seven feet high, windowless, with an iron-lattice slab for a door and flues for ventilation near the ceiling . . . in keeping with the external design, all inmates wore uniforms of coarse and solid-colored material. No sooner did they enter the institution than they were stripped, washed, their hair cut to a standard length, and put into common dress. Managers appropriately claimed that the refuge's main object, that of reformation, is never lost sight of, in any of its regulations, and in all its discipline. From the entrance of the child, he becomes subject to a routine of duties . . . order and method (Rothman, 1971:266; quoted from *Boston Asylum and Farm School*, 11: 1845).

The regularity of the institution's physical design was expected to influence juveniles and, this, combined with the scheduling of the daily routine, condition them to conform to societal norms. The institution experience, then, was to isolate offenders from all that might harm them and, at the same time, provide a well-ordered existence, which would instill all the virtues necessary for a law-abiding life in the community.

The routine of these asylums—like juvenile institutions—exemplified the ideas of righteous living and of leading a narrowly proper existence. Bells were often used to awaken the inmates and to announce each programmed activity of the day. From one area of the institution to another, residents were lined up for periodic head counts, marched to all activities, and even sent to pray in ranks. If youths did misbehave, punishment was certain to follow and involved deprivation of privileges, a bread and water diet, solitary confinement, ball and chain, whip, or any combination deemed appropriate by the keepers (Rothman 1971: 225-226).

FROM THE 1850s THROUGH THE 1970s

By the 1850s, confidence had waned in the ability of these houses of refuge to teach their moral program, and institutional directors were beginning to argue that custody was all they had to offer. The treatment regimen was disappearing as regulated routine became difficult and then impossible to maintain. State legislatures in the pre-Civil War era allocated their funds elsewhere, while towns and cities continued sending their hard-core juveniles to populate the houses of refuge and recently built reformatories. The overcrowded institutions, the inadequate numbers of staff, and the deteriorated buildings confined large masses of residents for whom no rehabilitation programs were developed. Further, a number of factors, including the mixing of different types of juveniles and a large influx of immigrants, made the task next to impossible.

The industrial or training school was the next innovation in the treatment of juvenile offenders. Using the cottage system, which generally involved a series of small house-type structures within a compound, training schools were opened in the 1840s and 1850s and by 1900, thirty-six states had them (*Task Force Report: Juvenile Delinquency* 1967: 3). The hope was that cottage "parents" could create a home-like atmosphere in these training schools and that the asylum-like effect of the houses of refuge and reformatories could be overcome. These institutions placed considerable emphasis on hard work. Youths, for example, were expected to farm land and take care of livestock.

Barbara M. Brenzel's study of the State Industrial School for Girls in Lancaster, Massachusetts, the first state reform school for girls in the United States, revealed the growing disillusionment in the mid- to late-nineteenth century regarding training schools. Intended as a model reform effort, Lancaster was the first "family-style" institution on this continent and embodied new theories about the reformation of youths. However,

> an examination of a reform institution during the second half of the nineteenth century reveals the evolution from reformist visions and optimistic goals at mid-century to pessimism and 'scientific' determinism at the century's close (Brenzel 1983).

Brenzel added that "the mid-century ideal of rehabilitative care changed to the principles of rigid training and custodial care by the 1880s and remained so into the early twentieth century" (Brenzel 1983:5).

In the twentieth and so far in the twenty-first century, only minor modifications have taken place in how society deals with institutionalized delinquents. As the number of juvenile offenders increased, the types of juvenile institutions multiplied. They included forestry and honor camps (minimum security), educational and vocational training schools (medium security), and end-of-the-line training schools (maximum security).

Therapeutic technologies, considerably more advanced now than before, have attempted to deal with clients' psychological and behavioral problems by initiating individualized group treatments.

Juveniles are able to graduate from state-accredited high school programs while attending training schools, and some youths are permitted to work in the community during the day. Weekend home visits, too, are part of the treatment program in many institutions. Yet, little evidence exists that such programs are sophisticated enough to prevent recidivism (Robinson and Smith 1969, Hood 1967).

Juvenile facilities were unquestionably designed to protect society from those considered dangerous. Barriers to the outside emphasized that the participants were limited to members of their own kind, and little emphasis was placed on helping inmates develop normal relationships. Most states continued to dwell upon institutionalizing their juvenile offenders because citizens remained dedicated to the concept of "locking them up and throwing away the key."

A gradual movement toward deinstitutionalization, however, has taken place in recent decades. Probation has certainly played a significant role in this movement, and many delinquents are now kept in the community under the supervision of a probation officer. As long as juveniles comply with their probation terms, they can avoid institutionalization. Foster homes and community treatment centers, in addition, have become important alternatives to incarceration. California, specifically, was involved in a process of deinstitutionalization during the 1960s through the 1970s. Upon discovering that community resources are a great deal more economical and as successful, the California Youth Authority began placing more and more of its youths in community treatment programs (Warren 1972).

CLOSING OF TRAINING SCHOOLS IN MASSACHUSETTS

The movement toward deinstitutionalization was clearly stimulated by the shocking news that Massachusetts was closing all of its juvenile institutions. In August 1969, the governor of Massachusetts signed into law an act which laid the groundwork for this dissolution (Rutherford 1974: 5). The training schools were dismantled, partly because of scandals and disclosures made in Massachusetts since 1965. The inadequate treatment of these youths was expressed in one study:

> The treatment of youths inside the institutions was at best custodial, and at worst, punitive and repressive. Marching, shaved heads, and enforced periods of long silences were regular occurrences. Punitive staff used force, made recalcitrant children drink water from toilets, or scrub floors on their hands and knees for hours on end. Solitary confinement was also used extensively and rationalized as a mode of treatment for those who needed it (Bakal 1973: 154).

Other features of the system were also faulty. Autonomous institutions caused little genuine communication between the central authority and its institutional subdivisions. Officials went their own way, hired the staff they wanted, and initiated the procedures they felt most conducive for handling the age groups assigned them. Lack of funds prohibited the hiring of qualified staff, and those already in the system appeared unlikely to accept any new programs with either enthusiasm or commitment (Bakal 1973: 154).

Not only were institutional programs lacking, but coordination among facilities and the probation and parole system was "disjointed and incoherent." The latter served more as a police force than as a champion for its clients. The result was identical to that caused by many similar institutions; youths were often more delinquent and bitter after their stay than before entrance into the system. Children who started their deviant careers merely as truant or incorrigible often ended up as hardcore offenders confined to adult penal facilities, an outcome clearly working both to their disadvantage and to society's.

Jerome G. Miller's *Last One Over the Wall: The Massachusetts Experiment in Closing Reform Schools* concluded that training schools are "impervious to reform" because they have a hidden task of holding a society together. Society, according to Miller, is understandably reluctant given this hidden task to embark boldly on a policy of mass deinstitutionalization. He also claims that there are a number of reasons why innovation, or change, is difficult in training school and that training schools too frequently dispense punishment and call it treatment (Miller 1991).

THE RESURGENCE OF TRAINING SCHOOLS

The idea of deinstitutionalization became popular in numerous states, and commitments to training schools declined in nearly every state. Kansas, Minnesota, North Dakota, Oregon, South Dakota, and Utah were soon placing nearly as many juveniles in resident and day treatment programs as they were assigning to training schools.

In the mid- and late-1970s the deinstitutionalization movement became stalled. A "get-tough-with-crime" mood in society contributed to the increased use of institutionalization, first in adult corrections and then in juvenile corrections. The public's notion, shaped largely by the media, that violent youth crime was rampant also influenced the return to institutionalization as a means to win the War on Crime.

Several efforts have been launched, however, to bring reform to training schools. First, some of the older and larger training schools in the nation were closed. For example, the Fairfield School for Boys, the oldest and largest training school in Ohio holding at one time more than one thousand youths, was closed in the early 1980s. Second, the passage of the 1974 Juvenile Justice and Delinquency Prevention Act prohibited the placement of status offenders with juvenile delinquents in long-term institutional placements. The consequences of the 1974 ruling and its various modifications have been the expansion of privately administered juvenile facilities to provide for the placement of status offenders and non-criminal youths. Third, a number of states in the 1970s began to convert their single-sex training schools into coeducational training schools.

The prevailing feeling at the time was that coeducational training schools provided more of a normalizing atmosphere than single-sex ones and, therefore, would have more positive consequences with youth. Fourth, upgraded staff training, as well as the growing acceptance of the

Table 1.1 Juvenile Residential Facility Census, 2004

	Facilities		Juvenile Offenders	
	Number	Pct.	Number	Pct.
Total	2,809	100%	94,875	100%
Public	1,187	42	65,197	69
State	500	18	35,822	38
Local	687	24	29,375	31
Private	1,612	57	29,558	31

Note: Total includes 10 tribal facilities holding 120 juvenile offenders.

Source: Sarah Livsley, Melissa Sickmund, and Anthony Stadky, *Juvenile Residential Facility Census, 2004: Selected Findings*. Washington, DC: Office of Justice Programs; National Report Series, 2009, p. 11.

accreditation standards of the American Correctional Association, were believed to improve both the quality of staff supervision and the management and control of residents. Fifth, there was a growing acceptance of grievance procedures for residents, and federal courts began to give more attention to the operation of juvenile correctional facilities. Finally, most states took steps to reduce or prevent the corporal punishment of institutional residents. Employees could be summarily fired in some states if charges of corporal punishment could be substantiated.

In the mid- and late-1980s, the increased use of public training schools was a major trend of juvenile corrections. In 1985, 49,322 juveniles were in public juvenile custody facilities, but by 1987, this figure had increased to 53,503 youths. In 2001, 104,413 youths were in training school placements; 73,328 of these juveniles were in public placements and 30,891 were in private placements (Sickmund, Sladky, and Kang 2004). However, from 2002 to 2004, the number of juvenile offenders in residential care decreased in forty states; on average, states held 11 percent fewer juvenile offenders in the 2004 census data than in the 2002 census data (Livsey, Sickmund, and Sladky 2009). See Table 1.1 on the prior page.

Another dynamic that may affect the size of residential care of juveniles in the future is that state budget cuts are forcing states to make cuts in their community-based programs for juveniles and, as a result, some of the juveniles previously placed in the community are sent to long-term juvenile facilities. The trend has been particularly identified in South Carolina, Tennessee, and Florida, but it may become more evident in other states (Davenport 2008).

Finally, besides being larger than in the past, training schools have also become more violent. Members of minority groups make up a greater proportion of juvenile correctional institutions; more juveniles are adjudicated to training school for drug offenses. Members of youth gangs are increasingly found in juvenile facilities and gangs sometimes dominate the residential culture. The use of the indeterminate sentence, especially the form in which institutional staff determines the data of release, is being increasingly replaced by mandatory sentences, by presumptive sentencing systems, and by sentencing guidelines matrixes.

EMPIRICAL CRITICISMS OF TRAINING SCHOOLS

Empirical studies have not been kind to training schools for males. Ken Wooden's investigative examination of training schools throughout the nation documented the brutal treatment residents received from staff in both private and public juvenile institutions. While eating, one resident requested permission not to eat any more. Staff denied him permission. When he vomited, he "was whacked on the head with a big serving spoon" and was made to do push-ups. According to the legal affidavit:

> After dinner, downstairs, the guard ordered Smith to do push-ups on the line. Smith felt sick again, asked the guard if he could go to the bathroom, was refused, and continued doing push-ups till he finally threw up again, this time on the floor. The guard ordered Smith to eat his own vomit. Smith kept refusing until the guard started kicking and hitting him. Smith was finally forced by the guard to eat his vomit until the floor was clean. He ate it all. When he was finally excused, Smith went into the bathroom and threw up (Wooden 1975: 113).

A number of studies have found that the culture generated by residents in both public and private facilities is exploitative and violent. Allen F. Breed's examination of the social structure among residents in the California Youth Authority's training schools identified the creation of a status hierarchy in every institution in which the strong dominated the weak (Breed 1963: 6-7).

Seymour Rubenfeld and John W. Stafford's study of a boy's training school in Washington, DC characterized the relationship among residents as a sadomasochistic struggle for privilege, power, and material goods (Rubenfeld and Safford 1963: 241-256). Sethard Fisher's examination of a small training school in California found that victimization and patronage were two of the major behaviors taking place. Victimization is defined as "a predatory practice whereby inmates of superior strength and knowledge of inmate lore prey on weaker and less knowledgeable inmates" (Fisher 1961:89). Patronage refers to residents' building "protective and ingratiating relationships with those more advantageously situated on the prestige ladder" (Fisher 1961: 89-90).

Barry Feld investigated the relationship between institutional orientation and violent inmate subcultures. He compared a sample of ten cottages from four institutions in Massachusetts before the training schools were closed and found that institutional orientation affected levels of cottage violence. Specifically, the more custody-oriented a cottage was, the more violent its residential subculture. Organizational orientation also affected violence indirectly through material deprivation. Residents of custody-oriented cottages had greater motivation to resort to violence than residents of treatment-oriented cottages because they had access to fewer resources (Feld 1977).

Clemens Bartollas, Stuart J. Miller, and Simon Dinitz in *Juvenile Victimization: The Institutional Paradox* focused on the victimization patterns found in institutional life. They found that 90 percent of the population of an end-of-the-line training school in Ohio was involved in exploitation. This study reported:

> The training school receives the worst of the labeled—the losers, the unwanted, the outsiders. These young men consider themselves to be among the toughest, most masculine and virile of their counterparts, and they have the societal credentials to prove it. Yet in much the same way that they themselves were processed, they create, import, and maintain a system which is as brutalizing as the one through which they passed. If anything, the internal environment and the organization and interaction at TICO are less fair, less just, less humane, and less decent than the worst aspects of the criminal justice system on the outside. Brute force, manipulation, institutional sophistication carry the day, and set the standards which ultimately prevail. Remove the staff, and a feudal structure will emerge which will make the dark ages seem very enlightened. In viewing the prospects, one almost is pushed to the Hobbesian position; surely there is little to be said for the Enlightenment thinkers with regard to the nature of the human character (Bartollas, Miller, and Dinitz 1976: 271).

Steve Lerner's more recent study of the California Youth Authority facilities found that inmate violence toward other inmates consistently has been reported at a level exceeding 2,000 incidents annually since 1982, involving 25 to 30 percent of the population. The open dormitories at the Youth Authority, according to Lerner, had become so vicious with the dense overcrowding that many youths feel they have to join a gang to purchase protection. The conclusion of this study is that "a young man convicted of a crime cannot pay his debt to society safely" (Lerner 1986: 12).

In 2009, the Center on Juvenile and Criminal Justice urged California to shut down the state prison system for the state's 1,600 youthful offenders, and turn the population back to county probation departments that have empty beds in new and refurbished juvenile halls. They claim that the youth prison system has become too expensive and too mired in abusive practices to be effective. California's Little Hoover Commission and the Legislative Analyst's Office also have concluded that given adequate time and resources, counties could house even the most troubled juvenile offenders in far cheaper and more effective institutions. Yet, the head of California's Division of Juvenile Justice, Bernie Warner, believes there must always be a state system for the most serious, violent, gang-involved youth offenders, most of whom need specialized treatment for crimes as serious as murder and sexual assault (Macallair, Males, McCracken 2009).

M. A. Bortner and Linda M. Williams' 1997 study of "Unit Four" reveals the promise and the reality of what took place in a "model" juvenile training school program in Arizona. Created because of a class action suit against Arizona's juvenile correction system, this model program generated much excitement; but it failed, partly because of the presence of gang youth who were involved in the program over the period of its evaluation (Bortner and Williams 1997: 54-60).

The two major studies of training schools for girls are Rose Giallombardo's *The Social World of Imprisoned Girls* (1974) and Alice Propper's *Prison Homosexuality: Myth and Reality* (1981). Giallombardo examined three training schools for girls in various parts of the United States and found that a kinship system existed with some variation in each of the facilities, in which girls were involved in varying degrees of lesbian alliances and pseudo-family relationships. This pervasive pseudo-family membership organization was called the "racket," the "sillies," and "chick business" (Giallombardo 1974).

Propper examined three coeducational and four training schools for girls scattered throughout the East, Midwest, and South. Five were public and two were private Roman Catholic training schools. Residents reported homosexual behavior involving from 6 to 29 percent of the residents in the various institutions. She found that the best predictor of homosexual participation during the present term of confinement was previous homosexuality. In contrast to the Giallombardo study, Propper found very little overlap between pseudo-family roles and homosexual behavior. She also documented that residents were sometimes the victims of homosexual rape (Propper 1981).

Christopher Sieverdes and Bartollas' study of six coeducational training schools in a Southeastern state also raised questions about the quality of institutional life. They found that juvenile females felt more victimized by peers than did males, but they did not harass staff as much as males did. Although pseudo-families existed among girls, they were based much less on homosexual alliances than were those in all-girl training schools. Status offenders were the worst victims in these training schools and had the most difficulty adjusting to institutional life. White males and females experienced high rates of personal intimidation and victimization by African-American and Native American youths (Sieverdes and Bartollas 1981: 91-103, Bartollas and Sieverdes 1979: 534-43).

Privately administered training schools were increasingly used during the 1970s and 1980s, but, consistent with other types of training schools, the majority of the studies have raised considerable reservations about the efficacy of these facilities. Howard W. Polsky examined a cottage in a residential treatment center in New York and found that the staff in Cottage Six were unable to prevent inmate leaders from exploiting weaker peers. He also found that the tougher the youth, the higher he ranked in the peer social hierarchy. Similar to the Bartollas et al.'s studies, those at the bottom of the status hierarchy found life extremely emotionally debilitating (Polsky 1963).

Bartollas and colleagues have examined the quality of institutional confinement in private facilities in several studies. Sieverdes and Bartollas examined a private facility for males in a Southeastern state and found that the attitudes of residents were no more positive than the attitudes of male and female residents confined in the coeducational institutions of this state (1981).

Even more disturbing was the finding that sexual victimization was rampant in this facility (Bartollas and Sieverdes 1979). David Shichor and Bartollas' investigation of the patterns of public and private juvenile placements in a large probation department in southern California revealed that few differences existed between juveniles sent to private and public placements. Those sent to private placements had more personal problems, and those sent to public placements appeared to be somewhat more delinquent, but the two populations did not differ markedly.

Significantly, this study reported that hard-core delinquents were not separated from those who had committed minor offenses (Shichor and Bartollas 1990: 286-99). Bartollas and Shichor's comparison of a state training school for males in the Midwest and of a highly regarded coeducational private placement in the same state found that the length of stay in the private facility averaged nearly twice as long as at the state training school. They also found that the enforcement of excessive rules in the majority of cottages in the private placement seemed to create a rigid cottage structure and living environment (Bartollas and Shichor 1990).

One of the most positive studies of private placements was Peter W. Greenwood, Susan Turner, and Kathy Rosenblatt's evaluation of the Paint Creek Youth Center in southern Ohio (1989). This evaluation claimed that Paint Creek is superior to the traditional training school setting because it is small (thirty-three beds) and expects staff and peers, rather than fences and locked doors, to maintain security. Paint Creek also features a comprehensive and integrated therapeutic approach emphasizing accountability, social learning, and positive peer culture. A sequence of programs providing increased responsibilities and privileges contingent on positive behavior within the program, as well as the implementation of a family therapy program, are two aspects of this comprehensive therapeutic approach.

In addition, Paint Creek residents receive an intensive aftercare program upon their return to the community. In comparing a sample of youths who were randomly assigned between Paint Creek and Training Institution for Central Ohio and other Department of Youth Services institutions, Greenwood et al. found that those who had been assigned to Paint Creek were less likely to be rearrested and to be recommitted to a correctional institution on new charges than those who had been assigned to the Training Institution for Central Ohio and other Department of Youth Services facilities (Greenwood, Turner, and Rosenblatt 1989).

KEY ISSUES IN JUVENILE INSTITUTIONALIZATION

In this historical and empirical sketch of the hopeful beginnings, the partial dissolutions, and the reemergence of juvenile institutions, the theoretical considerations have been kept separate. What, then, are the crucial theoretical issues that are pivotal in evaluating juvenile correctional institutions?

Institutional Management

Crowding, the influx of a drugs or alcohol, the increased commitments of street gangs, and the reduced popularity of rehabilitation all mandate that careful attention be given to the management of juvenile correctional institutions. This matter of management, of course, is one of the major themes of this book.

Institutional Control

One of the most intriguing aspects of prison life is the way informal power of the confined mitigates the formal authority of staff (Morris et al. 1961; McCleery 1961; McCorkle 1956; McCorkle and Korn 1954; Sykes 1958). The legitimate authority of the staff often blends into and sometimes becomes subservient to that of prisoners. Strong inmates often terrorize staff as effectively as they do other inmates. Staff find their orders laughed at, ignored, subverted, or in some manner refused.

Even though youths are younger, smaller, more dependent, and usually kept under closer surveillance than are adults, they also resent the authority and control of staff and do everything possible to attenuate that control. When staff are faced with resistant youths, they are aware that they must find ways to maintain control. One option is to treat residents fairly and teach them how to have their needs met in more pro-social ways. Or, staff can use corporal punishment, or apply "instant therapy," to change youths' attitudes. Additionally, they can prolong the length of institutional stay for negative behaviors. Highly desired jobs are also sometimes given to the strong in exchange for keeping the institution quiet; new residents are bartered to older ones for help in running the institution (Polsky 1962, Bartollas, Miller, and Dinitz 1976).

Decline of Ideology

In 1974, the late Robert Martinson stunned correctional personnel and the public in general by announcing that "With few and isolated exceptions, the rehabilitative efforts that have been reported so far have had no appreciable effect on recidivism" (Martinson 1974). This was quickly translated into the conclusion that "nothing works" in correctional treatment. Martinson's pronouncement, along with a 1975 book coauthored with Douglas Lipton and Judith Wilks—*The Effectiveness of Correctional Treatment*—persuaded many that the time had come to bury the rehabilitation model and to move on to more fruitful endeavors (Lipton, Martinson, and Wilks 1975). The instantaneous popularity of the "nothing works" thesis sparked an intense and spirited debate.

Treatment has regained some of its previous popularity (Palmer 1992), but there are presently few training schools which place the same emphasis on treatment as they did twenty years ago. What is more typical is for the rehabilitation model to be replaced by some form of a control model. Some training schools, especially those which work with hardcore delinquents, use few treatment programs.

A major problem involved with the demise of the rehabilitative ideal is that no other ideology has arisen to replace it. An important issue of juvenile institutionalization, then, is the effect of the demise of ideology on the quality of juvenile confinement. What, in fact, has taken place is that the process of institutionalization is increasingly seen as one of warehousing youths. The end of ideology in these facilities has too frequently resulted in a demoralized staff that sees no major purpose or end result in working with youth. One response from staff is that "we don't do anything with kids in this institution except hold them."

Institutional Violence

One of the most telling issues concerning the efficacy of juvenile institutionalization is the high degree of violence that takes place in some of these facilities. As reported by the studies cited earlier in this chapter, many juveniles neither feel safe nor actually are safe during institutional confinement. They may be brutalized by aggressive peers or by disillusioned or embittered staff. Residents may choose to strike out at staff, or they may direct their feelings of violence toward themselves in self-destructive ways.

The constant threat and occasional use of violence vividly bring home the terrifying nature of this social world. If new residents lack physical strength, they must either outsmart and out talk those who attempt to exploit them. Or, they must feign toughness so convincingly so as not to be challenged. Should this performance fail, new youths may be subject to the most devastating blow of all—sexual exploitation.

There is reason to believe that violence will become an even more salient issue with the present overcrowding of juvenile facilities, with the influx of drug-trafficking youth-gang members, and with the decline of treatment ideology and its accompanying reduced staff morale and involvement.

Disproportionate Minority Confinement

The Coalition for Juvenile Justice (formerly the National Coalition of State Juvenile Justice Advisory Groups) brought national attention to this problem of disproportionate minority confinement in their 1988 annual report to Congress. In that same year, Congress responded to this evidence of disproportionate confinement of minority juveniles by amending the Juvenile Justice and Delinquency Prevention Act (JJDPA) of 1974 by mandating that:

> states participating in the Formula Grants Program must address efforts to reduce the proportion of the youth detained or confined in secure detention facilities, secure correctional facilities, jail and lockups, who are members of minority groups if such proportion exceeds that proportion such groups represent in the general population (Hamparian and Leiber 1997).

The Juvenile Justice and Delinquency Prevention Act was reauthorized in late 2002 and took effect in October 2003. The first three mandates, for the most part, stayed the same. The fourth mandate was changed from disproportionate minority confinement to disproportionate minority contact (DC). The focus presently is on efforts to reduce minority contact with the system. Programs geared to delinquency prevention, as well as a multipronged approach to disproportionate minority contact are encouraged (Snyder and Sickmund 2006).

CONCLUSIONS

This review of the history of training schools, as well as their evaluation and salient theoretical issues, leads to the conclusion that juvenile correctional institutions reflect the public's worldview at any given time. Training schools traditionally have been ideologically driven, although presently an absence of ideology characterizes their operations. Some improvements have taken place, such as greater attention being given to due process than in the past, but the task of creating a humane and innovative facility, which will be a positive setting for confined youth, is a challenging one.

However, the authors, while recognizing the challenges and pitfalls that await those who want to make institutional care a meaningful experience for youth, approach this project with great enthusiasm. We will walk you through this exciting journey of creating such an institution in the chapters to come.

REFERENCES

Bakal, Yitzchak. 1973. *Closing Correctional Institutions*. Lexington, Massachusetts: D. C. Heath and Company.

Barker, Gordon E. and W. Thomas Adams. 1959. "The Social Structure of a Correctional Institution." *Journal of Criminal Law, Criminology and Police Science* 49: 417-499.

Bartollas, Clemens, Stuart J. Miller, and Simon Dinitz. 1976. *Juvenile Victimization: The Institutional Paradox*. New York: Halsted Press.

Bartollas, Clemens and David Shichor. 1990. "Juvenile Privatization: The Expected and the Unexpected." Paper presented to the Annual Meeting of the American Society of Criminology, Baltimore, Maryland.

Bartollas, Clemens and Christopher M. Sieverdes. 1979 Games Inmates Play. Unpublished manuscript. 1981. "The Victimized White in a Juvenile Correctional System." *Crime and Delinquency* 34: 534-543.

Bortner, M. A. and Linda M. Williams. 1997. *Youth in Prison: We the People of Unit Four*. New York: Routledge.

Breed, Allen F. 1963. "Inmate Subcultures." *California Youth Authority Quarterly*, 16:6-7.

Brenzel, Barbara M. 1983. *Daughters of the State*. Cambridge, Massachusetts: MIT Press.

Davenport, Jim. 2008. "Cash-Strapped States Cut Juvenile Justice Programs." Associated Press.

Feld, Barry C. 1977. *Neutralizing Inmate Violence: The Juvenile Offender in Institutions*. Cambridge: Ballinger.

Fisher, Sethard. 1961. "Social Organization in a Correction Residence." *Pacific Sociological Review* 5: 89.

Giallombardo, Rose. 1974. *The Social World of Imprisoned Girls: A Comparative Study of Institutions for Juvenile Delinquents*. New York: John Wiley and Sons.

Greenwood, Peter W., Susan Turner, and Kathy Rosenblatt. 1989. *Evaluation of Paint Creek Youth Center: Preliminary Results*. Santa Monica, California: Rand.

Hamparian, Donna and Michael J. Leiber. 1997. *Disproportionate Confinement of Minority Juveniles in Security Facilities: 1996 National Report*. Champaign, Illinois: Community Research Associates.

Hood, Robert G. 1967. "Research on the Effectiveness of Punishments and Treatments" in *Collected Studies in Criminological Research I*. Strasburg: Council of Europe.

Lerner, Steve. 1986. *Bodily Harm: The Pattern of Fear and Violence at the California Youth Authority*. Bolinas, California: Common Knowledge Press.

Livsley, Sarah, Melissa Sickmund, and Anthony Stadky. 2009. *Juvenile Residential Facility Census, 2004: Selected Findings*. Washington, DC: Office of Justice Programs; National Report Series.

Macallair, Daniel, Mike Males, and Catherine McCracken. 2009. *Closing California's Division of Juvenile Facilities: An Analysis of County Institutional Capacity*. San Francisco, California: Center on Juvenile and Criminal Justice. http://cjcj.org

Martinson, Robert, 1974. "What Works? Questions and Answers about Prison Reform." *Public Interest* 35:22-54.

McCleery, Richard. 1960. "Communication Patterns as Bases of System of Authority and Power," in *Theoretical Studies in Social Organization of the Prison*, Richard Cloward, G. N. Grosser, Donald R. Cressey, Richard McCleery, L. E. Ohlin, Gresham Sykes, and Sheldon L. Messinger, eds. New York: Social Science Research Council.

McCordle, Lloyd W. 1956. "Social Structure in a Prison." *Welfare Reporter* 8:5-15.

McCordle, Lloyd W. and Richard Korn. 1954. "Resocialization Within Walls." *Annals of the American Academy of Political and Social Science* 293:88-98.

Miller, Jerome G. 1991. *Last One Over the Wall: The Massachusetts Experience in Closing Reform Schools*. Columbus: The Ohio State University Press.

Morris, Terrence, Pauline Morris, and Barbara Belly. 1961. "It's the Prisoners Who Run this Prison." *Prison Service Review* 3:3-11.

Office of Juvenile Justice and Delinquency Prevention. 2009. *Disproportional Minority Contact: Technical Assistance Manual*, 4th ed. July. Accessed at www.ncjrs.gov/html/ojjdp/dmc_ta_manual/

Polsky, Howard. 1963. *Cottage Six: The Social System of Delinquent Boys in Residential Treatment*. New York: Russell Sage.

President's Commission on Law Enforcement and Administration of Justice. 1967. *Task Force Report: Juvenile Delinquency and Youth Crime*. Washington, DC: U.S. Government Printing Office.

Propper, Alice. 1981. *Prison Homosexuality: Myth and Reality*. Lexington, Massachusetts: D. C. Heath and Company.

Robinson, James and Gerald Smith. 1969. "The Effective of Correctional Programs." *Crime and Delinquency* 15:67-80.

Rothman, David. 1971. *The Discovery of the Asylum*. Boston: Little, Brown, and Company.

Rubenfeld, Seymour and John W. Stafford. 1963. "An Adolescent Inmate Social System—A Psychological Account." *Psychiatry* 26:241-256.

Shichor, David and Clemens Bartollas. 1990. "Private and Public Placements: Is There a Difference?" *Crime and Delinquency* 36: 289-299.

Sickmund, Melissa, T. J. Sladky, and Wei Kang. 2004. *Census of Juveniles in Residential Placement Databook*. Washington, DC: Bureau of Justice Statistics.

Sieverdes, Christopher M. and Clemens Bartollas. 1981. "Institutional Adjustment among Female Delinquents." *Administrative Issues in Criminal Justice*. Alvin W. Cohn and Ben Ward, eds. Beverly Hills, California: Sage Publications.

Snyder, Howard N. and Melissa Sickmund. 2006. Juvenile Offenders and Victims: 2006 National Report. Washington, DC: National Center for Juvenile Justice, Office of Juvenile Justice Programs and Office of Juvenile Justice and Delinquency Prevention.

Sykes, Gresham. 1958. *Society of Captives*. Princeton, New Jersey: Princeton University Press.

Warren, Marguerite Q. 1972. "The Community Treatment Project: History and Prospects" in *Law Enforcement Science and Technology*. S. A. Yefsky, ed. Washington, DC: Thompson Book Company.

Wooden, Kenneth. 1976. *Weeping in the Playtime of Others*. New York: McGraw-Hill.

CHAPTER 2

A PROFILE OF YOUTH COMMITTED TO JUVENILE RESIDENTIAL CORRECTIONAL FACILITIES

Juveniles in residential correctional facilities can make major gains in their education and coping skills if staff understand and respect them.

If juvenile facilities hope to improve upon their poor track record, administrators must make a more deliberate and concerted effort to understand the characteristics of youth committed to their facility. Are they dangerous and if so, why? Have they been victimized? Do they have mental health problems or chemical abuse issues? What are their needs? What is their delinquent history? Why do they have so much involvement in violence, drugs, and gangs? Why is there so much failure in school and lack of involvement with community institutions, such as churches, parks, clubs, and so forth? Why are recidivism rates above 50 percent for so many juvenile facilities?

The profiles of the youth who are served affect the type of physical facility and the level of security, the policies and procedures, the qualifications and training of staff, the ratio of staff to youth, and the services provided to youth. Thus, facilities must be better prepared to provide age-appropriate and needs-appropriate structure, support, accountability, and services.

However, confined youths will not make these internal changes if their needs and issues are ignored. They cannot make needed changes if their learning styles are ignored. They will not make needed changes if the facility in which they are living is not safe, for they will be too busy and preoccupied using their well developed "street smarts" (intimidating, joining gangs, running, carrying weapons, and using drugs) to keep themselves safe. They will not make needed changes if they are disrespected, for they will not listen or learn from someone who disrespects them.

The nursing supervisor at the Hillcrest Training School in Cincinnati said:

> There is no value in shaming a youngster. They don't need to be told that they are a jerk. They have a whole life of others finding things wrong with them. If you do that, the kid will just shut you out. This is not the way to build a relationship with this youngster (Hillcrest Training School Interviews 2006).

The great educator Jean Piaget said, "Instructors teach their subjects, but teachers understand how children learn" (Piaget 1997). Jawanza Kunjufu goes several steps further in his book, *Countering the Conspiracy to Destroy Black Boys*. He states:

> You cannot teach a child whom you do not love. You cannot teach a child whom you do not respect. You cannot teach a child whom you do not understand and you cannot teach a child you are afraid of and you cannot teach a child without bonding first, which results from love, respect and understanding (Kunjufu 1982).

Administrators who embrace these concepts lead successful residential juvenile correctional facilities. When they recruit new staff, or develop training for current staff, they place emphasis on the importance of understanding and respecting delinquent youth. They also place emphasis on respect and on the importance of forming appropriate and healthy relationships with these youth. If any correctional facility is to be successful at teaching new coping skills and new problem solving skills, time and effort must be put into understanding the youth with whom they are working. Only then will effective intervention strategies, services, security, and staffing levels be developed and implemented.

When administrators decide to take the time to learn about youth entering their facilities, they will find many resources and much information is available to enable them to begin to understand these youth. This will, in turn, support the development of appropriate services and structure.

Many different local and national organizations compile statistics and profiles. The typical youth being committed to residential juvenile correctional facilities today is a male non-Caucasian who is fourteen-to-sixteen years old and from a lower economic status, single-parent family. Most have failed at community programs because of acting out/assaultive behaviors. Most have diagnosable mental illness as well as chemical-abuse issues (Synder and Sickmund 2006).

CHRONOLOGICAL AGE

Youth committed to residential juvenile correctional facilities are as young as ten but more commonly between the ages of twelve and eighteen. Their average age is fifteen; some states maintain youth to twenty-one. In the United States, this average age is dropping. Most jurisdictions are dealing with younger offenders. This trend is also fueled by many states and jurisdictions lowering the age of youth who can be dealt with through the adult correctional systems thus removing them from the authority of juvenile courts. However, administrators must pay attention to the youth's age, addressing this broad chronological age difference in housing and programming. Since their average age is fifteen, these youths are adolescents who have adolescent characteristics.

- **Peers are powerful at influencing an adolescent's behavior.** Administrators must be cognizant of this fact. Decisions need to be made not to assign to the same living units low-risk and high-risk youth or very young and nearly emancipated youth. Program structure needs to minimize low-risk and high-risk youth being together. When they are together, it is important to ensure that they are supervised directly.

- **Adolescents will challenge authority.** If there are no structured/sanctioned outlets in the facility for youth to challenge authority, one can expect that disruptive behaviors and conflict with staff will be more frequent. This makes it much more difficult to develop a positive culture in that institution. For an administrators, this means that they must structure outlets that are designed to allow for these challenges. This is a great opportunity for an institution to teach legitimate legal ways to challenge rules and/or authority.

- **Adolescents are judgmental and see things as black and white.** Consistency and fairness in application of the rules and discipline of the institution is therefore paramount to them being accepted and followed. Since youths are interacting with different staff at all times of the day and night, it is critical that all staff working on different shifts and different days agree to apply rules and discipline in a uniform manner.

- **Adolescents have lots of energy.** Daily physical activity is extremely important and most times required by licensing agencies. Physical activity results in increased energy consumption and food intake. Too many facilities do not develop and maintain food services that consistently provide well-balanced healthy meals. A healthy, plentiful diet leads to youth who will be more attentive at school and more receptive at treatment meetings.

- **Adolescents are more likely to listen and learn with experiential, "hands-on" teaching methods.** James Baldwin once said, "Children are not good at listening to their elders but they never fail to imitate them" (Baldwin 1963). Whether it is mopping the floor, making their bed, or resolving conflict without violence, lecturing is an ineffective method of teaching these youth. For an administrator, this means staff training regarding "hands-on" teaching techniques.

DEVELOPMENTAL AGE

A majority of youth being committed to residential juvenile correctional institutions today have experienced significant trauma throughout their lives. More than half of the young women have been sexually abused. Most of the juveniles come from families where child protective services or other agencies have interceded. Many have experienced severe neglect. Many have witnessed, or experienced first hand, extreme violence. The result of this entire trauma is, of course, mental health issues—not the least of which is the fact that even though they may be fifteen years old chronologically, most are significantly delayed developmentally.

Many youngsters seem to have lost the capacity to assimilate new experiences and to learn new things. These youngsters have devoted much of their energy to surviving and staying safe in their communities. Administrators need to be aware of this fact because youth who are significantly developmentally delayed have not yet developed cause and effect thinking. Youths who lack this skill will not learn to improve their behavior by staff simply giving them poor grades, putting them in their room, or into some sort of isolation. Yet, during their stay, staff have an opportunity to teach new skills and to help youth realize alternative methods of dealing with the situation that led to the rule infraction.

GENDER

According to the National Council on Crime and Delinquency, approximately 85 percent of youth committed to correctional institutions are male (National Council on Crime and Delinquency 2007). However, the national trend shows an increasing percentage of females both in the justice system, and those being committed to facilities. Those facilities that have designed their program and structure based on the needs and characteristics of males are ignoring the unique needs of females being committed.

According to the 1998 publication, *Guiding Principles for Promising Female Programming*, girls demonstrate a need for the following things:

- Physical safety and healthy physical development

- Trust, love, respect, and validation from caring adults to foster healthy emotional development and to form positive relationships

- Positive female role models to develop identity as women

- Safety to explore sexuality at their own pace for healthy sexual development

- Acceptance, to belong, and to feel competent and worthy

Programs working with young women must meet these unique needs to be successful. Consideration of male and female pathways into illegal behaviors and their different responses to incarceration lead to different program needs. For young women, acting-out is often a post-traumatic adaptive response to trauma of physical and sexual abuse. National studies indicate as many as 92 percent of girls in detention have been victims of abuse (Acola and Dedel 1998). Administrators must be sensitive to this fact when developing staff training and programming. Staff that are assigned to work with young women must have strong relationship abilities and be able to set clear boundaries.

RACE-ETHNICITY

Nationwide, youth of color are disproportionately detained compared to white youth. The National Council on Crime and Delinquency reported in its January 15, 2007 publication that youth committed to correctional institutions have the following race/ethnicity designations;

38 percent African American (but 16 percent of the general population)
23 percent Latino or Native American
39 percent Caucasian (but 62 percent of the general population)

The national trend is that the percentage of non-Caucasian youth in facilities is increasing. Youth of color represented a greater proportion of the total juveniles in public facilities (65 percent) than private facilities (55 percent). Programming must be culturally specific to be effective. Since role modeling is essential to the learning of youth, it is also important that the facility have a diverse staff—staff with whom youth can identify (Bandura 1985). Another way of saying this is that a good representation of staff should look like the significant people in their family and community.

FAMILY

The family structure and the quality of family life have an important effect on the behavior of children. McCurley and Snyder's study found that youth ages twelve-to-seventeen who lived in families with both biological parents were generally less likely than youth in other families to report a variety of problem behaviors, such as sexual activity, running away from home, assault, and major theft (McCurley and Snyder 2007). The proportion of children under age eighteen living in two-parent households has declined in recent years (Snyder and Sickmund 2006).

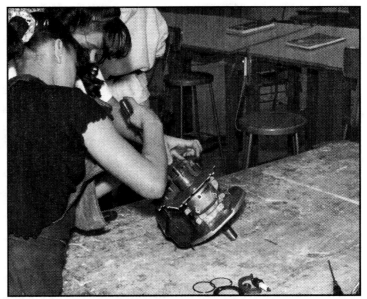

Young women taught non-traditional job skills will be better able to find a well-paying job to support themselves and their family when they leave school.

The economic well-being of children is also related to family structure. In 2002, more than half, or 52 percent, of children below the poverty level lived in single-mother families while about one-third lived in two-parent families (Snyder and Sickmund 2006). Family structure is further related to the proportion of children in households receiving public assistance or food stamps. In 2002, 5 percent of all children received public assistance and 11 percent received food stamps. However, of those who lived in single-mother families, 13 percent received public assistance and 29 percent received food stamps (Snyder and Sickmund 2006). Table 2.1 (on the next page) shows the percentage of children in various types of family arrangements who received public assistance or food stamps.

According to Barb Comstock, clinical psychologist from the National Child Traumatic Stress Network, youth committed to correctional facilities have the following profile:

- 33 percent had a parent who was deceased

- 20 to 30 percent had a parent who had been incarcerated

- 20 to 30 percent come from single mothers

- They have a high number of male family members associated with crime.

- There are chronic family health problems: immunizations are not current, dental work is needed (Comstock 1997).

Table 2.1 Percentage of Families Receiving Public Assistance or Food Stamps		
	Percentage of Children Receiving	
Family Structure	Public Assistance	Food Stamps
All Families	5 percent	11 percent
Two-Parent	2	4
Mother Only	13	29
Father Only	5	13
Neither Parent	12	15

Source: Howard N. Snyder and Melissa Sickmund, 2006. *Juvenile Offenders and Victims, 2006*, National Report. Washington, DC: Department of Justice, Office of Juvenile Justice and Delinquency Prevention.

Medical staff across the country would support what the head nurse at Hillcrest Training school details:

> One kid, when asked what his doctor's phone number was, told me 911. These kids have no private physician and 99.9 percent are on medical cards. They don't go to clinics. These kids go to the emergency room when they have something wrong with them. No one has really looked at these kids' bodies from head to toe and said, 'My God; do you know you can't hear? Do you know you can't see?' We get these kids, and they come in and argue about the 'E' at the top of the chart, and you try to tell them, 'Sweetheart, believe me, other people can see that 'E'" (Hillcrest Interviews 2006).

What an administrator needs to know is that more than 90 percent of youth committed to juvenile correctional facilities return to their family. Too many juvenile facilities "write off" these families because of all of their issues—housing, employment, chemical and mental health issues, poverty, and family criminality. Juvenile institutions must work to engage the families of these youth. They must work to form a partnership with the youth's family for the sake of the youth. In many cases, this will involve teaching the family new skills, and partnering the family with community agencies that can help with problems with which the family is struggling.

GANGS AND COMMUNITY

Most youth committed to residential correctional facilities are from economically disadvantaged neighborhoods with little or no capacity to address the intensive and varied needs they and their families have. Many times the youth's antisocial behaviors are tolerated. Traditional community institutions such as schools and churches have failed them. These neighborhoods often times lack adequate numbers of prosocial adult role models.

Gang involvement is common. Youth join gangs for many reasons: excitement, safety, or economics. It could be their chance to feel they are a part of something bigger than themselves—to belong. Perhaps, it is a chance to be respected or a chance to succeed and be recognized and affirmed.

Programming must, therefore, recognize the power of these gang and peer relationships must also teach noncriminal ways to achieve and succeed.

MENTAL HEALTH

The juvenile justice system has become the default system for many young people with mental health disorders who are not receiving appropriate treatment from the mental health system (Greenstein, Johnson, and Friedman 1992). Otto Greenstein and colleagues add: "We now know that youth in the juvenile justice system experience substantially higher rates of mental health disorders than for youth in the general population" (Greenstein, Johnson, and Friedman 1992).

According to Cynthia R. Pfeiffer of Cornell University, an estimated 65 to 75 percent of youth in correctional facilities have a psychiatric disorder and suicide rates in juvenile detention and correctional facilities are four times higher than youth in the general population (Pfeiffer 2006). The diagnosis that is most frequently found is disruptive disorders, followed by substance abuse disorders, anxiety disorders, and mood disorders. Among a sample of incarcerated youth, girls reported significantly higher levels of physical punishment and sexual abuse and higher levels of psychological distress such as post-traumatic stress disorder and depression than boys (Wood 2002).

As one young woman, Melissa T., wrote:

When I look at this girl I see sadness,
Tear falling,
Resorting to madness,
When I look at this girl I see wonder,
Wonder if she will follow through,
And continue to do what she wants to do,
When I look at this girl I see love,
But, not love for life.
Love for death (Diver City 2006).

Administrators need to understand that providing traditional mental health services is only one part of maximizing success with these youth. Programming and structure must accommodate their abilities and their limitations that result from their mental illness. For example, traditional juvenile correctional facilities will often use room time and segregation as the first choice for dealing with a youth's misbehavior. For a clinically depressed youth who has a suicidal ideation or has attempted suicide, this method of control not only is ineffective but counterproductive to the youth's safety and progress in the program because it can exacerbate his or her depression and lead to tragedy—successful suicide.

CHEMICAL ABUSE

Various studies have indicated a high percentage of youth in correctional institutions who use and abuse chemicals. A study of 1,800 incarcerated youth in Chicago, found 51 percent of the males and 47 percent of the females had a substance abuse disorder (Nissen, Butts, Merrigan, and Kraft 2006). Most juvenile institutions including training schools have experienced a surge in juveniles with a history of methamphetamine use and its attendant health problems.

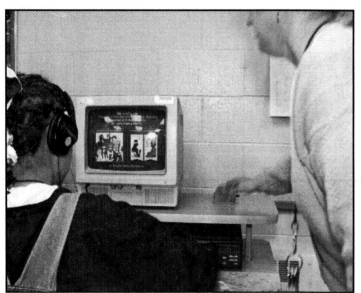

Special education may be needed by half of the youth entering juvenile residential facilities.

These youth have learned that drug abuse ameliorates their continued pain. Without access to mental health interventions, they medicate their pain by the means that are available to them—in many cases using drugs that are illegal and obtaining money for those drugs through criminal behaviors.

Treatment of their chemical use and abuse must, therefore, be coordinated with treatment of their mental health and criminal behavior issues.

EDUCATION ISSUES

Youth admitted to residential juvenile correctional facilities today are behind in their basic academic skill levels. They have a history of poor academic performance fueled by truancy, learning disorders, behavior disorders such as attention deficit hyperactivity disorder (ADHD), physical problems (such as discussed earlier with poor sight), Fetal Alcohol Syndrome (FAS), and lack of family support. Often, youth who come from violent living situations spend much of their energy on staying safe. They have not developed good listening skills.

Most have trouble sitting still for long periods of time—something that traditional education requires. Many have not been in school in years or have developed school phobias. They have learned in their local schools that if they act out enough in school, they will take control and avoid problems. They choose to act out and get expelled rather than face the various challenges the school presents, whether it is fear of peers, of failure, or of teachers.

Juvenile residential correctional facilities across the country are reporting 50 percent or more of their admissions are in need of special education. Virtually all are in need of remedial math and reading to even get close to their cohort's proficiencies.

For administrators, the youth's educational deficits mean they will require some very specialized and intensive educational programming. For example, highly trained special education teachers are needed. Disruptive behavioral issues that many of these youth exhibit in a classroom setting exasperate these educational deficits. Some of these acting-out behaviors are caused by their mental and physical health issues. Help must come from the administrators of the facility:

- To encourage, support, and provide things such as small class size with institutional staff available to help with enforcing good behavior

- To implement policies and staff training reflecting and supporting high expectations of good behavior in the classroom

- To continually encourage and demand good communication between the staff of the living units and the teachers at the school

- To ensure that the youth arrive at school on time with a good night's sleep and a good breakfast

- To expect support from the living units for after school follow-up with things such as homework and with processing the day's accomplishments

- To provide rewards for good behavior and consequences for bad behavior

VIOLENT AND DISRUPTIVE BEHAVIOR

A national profile of youthful offenders reveals that less than 1 percent of juveniles who come into contact with the police are placed in out-of-home placements (see Figure 2.1). Those researchers and theorists employing the current trend of evidence-based practices tell us that correctional interventions will be most successful if the most intensive secure residential facilities are reserved for the highest risk youth.

Using the research on evidence-based practices in designing programs that work with delinquent youth has become the norm for planners and correctional administrators. One of the tenets of evidence-based practices is "targeted interventions." This principle essentially states that a jurisdiction's most expensive and intensive resources should be directed to the youth who pose the highest risk to reoffend. Driven by the high cost of secure residential beds and supported by this evidence-based research, juvenile correctional facilities are seeing much higher percentages of serious, chronic, gang-involved violent offenders.

Youths entering correctional facilities have experienced the world as dangerous and frightening, with little or no support from responsible adults. They have a pervasive sense of not being cared for. Each youth has his or her own story of neglect and or abuse. Mark's first memory was waking up in a garbage can where his crack-addicted mother's boyfriend had thrown him. Jesse spent the first three years of his life rarely touched by human hands, as he had been placed in a playpen on top of a refrigerator to live. Lamar remembers waking up each day foraging for food and hoping his mother would come home sometime to check on him. Serha remembers her mother's various boyfriends making bedtime a time of horror, as she was sexually abused almost daily (Interviews 2001).

These youth are survivors and have learned to get their needs met and to protect themselves from real and perceived dangers by acting out violently, threatening, carrying weapons, and joining gangs. The young women, more often than the young men, turn their shame, anger, and violence inward to themselves resulting in depression, a suicidal ideation, suicide attempts, and successful suicide.

James Garbarino, a noted author and psychologist, believes moral reasons partly explain their negative behavior:

> While to an outside observer, the violence these boys commit often seems to make no sense or to evidence a total breakdown in morality: this is not the case if we can see the world through their eyes. Boys often commit acts of violence because they get a moral idea in their heads, usually something to do with revenge or injustice or

Continued on page 25

23

Figure 2.1 National Profile of Youthful Offenders

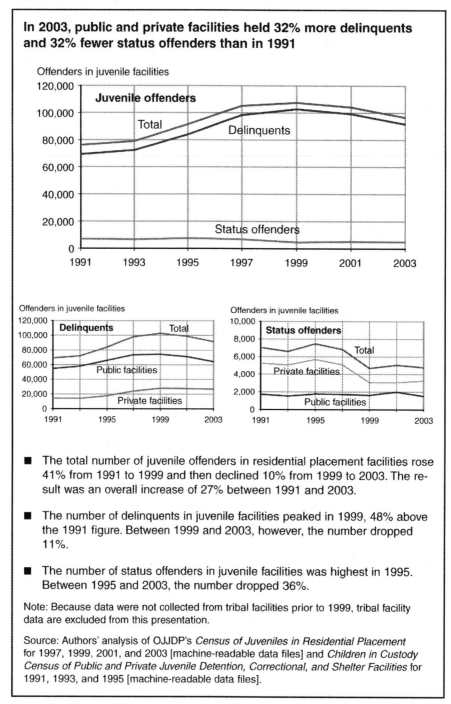

In 2003, public and private facilities held 32% more delinquents and 32% fewer status offenders than in 1991

- The total number of juvenile offenders in residential placement facilities rose 41% from 1991 to 1999 and then declined 10% from 1999 to 2003. The result was an overall increase of 27% between 1991 and 2003.

- The number of delinquents in juvenile facilities peaked in 1999, 48% above the 1991 figure. Between 1999 and 2003, however, the number dropped 11%.

- The number of status offenders in juvenile facilities was highest in 1995. Between 1995 and 2003, the number dropped 36%.

Note: Because data were not collected from tribal facilities prior to 1999, tribal facility data are excluded from this presentation.

Source: Authors' analysis of OJJDP's *Census of Juveniles in Residential Placement* for 1997, 1999, 2001, and 2003 [machine-readable data files] and *Children in Custody Census of Public and Private Juvenile Detention, Correctional, and Shelter Facilities* for 1991, 1993, and 1995 [machine-readable data files].

wounded pride or glory. The armed assaults on their classmates committed by the boys in Jonesboro and Padula probably made sense to them before the fact, as they contemplated and planned their actions. In this way, there is no such thing as a "senseless act of violence." This does not mean that we simply accept their motives as legitimate, of course, but it does force us to look beyond shock, horror, and indignation to see the root of the problem (Garbarino 1998).

Staff must affirm these youth. They need to keep some pride in who they were and where they came from. They need to hear repeatedly how smart, clever, strong, and functional these survival skills (not trusting adults, joining gangs, being angry, intimidating, accommodating, withdrawing, and using drugs) were when they were young in their hostile environment. More importantly, they need to know that those very defenses are now barriers, hindrances to learning new skills and getting help from others. It is important for youth to know that they do not have to go through life fearful, angry, and poor. They need to know there is a better world for them. There is reason to hope. They can change.

Recent research by national organizations and private organizations speak of "protective factors" that are inherent in the individual such as "resilient temperament" that helps a child bounce back in adverse circumstances (Office of Juvenile Justice and Delinquency Prevention 1995). The Search Institute, an independent nonprofit organization whose mission is to provide leadership, knowledge, and resources to promote healthy children, youth, and communities, has created a list of "developmental assets," which are helpful in working with these youth to begin to understand the strengths they have upon which they can build their new life (www.search-institute.org/assets/).

CHALLENGES FOR ADMINISTRATORS

There is no simple "one size fits all" description of delinquent youth committed to residential juvenile facilities. What is simple and straightforward is that we must take the time to understand the profile of these youth if we are to provide interventions and programming that are effective.

Effective programming structure and services must take all of these characteristics into account. Administrators who pick and choose one or two characteristics from the youth's profile to structure their programming usually fail both in protecting the youth who are in residence but also fail in protecting the public.

The traditional medical model for mental health interventions will fail if applied separately from the other profile realities. Many of the youth now entering facilities have either not been accepted or have been expelled from mental health programs for assaultive behaviors, threatening behaviors or running behaviors (not showing up for appointments, and so forth). This "medical model" generally views the youth as a victim, someone to be cured.

These mental health providers have the general view that adolescent offenders, no matter how serious their offending behaviors, should be treated as victims. The reasoning for this is that they have been traumatized, abused, and neglected. Accordingly, they must be diagnosed, have mental health assessments, and have their "disease" treated. There have been some mixed successes in treating chronic, serious, or violent youth with this medical health approach, but it is most often met with failure and frustration. We contend that the reason recent research, using meta-analysis to debunk mental health interventions, is probably correct is that institutions chose to ignore the other characteristics of the youth with whom they were working.

In a large Midwestern juvenile residential correctional institution, a beautiful plaque with a picture of a social worker hangs prominently in the reception area of the administration building. This social worker was brutally raped and murdered by one of the youth on her caseload. The murder occurred during normal working hours, in the social worker's office, just down the hall from the living unit that was fully staffed. Subsequent investigation revealed that this social worker ignored security protocols and routinely met individually with youth in her office.

Her training and education was in psychology and social work. This social worker unfortunately ignored the fact that this youth was dangerous in addition to being a victim. Decisions were subsequently made to fire administrators, severely cut social work and psychological services, and hire more correctional officers. This change in policy and administration did little to stop the problems that this facility continued to encounter. In fact, this facility is currently under a federal consent decree for not providing adequate mental health services.

Success depends on understanding and treating the whole child. Success depends on addressing each of the profile characteristics of the committed youth. In the case of this facility, they went from ignoring the dangerous aspect of the youth to ignoring the mental health needs of the youth. Traditional correctional practices focusing on security while ignoring the realities of the youth being committed will, just as this large Midwestern training school, end in failure.

At the same time, we contend that it is a mistake to treat delinquents as mini-adults. Treating youth as "mini-adult criminals" requires correctional practices such as:

- Using segregation as the primary tool for discipline

- Teaching by didactic methods such as lectures

- Relying on authority and the role of a guard instead of relationships to gain compliance to rules

- Making compliance to rules and immediate behavior control the focus of staff's interventions

- Implementing mental health strategies that focus on fixing the youth rather than empowering them to build on their own strengths to get healthy

- Seeing the family and the community as tangential to their mission or even as an obstruction to their mission

Figure 2.1 shows the 2008 policy resolution on juveniles passed by the American Correctional Association. It provides sound directions for administrators of juvenile residential facilities.

Feature 2.1 ACA's Public Correctional Policy on Juvenile Justice

Introduction

Children and youths have distinct personal and developmental needs and must be kept separate from adult offenders. The juvenile justice continuum consists of prevention, diversion, detention, probation, residential and aftercare programs. The best interests of the individual youth must be balanced with the needs of the victim and the community.

Policy Statement

The juvenile justice system must provide a continuum of services, programs and facilities that ensure maximum opportunity for rehabilitation and are consistent with public safety. These should place a high priority on providing individualized care and rehabilitative services to juvenile offenders throughout the juvenile justice system. To implement this policy, juvenile justice officials and agencies should:

A. Increase public awareness of why it is in their best interest to promote, support, participate in and fund those programs that have proven effective in preventing delinquency and producing healthy, positive, and socially responsible children and adolescents

B. Establish and maintain effective working relationships with those who can have an impact on the juvenile to achieve the fullest possible cooperation in making appropriate decisions in individual cases and in providing and using services and resources

C. Provide a range of non-residential and residential programs and services in the least-restrictive manner, consistent with the needs of individual offenders and the protection of the public

D. Engage the family whenever practical, appropriate, and therapeutic to the youth, in the development and implementation of his or her treatment plan

E. Use a juvenile classification system to identify the risk and needs of the juvenile offender, and develop and implement an individualized treatment plan based on this assessment

F. Advocate for the separation of status offenders from adjudicated delinquent offenders in the same facilities

G. Provide a range of non-secure and secure short-term detention options pending adjudication

H. Advocate for the separation of adjudicated from pre-adjudicated youths in the same housing units

I. With the involvement of the youth and prior to release from custody, develop a transition plan that includes educational and/or vocational programs for aftercare/reentry and ensure that these reentry services are available and provided when the youth returns from residential placement

Continued on page 28

27

ACA's Public Correctional Policy on Juvenile Justice, *continued*

J. Establish written policies and procedures that will protect the rights and safety of the juvenile, the victim, and the public in as balanced a manner as possible

K. Establish procedures to safeguard the accuracy and use of juvenile records and support limitations on their use according to approved national standards, recognizing that the need to safeguard the privacy and rehabilitative goals of the juvenile should be balanced with concern for the protection of the public, including victims

L. Develop performance-outcome measures from which program effectiveness and system operations can be assessed and adjusted when needed; and

M. Implement research and evaluation initiatives that will measure the effectiveness of juvenile justice programs and disseminate findings to the field

Source: Originally passed August 23, 1984. Re-ratified January 17, 1990; January 10, 1993; January 14, 2002; and January 24, 2007.

Conclusions

Youth entering residential juvenile correctional facilities today have frequently committed serious criminal activities. Many of these youth are dangerous, but they are also needy adolescents who have been neglected, abused, and traumatized with resultant school problems, mental health issues, and chemical abuse issues. Administrators who understand this profile will be able to design and implement more effective services, structure, and interventions.

Understanding the profile will ensure appropriate policies and procedures are put into place. The staff qualifications and training needs will be more apparent. They will help determine the ratio of staff to youth and what services are critical to provide.

REFERENCES

Acoca, L. and Dedel, K. 1998. *No Place to Hide: Understanding and Meeting the Needs of Girls in the California Juvenile Justice System.* San Francisco, California: National Council on Crime and Delinquency.

American Correctional Association. 2007. *Public Correctional Policy on Juvenile Justice.* Alexandria, Virginia: American Correctional Association.

Baldwin, James. 1963. *Nobody Knows My Name.* New York: Vintage Books.

Bartollas, Clemens, Stuart J. Miller, and Simon Dinitz. 1976. *Juvenile Victimization: the Institutional Paradox.* New York: Halsted Press.

Garbarino, James. "Interview with James Garbarino." *All Things Considered.* March 1998.

Greenstein, Otto R., J, Johnson, M. Friedman, and R. Friedman. 1992. "Prevalence of Mental Disorders among Youth in the Juvenile Justice System" in *Responding to the Mental Health Needs of Youth in the Juvenile Justice System*, J. Cocozza, ed. Seattle, Washington: National Coalition for the Mentally Ill in the Criminal Justice System.

Hillcrest Training School Interviews. 2006.

Kunjufu, Jawanza. 1982. *Countering the Conspiracy to Destroy Black Boys.* Chicago: African American Images.

Leary, Alex. 2006. "State Closes Door on Boot Camps." *St. Petersburg Times*. April 12.

Loughran, Ned and John Platt. 2006. *Safety and Welfare Plan: Implementing Reform in California*. Sacramento, California: Department of Corrections and Rehabilitation, Division of Juvenile Justice.

Marks, Alexandra. 1999. "States Fall Out of Tough Love with Boot Camps." *The Christian Science Monitor*. December 27.

McCurley, C. and H. Snyder. 2007. "Risk, Protection, and Family Structure." Office of Juvenile Justice and Delinquency Prevention, *Juvenile Justice Bulletin*. Washington, DC: Office of Juvenile Justice and Delinquency Prevention.

Murray, Christopher, Chris Baird, Ned Loughran, Fred Mills, and John Platt. 2006. *Safety and Welfare Plan: Implementing Reform in California*. Sacramento, California: Department of Corrections and Rehabilitation: Division of Juvenile Justice.

National Council on Crime and Delinquency. 2007. *And Justice for Some*. San Francisco, California: National Council on Crime and Delinquency.

National Council of the Juvenile and Family Court Judges Association. 2003. *Family Justice Today* 54:17

Nissen, Laura Burney, Jeffrey A. Butts, Daniel Merrigan, and Katherine Kraft. 2006. "The RWJF Reclaiming Futures Initiative: Improving Substance Abuse Interventions for Justice Involved Youths." *Juvenile and Family Court Journal* 57:39.

Office of Juvenile Justice and Delinquency Prevention. 1995. *Guide for Implementing the Comprehensive Strategy for Serious, Violent, and Chronic Juvenile Offenders*. Washington, DC: U.S. Government Printing Office.

Payne, Ruby K., Philip Devol, and Terie Dreussi Smith. 2002. *Bridges Out of Poverty: Strategies for Professionals and Communities*. Highlands, Texas: Search Institute.

Pfeiffer, Cynthia R. 2006. "Our Turn: The Most Vulnerable Among Us—Our Children." *Advanced Suicide Prevention*, 1. Search Institute, *www.search-institute.org/assets/*

Snyder, Howard N. and Melissa Sickmund. 2006. *Juvenile Offenders and Victims: 2006 National Report*. Washington, DC: Office of Juvenile Justice and Delinquency Prevention.

Snyder, Howard N. and Melissa Sickmund,. 2006. *Juvenile Offenders and Victims: 2006 National Report*. Washington, DC: U.S. Department of Justice, Office of Justice Programs, Office of Juvenile Justice and Delinquency Prevention.

Sullivan, Patrick. 2010. *Creating Treatment Environments for Troubled Youth: Evidence-Based Design*. Alexandria, Virginia: American Correctional Association.

CHAPTER 3

MANAGERIAL STYLES AND INSTITUTIONAL CONTROL

Teamwork among staff and between staff and residents leads to a win-win for everyone.

The management styles of correctional administrators will, in a large degree, affect the quality of life that takes place within those institutions. The top administrator, or superintendent, can affect the operation of the institution in a number of ways: the allocation of resources, the types and quality of training provided for staff, the evaluation criteria, the rewards associated with good performance by staff, and, ultimately, the management and structure of the program (Caeti, Hemmens, Cullen, and Burton, Jr. 2003: 385).

There has been much more concern with the management of adult prisons than there has been with the management of juvenile correctional institutions. Part of the reason for this is the belief that adult prisons must be managed well, because they have larger physical plants and house more dangerous inmates for longer periods of time. Part of the reason also rests with the decades-old assumption in juvenile corrections that the basic role of these facilities is to rehabilitate youths, and it did not require a particularly sophisticated management philosophy or style to accomplish this goal.

This chapter has five parts—the first reports on a national survey of juvenile correctional administrators that examines their attitudes on several issues and their managerial problems; the second examines efforts in the past to manage juvenile facilities; the third discusses the importance of a homelike or normalizing environment; the fourth recommends important aspects of management style in a juvenile facility, and the final part examines the accreditation process and its important role in the management of juvenile residential facilities. All administrators, of course, must shape their management style, based on their philosophy, goals and objectives, and personal experiences.

NATIONAL PROFILE OF JUVENILE CORRECTIONAL ADMINISTRATORS

In a 2003 study, Tory J. Caeti, Craig Hemmens, Frances T. Cullen, and Velmer S. Burton, Jr., collected a complete listing of juvenile treatment facilities in the United States from the American Correctional Association. The sent a questionnaire to 406 identified treatment facilities, and received 258 usable questionnaires, resulting in a 63.5 percent response rate.

Comparison of the Backgrounds of Juvenile Facility Directors and Prison Wardens

Twenty percent of the directors of these juvenile facilities were women, and 80.2 percent were white. There were striking differences between the backgrounds of prison wardens (data collected by Cullen, Latessa, Burton, and Lombardo 1993) and the juvenile directors in this study. Juvenile facility directors tended to have less experience in the military, to be less likely to have worked in a beginning custodial position (correctional officer in the adult system and child care position in the juvenile system), and to be more likely to have worked in a treatment position.

Moreover, the juvenile directors had worked for long periods of time in their current facility but for less overall time in corrections. According to the authors of this study, the most striking difference in the comparison of the two groups was that wardens supervised an average of 862.1 inmates, while juvenile directors supervised an average of 118.6 residents (Caeti, Hemmens, Cullen, and Burton, Jr. 2003: 390-391).

Job Attitudes and Beliefs

The juvenile facility directors tended to report greater emphasis on rehabilitation and less emphasis on custody than prison wardens. In rank ordering the four primary goals of corrections (rehabilitation, deterrence, incapacitation, and retribution), most directors ranked the number one goal of their facilities as rehabilitation. This was followed by deterrence, incapacitation, and retribution. Significantly, only 1.9 percent ranked rehabilitation fourth. Prison wardens ranked retribution first, followed by deterrence, rehabilitation, and incapacitation. Juvenile directors tended to be much more positive on items concerning rehabilitation and less positive on punitive items when compared with prison wardens (Caeti, Hemmens, Cullen, and Burton, Jr. 2003: 394-395).

Both groups of administrators reported a strong concern for maintaining security and for keeping inmates/residents busy by having them work. Yet, to be expected, juvenile directors placed less importance on preventing escapes and punishing residents than did wardens. Juvenile directors, more than wardens, reported that the greatest influence over day-to-day activities of the facilities came from within the institution. Juvenile directors usually strongly agreed with the statement that they could trust staff to handle matters while they were away from the institution. They also tended to disagree with the statement that institutional control is slipping out of their hands (Caeti, Hemmens, Cullen, and Burton, Jr. 2003: 396).

In terms of job satisfaction, juvenile facility directors were a little less satisfied than prison wardens, but more so than correctional officers in adult prisons, and much more satisfied than the general public. The factors of salary, years in juvenile corrections, and job-related stress all affected the degree of job satisfaction. One of the most important findings of this survey is that support for rehabilitation increased job satisfaction (Caeti, Hemmens, Cullen, and Burton, Jr. 2003: 397).

PREVIOUS STYLES OF MANAGING JUVENILE FACILITIES

Several studies of the management of juvenile facilities have been documented in the twentieth century. They include the role of charismatic leadership and the development of the Borstal System in England; (2) David Street, Robert D. Vinter, and Charles Perrow's study of organizational goals and their effect on training schools in Michigan; (3) Dr. Jerome Miller's principles of reform that he used to close the training schools in Massachusetts; (4) an analysis of the management styles found in a thirty-year study of a maximum-security training school in Ohio; and (5) M. A. Bortner and Linda M. Williams' study, "Unit Four," which focuses on organizational change in an Arizona training school cottage.

The Borstal System in England

Sir Eveyn Ruggles-Brise is credited with developing the Borstal system for youthful offenders in England. The principles of the system are important because they influenced the set up of similar programs in the United States and in the British oversees dominions. Briefly, the Borstal system called for the youth's reform by individualization mentally, morally, and physically. There would be physical drill, gymnastics, and technical and literacy training. Good conduct would be rewarded. The staff was selected for characteristics that were likely to influence youths of the kind that Borstal had to work with. Soon after the beginning of the program, authorities decided that the minimum period of exposure to Borstal should be at least a year. In 1908 Parliament passed legislation authorizing the system along the lines that Ruggles-Brise recommended (Ruggles-Brise 1921).

The Borstal system proceeded on this plan until 1921, when the remarkable personality of Alexander Patterson was added to the Prison Commission. He was one of a kind. The son of an affluent family, he attended a public school and went on to Oxford University like hundreds of others headed for conventional careers in the civil service or politics. At the age of twenty-one, he graduated from Oxford and settled in Bermondsey, one of London's worst slums, as a member of the staff of the Oxford Medical Mission. He lived in Bermondsey for twenty years, organizing boys' clubs and recruiting Oxford students to work with him and later, when he became a prison commissioner, to take on assignments in the Borstal system (Ruggles-Brise 1921).

Patterson's work in the Borstal system was notable for at least four achievements. First, as much as possible, he removed the appearances and the procedures of the British prisons from the Borstals. The governor was still called "the governor," but the assistant governors served the role of housemasters in an English public school. The prison officers were taken out of uniform, and so were the lads, who were allowed to wear civilian clothes instead of the convict's demeaning uniform (Ruggles-Brise 1921).

Second, having removed as many of the earmarks of prison as he could, he went on to bring in young university men to fill the posts of governors and housemasters. To induce scions of the upper and middle classes to choose a career in penology was an astonishing innovation. As in the United States, prison work in England did not enjoy even modest occupational prestige. Patterson's peculiar magnetism changed that. The governor of one of the largest prisons in England explained how he was recruited.

He had worked in Patterson's settlement house in Bermondsey during a university vacation. Shortly after his return to Oxford, he heard a knock on the door of his college room, and there was Patterson. He said, "I need you as a housemaster at a new Borstal. I want you to report to my office in London next Monday." The startled young student protested that he was only in his second year at Oxford but perhaps could come during the next vacation. "That's not soon enough," Patterson replied. "I need you full time, beginning next Monday." To the mystification of the college authorities and the dismay of his parents, he left Oxford, reported the following Monday, and continued in the Borstal system and later in the Prison Commission for the succeeding forty years (Ruggles-Brise 1921).

Patterson's third innovation was a training program for prison and Borstal staff at Wakefield in the north of England. For years there had been much discussion of whether training of prison staff was needed, and, if so, exactly what training was required. The prison staff college was opened in 1935 to train likely candidates for promotion—not a popular new departure among prison officers accustomed to promotion by seniority. Eventually, the training program was expanded to include a six-week curriculum for all new recruits for prisons and Borstals and a six-month course for new assistant governors and housemasters. It was still the time of the British Empire, and colonial prison personnel were invited to attend and did (Ruggles-Brise 1921).

Patterson's fourth and surely his most significant contribution was the Borstal mystique. He had a flair for aphorisms: "You cannot train a man for freedom in conditions of captivity." He added:

> The Borstal System has no merit apart from the Borstal staff. It is men, and not buildings who will change the hearts and ways of misguided lads. Better an institution that consists of two log huts in swamp or desert, with a staff devoted to their task, than a model block of buildings . . . whose staff is solely concerned with thoughts of pay and promotion (Ruggles-Brise 1921).

This managerial style of leadership is built around a charismatic personality, who is able to engage staff, develop humane principles, and normalize what takes place within the Borstal setting. Seeing himself as a reformer and with absolute commitment to his vision of what a Borstal should be, Patterson was able to transform how delinquent juveniles in England were handled and, in turn, influenced the development of juvenile corrections in the United States.

Organizational Goals and How They Affected Institutional Life in Michigan

Some believe that the role of the manager is to develop organizational goals to accompany the institution's mission. In one of the most important studies of juvenile corrections, Street, Vinter, and Perrow (1996) identified the organizational goals of obedience/conformity, reeducation/development, and treatment in the management of several private and public training schools in Michigan. They found that staff in obedience/conformity institutions kept residents under surveillance, emphasized rules, reacted punitively, and did not become involved with them. Staff members in reeducation/development institutions, in contrast, demanded conformity, hard work, and intellectual growth, but they were more willing to reward positive behavior and to develop relationships with residents. Staff members in treatment institutions were the most involved with residents since they interacted more with them and also put more energy into working with their problems (Street, Vinter, and Perrow 1966).

In sum, while no recent studies of organizational goals and institutional mission are available, there is strong support for the belief that the organizational goal affects what takes place for both residents and staff in the institutional context.

Reform of Juvenile Corrections in Massachusetts

From 1969 to 1973, Dr. Jerome Miller was head of the Massachusetts Department of Youth Services. Miller closed the reform schools in Massachusetts and replaced them with a few small, secure units and a diverse array of community-based services. He describes the resulting antics and heroics of state house politicians and agency employees. He warns of the domination of human problem solving by either helping professionals or "pork barrel" elected officials (Lindgren 1992).

Miller describes the Massachusetts Juvenile Corrections System that he found and chronicles the Kafkaesque routines of "rabble management" and the too-frequent accompanying indecencies and violence heaped on the captives who were supposedly there to be helped. His book is replete with accurate accounts of a youth's life under a repressive regime:

> Talking seemed like a deviant act, and the silence overwhelmed my puny stabs at civility. . . . the dilemma of the institution. It must handle all inmates alike. It was demeaning ritual: an exercise in symbolic castration with no resolution. It was an unwritten rule . . . the chasers would beat the runners when caught. In return they were given favors which ranged from extra cigarettes to consideration for parole. The difficulty of getting any humane response from government bureaucracies increases exponentially when, in addition to being poor, the client is delinquent or criminal (Miller 1991).

Miller creatively and courageously acted to change these realities. He described and implemented several principles:

1. Reform the "deep end" first. Eliminate large rural institutions and replace them with smaller urban-based alternatives for the "worst kids." If the "least-deserving" youth are treated with fairness and decency, the rest of the system will follow.

2. Ensure that the funds follow the youth to the community, otherwise the alternatives to institutions will become supplements, only increasing costs and capacity and unnecessarily isolating more youth.

3. Stay personally connected to the youth. Seek to understand and respect the uniqueness of each person and his or her life story. Fuller understanding will lead to responses that are more humane.

4. Develop a diversity of alternative responses to youth misbehavior, and a meaningful and dynamic process for matching youth and programs. Allow each youth to influence the choice of programs. Negotiate and renegotiate the options.

5. Delinquents are powerful resources for reform propaganda. Encourage youth to come and go in administrative offices. Administrators must constantly return to bedrooms, dormitories, and cells, and constantly put their charges before the press, the politicians, and the public to complete the picture and demonstrate that delinquent youth are more, much more, than their worst actions.

6. Seize the moment. True reform is much more a matter of messy increments through risk taking, creative fund management, and manipulation of personnel rules and staff appointments than master planning and smooth administration.

7. Build broad coalitions. Seek support from not only the usual child advocacy and justice reform groups, but also rely heavily on groups such as the League of Women Voters. Accept all invitations from service clubs, civic and professional groups, churches, schools, and the media (Lindgren 1992).

It is now more than four decades since Miller concluded that his days were numbered in Massachusetts and submitted his resignation. Was he successful? Did the reforms hold? Are the juveniles better off? Are the people of Massachusetts safer because of his reforms? What have other state officials learned from the "Massachusetts Experiment"? Miller repeats several times that he was neither a competent nor an effective manager. One must conclude, however, that given the obstacles, he was one of the most, if not the most, successful inside reformers of American juvenile corrections. Yet, Miller's accomplishments are not the types of successes that appeal to most public administrators. At the end of his tenure, he was about to lose his job. The leading practitioner organizations have never formally recognized his accomplishments. To the contrary, the National Conference of Superintendents of Training Schools and Reformatories formally censured him by a vote of 58 to 2 (Lindgren 1992).

Styles of Management:
A Thirty-Year Study of a Maximum-Security Training School in Ohio

Miller, Bartollas, and Dinitz's unpublished 1989 follow-up study of the 1976 *Juvenile Victimization* book traced the management styles used by superintendents at Training Institution Central Ohio from its establishment over a thirty year period. Superintendents at the Training Institution Central Ohio have varied from those who were enormously popular with staff to those who were widely despised.

Other than one who held the position for seven years, they usually held their jobs for around two years. Most were dismissed, usually for excessive runaways, but two are continually identified by staff as "the best we ever had." Although some administrators prided themselves on getting to know residents, few residents typically had much contact with them. In examining the various superintendents who were appointed by the governor to manage what has always been regarded as a tough institution, three fundamentally different management styles emerged. Each management style had wide influence on staff morale, on the degree of institutional control, and on the emphasis placed on rehabilitative programming (Bartollas, Miller, and Dinitz 2007).

The three management styles that surfaced in interviewing staff, some of whom have been Training Institution Central Ohio employees since the institution was established in 1961, were charismatic, bureaucratic, and technocratic. Charismatic managers depend upon the force and the credibility of their personality to effect organizational change and decision-making. Bureaucratic managers rely on procedures, directives, and departmental supervision to maintain organizational processing and to expedite decision-making. Technocratic managers, on the other hand, use managerial principles, accreditation, computer technology, and internal and external security hardware to effect institutional efficiency and accountability.

An examination of Training Institution Central Ohio superintendents suggests that these management styles can be further divided into five categories: (1) charismatic control, (2) charismatic reform, (3) bureaucratic control, (4) bureaucratic reform, and (5) technocratic control. We will discuss each of these.

Charismatic Control. The two most popular superintendents in the history of the Training Institution Central Ohio were managers whose style of leadership could be characterized as "charismatic control." Both administrators communicated, in somewhat different ways, their message, "I'm the Man, and I'm in control." One of these administrators quickly gained the respect of staff by being a good communicator, by giving them responsibility, and by expecting them to be accountable. He held frequent staff meetings and, with the force of his personality, had remarkable skill in motivating and controlling staff. Part of his control strategy was to incorporate the military model, which he had used at the Fairfield School for Boys. Residents marched everywhere, received short military-style haircuts, and wore grey uniforms and black shoes. However, the key to his control philosophy was to place responsibility for control on staff and to hold them accountable for cottage problems. The latent danger in this approach was realized with the widespread use of physical force for misbehaving youths.

Charismatic Reform. The third well-respected superintendent in the history of the Training Institution Central Ohio pursued a different type of leadership style. Becoming superintendent in 1978, he also had a charismatic personality and was able to motivate many staff to follow him. Staff characterized his administration by saying, "one of the nicest guys in the world," "he couldn't say no to anybody," and "it was really a great place to work in those days under him." Yet, his reform emphasis ultimately alienated many staff because of its inability to control residents and eventually led to his termination because of the high numbers of institutional runaways.

His ideology of reform and the freedom it permitted, especially in youths going off campus, generated far too many runaways. He believed that if projects were created that residents looked forward to doing, they would behave themselves so that they would be able to be involved in these projects. His method of control, then, was based on a reward system for residents.

Bureaucratic Control. Two superintendents used a bureaucratic style of management. Although neither was well-liked, one particularly generated negative feelings from all levels of staff. One became superintendent in 1970 and resigned in 1972. His administration was characterized by three features, none of which endeared him to line staff. First, they viewed him as weak and insecure, which was heightened by the realization among supervisory staff that he was afraid to or did not have the authority to make decisions on his own.

Second, African-American staff felt that the superintendent did not respect them. Some staff members even blamed the formation of the union among line staff at this time on the fact that staff felt they needed protection from the superintendent.

Third, many youth leaders believed that the superintendent would take the words of residents over their own. Although there was little evidence to support this assertion, it was widespread and contributed to the staff's loss of support and loyalty. What partly may explain this view is the director of guidance during this time was extremely permissive toward residents, and the superintendent was blamed for sanctioning this permissiveness.

However, the negative feelings of staff at their most intense point toward this superintendent did not begin to match the antagonism they felt for the other bureaucratic one. She, of course, started out with a big strike against her; she was the first female superintendent. Nearly all of the staff agreed that there was no way a female could run the institution, and most staff also shared the belief that they were not going to take orders from a female.

She emphasized paperwork more than previous administrators had done. Staff soon felt overwhelmed by what they regarded as an avalanche of paperwork. Everything had to be documented, and rules and procedures were developed and applied to more areas of institutional life. The skyrocketing population of the institution was even more unbearable. Staff, including social workers, felt that they no longer had time to work with residents because of the amount of paperwork they were required to do.

A fair assessment of her administration was that the superintendent and staff took each other on. She did not trust staff, centralized all authority through her, and was quick to administer discipline. Staff, in turn, did not like or respect her. They generally felt that she was arrogant, unreasonable, punitive, and went out of their way to confront her. A number of staff walked off the job, because they believed that they were being treated unfairly, and because they were required to work single coverage in a cottage. According to one staff, she "fired at least thirty people for walking off the job. They brought the staff from over at Buckeye Ranch to work here." Incidentally, they all received their jobs back six or seven months later when they successfully appealed through the civil service review process.

Bureaucratic Reform. One superintendent best exemplifies the "bureaucratic reform" style of leadership. He advocated reform because he believed in humane treatment of residents and virtually outlawed physical force unless it took place for self-defense or protection of another staff member. He combined the cottage life and guidance department, which gave treatment a much more dominant role than it had with previous administrators. He also established other restrictions on how staff would deal with residents, started the pre-release program, did away with the marching that had previously characterized the movement of residents from one area to another, and implemented a no-smoking policy among residents.

His bureaucratic role was expressed in his tendency to stand behind rules and procedures rather than the force of his personality. He was a very small person, and some felt that his size did not prepare him to deal with staff. Although he moved around the institution a lot, he appeared to be more concerned with cleanliness rather than staff interactions. For example, one security supervisor noted, "He was around the institution a whole lot, but he was always picking up cigarette butts and pieces of paper. He put signs and posters up every place."

He clearly was not comfortable at the Training Institution Central Ohio, nor were staff comfortable with him. When this superintendent came to the Training Institution Central Ohio, he found a dedicated staff who were used to working under a hard-nosed and control-oriented administrator. The reduced control over residents, the increased problems with AWOLS, and his greater reliance on rules and restrictions all contributed to reduce the morale and engagement of staff.

Technocratic Control. A previous youth leader in the institution was appointed superintendent in 1986 much to the surprise of institutional staff. He was not respected, liked by his peers, or valued by supervisors. Staff had grave concerns about his competence and integrity. The superintendent, in turn, quickly responded to what he perceived as lack of loyalty by becoming reactive and punitive in his treatment of staff and, as a result, became known as "the write-up superintendent." One senior staff member expressed it this way, "He's punitive. He always goes for the throat. He wants to put you on the streets for six months to a year. He's not a fair person."

On top of their questions about him was the reality that the facility was totally out of control. Staff felt beaten down and did not see how control and order could be restored. Furthermore, the pending retirement of several key "old-timers," as well as the recent resignation of other staff, left the institution in a potential leadership crisis.

What appeared to be a continual problem with crisis-centered management—so typical of large maximum-security adult prisons—suddenly shifted into a technocratic model of correctional administration. Several events contributed to this change from crisis-centered management to what can be considered an efficiency model of correctional administration.

Administrators had various security hardware installed. This provided greater control over residents and security for staff. The razor-wire fence had been built shortly before he became superintendent, and this fence, which resembled that in a medium-security adult prison, made the Training Institution Central Ohio a much more difficult place from which to escape. In addition, as a result of a savage attack on the institution's nurse, each staffer with direct contact with residents received a "man-down" monitor. Staff in trouble could set off these monitors or they would be set off if a staff member fell or was thrown to the ground. Plans were also developed to implement a closed-circuit TV system to observe the movement of residents throughout the facility and to install a much better equipped control center. Finally, new systems for moving residents from cottages to dining, school, and recreational areas were started.

This technocratic model of correctional administration emphasizes efficiency, perceives administrators as professional mangers, is strongly committed to accountability and responsibility, develops rules that are regarded as sacrosanct, and is concerned with the overall order of institutional operations. It places little value on correctional reform, or rehabilitative philosophy and, instead, contends that if reform is not feasible, then it is at least possible to create a clean environment.

There have been essentially three approaches to correctional administrations at the Training Institution Central Ohio—the "shake-up" model, the "fix-it" model, and the "efficiency" model. Superintendents who were either charismatic-control or bureaucratic-control leaders followed a "shake-up" model, in that they attempted to bring order to the disorder they perceived. They began by shaking up the disorder, but their end objective was residents' predictability, consistency of operations, and institutional calm.

"The fix-it" model was advocated by charismatic-reform and bureaucratic-reform leaders who wanted to realize positive benefits to a resident's life. The purpose of confinement, according to these reform proponents, represented the acceptance of a rehabilitative agenda.

Finally, the "efficiency" model, a new approach to administering adult prisons, was partially implemented at the Training Institution Central Ohio prior to and during the process of this follow-up study. The technocratic model based on efficiency is concerned that everything has to look right, that rules and procedures are followed, that the institution is secure, and that power is decentralized into smaller units.

Establishment of Unit Four—A Model Cottage in an Arizona Training School

M. A. Bortner and Linda M. Williams examined a model program in a training school, initiated in response to a class-action lawsuit against Arizona's juvenile correctional system. This reform effort brought a new vision of institutional care for juveniles. It insisted that only youths who represented a threat to public safety or those for whom alternative efforts had failed would be included. It also emphasized accountability and guidance for youth, including providing them with essential skills for survival in society (Bortner and Williams 1997: 176).

The program prioritized rehabilitative change and successful reintegration into society. As a result, coercive methods were replaced by an atmosphere in which residents were afforded dignity and respect. Instead of "doing something for" residents, as many treatment efforts attempt to do, or of "doing something to them" in the name of punishment, this change effort intended to provide opportunities and skills so that residents could do something for themselves and the community. It offered much to residents—"respect, skills, new chances. It also required much of them—respect for others, genuine efforts to understand themselves and others, and a commitment to change" (Bortner and Williams 1997:177).

The program generated great enthusiasm from residents, staff members, and administrators during its first six months of operation, and there were many encouraging signs that it was having a positive effect on residents. However, it was not long before this reform effort began to decline and its demise took place by the end of the second year of operation. Many factors contributed to the demise of this program. The youths' educational needs were not fully addressed; the treatment services were not delivered as planned; security staff resisted them; and inadequate and uneven training of staff damaged the delivery of services. Also, staff had a widespread perception that the promised working conditions did not improve for them; and that the central administration's support for the program was often inconsistent and inadequate (Bortner and Williams 1987: 93-135).

On the individual level, youths' commitments to drug use and trafficking, as well as gang membership, ultimately circumvented any real commitment to a positive peer culture. On the political level, the strong need for punishment of both youthful and adult offenders resulted in reduced resources being allotted to this pilot program. On the institutional level, staff were not adequately trained. They were not engaged in the program and did not receive sufficient rewards to continue their commitment to this reform effort.

Despite all of these examples of management-pursued reform, the hoped-for outcome within juvenile residential facilities was no easy matter. In Feature 3.1, Jay Lindgren provides some of the difficulties of bringing meaningful change to juvenile residential facilities or an entire juvenile correctional system.

Feature 3.1 Reflections on a Career in Juvenile Correctional Service

By Jay Lindgren

My forty-year career as correctional-human-service practitioner-bureaucrat has been variously enlightening, disheartening, and inspiring. My full-time assignments for the first half of what is turning out to be an incredible journey were in my native Minnesota. My career began in 1967 at a remote state youth facility where my staff and I worked hard to counteract the anti-therapeutic culture that often arises in large isolated institutions.

I left that institution to develop and direct community-based, not-for-profit residential programs for adult and juvenile offenders where I learned the importance of natural relationships and accessible locality as contexts for pro-social change. In that position, I learned that the majority of even the "worst offenders" had incredible strengths but that the process of bridging the gap between incarcerated youth and their distant natural supports faced very difficult bureaucratic and cultural barriers. That innovation for chronic and violent juvenile offenders also suffered from the common obstacles confronting grant-funded projects. We thrived under a progressive commissioner whose more traditional successor declined to seek sustaining funds for activities that fit neither in the institution nor community service bureaucratic divisions.

I then accepted a second state corrections position at the central office where I approved juvenile institution treatment plans, releases, and revocations, and represented the commissioner on youth policy matters. From this position I was able to observe and often influence the bridging of fragmented services and supports for youth offenders. *Continued on page 41*

In 1988, I accepted an invitation from Ron Jackson, the Texas Youth Commission Executive Director, to serve as his deputy where our dedicated staff worked to realize the final requirements of the landmark *Morales v. Thurman* final federal consent decree. After hearing Allen Breed, one of the overseers for the federal court, hail our reforms in the early 1990s as a "renaissance" and Federal District Judge William Wayne Justice subsequently applaud Jackson's achievements as extraordinary, I have been disheartened to read recent newspaper accounts of youth and staff injuries and allegations of abuse and cover-up within the Texas Youth Commission.

In 1994, it appeared to me that then Governor George Bush and the Texas Legislature were fundamentally undermining the reforms of the 1980s and early 1990s as they mandated the Youth Commission to rely on remote mega-institutions unsuited for the habitation of youth. As a result, in 1995, I left the Texas Youth Commission and accepted an offer from Governor Lincoln Almond to direct the Rhode Island Department of Children, Youth and Families—the scandal riddled state agency responsible for child protection and mental health, and youth detention, probation, and corrections.

In the spring of 2005, the new Governor, Donald L. Carcieri, replaced me. I did not dispute the governor's need to have a person that he could trust and would fully support him in that persistently controversial chair. I was, however, deeply disappointed to leave when the youth correctional system appeared to be at the brink of the fundamental reforms that had eluded us for nearly a decade. I worried too that this governor, much like our President, saw many of my fellow public servants and me as problems to be conquered or ignored rather than professionals to be heeded and led.

In addition to my full-time positions in three states, I was a participant observer of reforms in two others jurisdictions. While still working in Minnesota, I had the good fortune to consult with Ellen Schall and her management team as they led substantial reforms within the New York City Department of Juvenile Justice. I also began visiting Massachusetts in the early 1970s at the peak of Jerome G. Miller's led reforms. I subsequently followed the published studies of these reforms and revisited Massachusetts several times during the 1980s and 1990s.

Through the lens of my direct experiences in these multiple and diverse bureaucracies, I have learned that fundamental and sustained reforms are difficult to achieve. As I look back and observe present day crises and opportunities, I believe Jerome Miller remains a wise force with whom all correctional leaders should contend. In Massachusetts, Miller was a rebel with a cause. His autobiography of that period remains essential reading for anyone concerned with public policy toward those who violate our laws.

At the time Miller wrote his book, I concluded that his view of American juvenile corrections administration was overly pessimistic and narrow. For example, he lamented that some of his Massachusetts reforms were weakened in favor of smooth management. Miller is correct over time: if constant vigilance with ability to act is lacking, there will be deterioration within even the small secure and privately run non-secure programs, much as there is in the larger institutions. However, in criticizing smooth management, Miller appeared to ignore what was happening to management theory and practice across the country. Organizational development experts such as Edward Deming, Peter Drucker, Peter Senge, Russell Ackoff, and Tom Peters conceptualized and taught many of the principles described and practiced by Miller. Companies such as Xerox and Ford had effectively applied these principles in corporate America.

Continued on page 42

Feature 3.1   Reflections on a Career in Juvenile Correctional Service, *continued*

There are many styles of effective leadership. Perhaps that is why Miller disregarded the accomplishments of his successors and many of his colleagues in other states and why professional organizations have been hostile or indifferent to Miller's accomplishments. The metaphor offered to me by the Wharton School's Tom Gilmore is illuminating. Gilmore points to the two extreme running events in track: the dash and the marathon. Many career bureaucrats are marathon runners and see reformers as superficial and quixotic in their stance and, in the long-run irresponsible. Impatient reformers like Miller, however, see the marathon runners as foot-dragging and resistant.

Those who strive to lead quality organizations need Miller's principles and courage. They must also lead those who are in for the duration. Much of what has happened within the practice of management in this country recognizes that quality services require constant vigilance, rigorous measurement and systematic feedback of outcomes, continuous improvement and open responsive connections with consumers. In addition, lasting reform requires that staff and key stakeholders from the juvenile court and legislatures are brought along. This Miller failed to do, a particularly serious flaw in an organization with police power over its customers.

Source: E-mail sent to the authors in 2007 and used with permission.

NORMALIZING ENVIRONMENT

The 1994 Juvenile Justice and Delinquency Prevention Act (JJDPA) and its various amendments emphasized the need for smaller community-based programs and facilities, which would provide residents with homelike environments (JJDPA 1974).

Table 3.1 Design Elements of Homelike and Institutional Facilities

Homelike Design Elements	Institutional Design Elements
	Larger rooms
Wood doors	More doors—often steel
Wood doorways	
Wallpapered walls	Rough textured walls (brick, block)
Painted wall board	
Stained wood paneling	
Carpeted floors	Brick, tile, vinyl floors
Art work on walls	
Personal items	Metal receptacles, toilets, lavatories
More living room light fixtures	Fewer lighting fixtures
	Fluorescent lighting
	More fire alarms

Source: Patrick M. Sullivan. 2010. *Creating Treatment Environments for Troubled Youth: Evidence-Based Design.* Alexandria, Virginia: American Correctional Association.

The characterization of homelike may be difficult to define; yet, the description of a setting that provides a safe environment, personal space, and the symbols that describe family relationships, values, and heritage is a good start. Clearly, homelike does not represent block grey walls with small "slit" windows (Sullivan 2010). Table 3.1 summarizes some of the design elements which are related with homelike and institutional facilities.

According to Patrick Sullivan, FAIA, an architect who has designed many innovative juvenile facilities, homelike has several characteristics.

- **Privacy:** Privacy has meaning, as the opposite of being public. Teens need some opportunity to have personal space and solitude.

- **Choice:** Some choices are necessary. The number of these choices can increase for individuals demonstrating responsible behavior. There may be choices in items such as food, free time, and related activities.

- **Territory:** A homelike environment ensures safety and protection from predatory peers.

- **Quiet Places:** The noise in some environments can be so stressful that it keeps both staff and residents from dealing with anything but their lowest-level needs. This noise can be a constant annoyance. The design of the building can do much to reduce the noise and confusion of the environment (Sullivan 2010).

RECOMMENDATIONS FOR JUVENILE FACILITY MANAGEMENT

The few studies that are available do not reveal how to manage a juvenile residential facility humanely and effectively. Given the widespread criticism of juvenile residential facilities, it is clear that publications are needed to provide guidance to administrators of these facilities. Indeed, the purpose of this publication is to fill such a void in the literature.

We provide a number of recommendations for institutional leadership. These recommendations are intended to be broad strokes. Obviously, much has to be done to implement these managerial goals and objectives in institutional life. The remaining chapters of this book will focus on the implementation of these recommendations.

- **Pursue excellence in the facility.** Successful administrators set high standards. They not only expect excellence, they demand it. They reward good performance but do not condone mediocrity. They have little tolerance for error, poor judgment, or inefficiency. They have no tolerance for abuse of youngsters under their care. This pursuit of excellence is found in everything that takes place in the institution.

- **A meaningful institutional program requires a carefully thought-out plan of action or strategy.** Administrators must determine where they want to go (their vision) and understand how it is possible to get there (implementing the vision).

- **Management should be proactive.** Proactive management begins with control. Without control of the institution, nothing positive can be accomplished. An anticipatory and preventative approach is fundamental to maintaining institutional control. A proactive approach requires seeing emerging trends and issues that should be addressed early. This approach does not permit problems to simmer any longer than necessary. Yet, this approach further requires the ability to distinguish those issues that are ephemeral, and to avoid acting precipitously. Clear and effective communication is a requirement for proactive leadership. This means that both staff and residents clearly understand what the rules are, what is expected, and what the consequences of unacceptable behavior would be. Staff must clearly understand the importance of being accountable, paying attention to detail, and following the schedule.

- **Professionalism should be held up as a goal to all staff.** Staff development and training are important steps in staff seeing themselves as professionals.

- **Cleanliness and orderliness of the facility are absolute necessities.** Cleanliness shows that the staff are in control.

- **The institutional environment must be safe for youths and staff.** If an institution is not a safe environment, little positive can be accomplished.

- **Both residents and staff must be treated with dignity and respect.** The norm for staff is that they treat residents as they would want their own sons or daughters to be treated.

- **Good programming by committed staff must be available for those youths who want to make positive changes in their lives.** Treatment programs must be delivered effectively to those interested residents, especially those with addictions and anger management.

- **Effective systems of accountability for both staff and youths are necessary.** Sufficient consequences are required for inappropriate behavior, especially when rules are broken.

- **The services that are promised must be delivered to youths when they are scheduled to be delivered.** It is important that the system is predictable and can be trusted to do what was promised.

- **The quality of life within the facility must include both internal and external control; the absence of this control within the facility will destroy the program.**

- **Facilities, as much as possible, should have the following characteristics:**

  - They are as close as possible to juveniles' families.
  - They are smaller with personalized services.
  - They are family friendly.
  - They are managed in a caring manner.

- **The administrator's task is to always strive to attain a normalizing, or a homelike, environment.**

- **Staff must be rewarded for positive contributions to the program, including giving them raises, recognition, and promotion.**

- **The administrator must be a model of integrity in every way, both inside and outside the facility.**

- **Accreditation is an important process in a juvenile residential facility offering humane confinement and mission effectiveness.** The accreditation program offered by the American Correctional Association (ACA) provides a benchmark for institutional administrators for what is effective and what needs to be improved.

STANDARDS AND ACCREDITATION

Standards can be seen as practices that have proven to be successful. They are not enforced by law but establish a background for the recommended operations of juvenile programs. They provide guidelines for the development of staffing plans, treatment programs, effective policies, and area requirements. Standards provide the basis for accreditation reviews in terms of the policies, procedures, and physical conditions of an agency's treatment program (Sullivan 2010).

In 1978, the American Correctional Association began a process of juvenile accreditation that currently includes 80 percent of all state departments of corrections and youth services as active participants. The ACA and the Commission on Accreditation for Corrections (CAC) are private, non-profit organizations that administer the only national accreditation programs for all components of juvenile corrections. The purpose of accreditation "is to promote improvement in the management of correctional agencies through the administration of a voluntary accreditation program and the ongoing development and revision of relevant, useful standards" (ACA 2009).

This publication strongly recommends juvenile residential facilities pursue the process of accreditation by the American Correctional Association. *The Performance-Based Standards for Juvenile Correctional Facilities* sets forth this accreditation in six aspects: (1) safety, (2) security, (3) justice and order, (4) care, (5) programs and services; and, (6) administration and management (2009). Among these standards are the following:

- Under safety, "juveniles, staff, and the public are protected from injury and illness caused by the physical environment."

- Under security, the facility uses a combination of supervision, inspection, accountability, and clearly defined polices and procedures in the use of security practices and equipment to promote safe and orderly operation.

- Under justice and order, the institution is to "maintain an orderly environment with clear expectations of behavior and systems of accountability that treat juveniles fairly and respect their legal rights" and "alleged rule violations, which may result in major sanctions including loss of liberty, are handled in a manner that provides juveniles with appropriate procedural safeguards. Juveniles comply with rules and regulations. There are rewards for positive behavior and sanctions for failure to comply with facility rules."

- Under care, several things occur: juveniles are served nutritious meals, they are provided a continuum of health and mental health services, and receive substance-abuse and chemical-dependency services.

- Under programs and services, juveniles must receive a screening and assessment at admission, and then be classified to the most appropriate level of programming, and receive these program services.

- Finally, under administration and management, the facility is required "to operate as a legal entity with well-developed goals, objectives, policies, and procedures" (American Correctional Association 2009).

These standards provide the minimum-level of care needed in juvenile correctional facilities in the United States. It is up to residential administrators to establish such standards as the benchmark of institutional care.

CONCLUSIONS

The first three chapters were designed to provide the background describing where juvenile facilities have been in the past, the profile of youngsters who are currently being sent to these facilities, and to examine management principles that have been previously used in juvenile institutions. This chapter further developed concepts of humane principles of institutional care and listed standards and recommendations for institutional management. This background will provide the context for the chapters to come, which include insights and suggestions on the institution's mission, staff development and training, the budget, specific forms of programming, and other aspects found in juvenile institutionalization.

REFERENCES

American Correctional Association. 2009. *Performance-Based Standards for Juvenile Correctional Facilities*. Alexandria, Virginia. American Correctional Association.

Bartollas, Clemens, Stuart J. Miller, and Simon Dinitz. 2007. "Managerial Styles and Institutional Control." *Youth Violence and Juvenile Justice* 5: 57-70.

Bortner, M. A. and M. Williams. 1997. *Youth in Prison: We the People of Unit Four*. New York: Routledge.

Caeti, T., J. C. Hemmens, F. T. Cullen, and V. S. Burton, Jr. 2003. Management of Juvenile Correctional Facilities. *The Prison Journal* 83: 383-405.

Cullen, F. T., E. Latessa, and V. S. Burton, Jr. 1993. Correctional Orientation of Prison Wardens: Is the Rehabilitative Ideal Supported? *Criminology*, 31: 69-92.

Lindgren, Jay. 1992. "Book Review: J. Miller, *The Last One Over the Wall: The Massachusetts Experiment in Closing Reform Schools*," In *Community Alternatives: International Journal of Family Care*. 4, 1: 161-166.

Miller, Jerome G. 1991. *The Last One Over the Wall: The Massachusetts Experiment in Closing Reform Schools*. Columbus, Ohio: The Ohio State University Press.

Ruggles-Brise, Sir. Evelyn. 1921. *The English Prison System*. London: Macmillan.

Street, D., R. D. Vinter, and C. Perrow. 1966. *Organization for Treatment: A Comparative Study of Institutions*. New York: Free Press.

Sullivan, Patrick M. 2010. *Creating Treatment Environments for Troubled Youth: Evidence-Based Design*. Alexandria, Virginia: American Correctional Association.

CHAPTER 4

WHY MISSION IS IMPORTANT

Education is often the gateway out of delinquency. The administrators should help staff provide guidance for consideration of post-secondary education as a way to open up opportunities.

The mission is the foundation of the juvenile residential correctional facility. It is important because it guides short- and long-term planning, operating budget and capital budget development, and overall priority setting. The mission drives what type of physical plant should be designed based on the resident's profile when creating a new facility or in modifying an existing facility. Facility location and the type of buffer required are predicated upon mission. Everyone's understanding and adhering to a clear mission will determine which staff the facility hires and how those staff work with committed youth.

Mission is the essential administrative tool for the development of a juvenile residential-treatment environment. Administrators use mission to inspire and motivate managers, clinicians, line staff, and other stakeholders. A mission statement, which is understood and accepted by stakeholders, can become the compass for the leader. It will help the administrator to sort through the seemingly endless and sometimes conflicting demands from stakeholders, to set priorities that are consistent with the purpose of the facility's existence. Whether it is implementing cost-saving measures or determining staffing or training needs, a well thought out mission will help leaders to ensure that their resources stay focused on what is important to their success. Mission statements cannot be left in a file cabinet. They need to be posted throughout the facility. The mission statement needs to be a part of everyday facility life.

The mission statement must define the institution's primary responsibilities to the community, the confined juveniles, and other major constituencies (Sullivan 2010). These responsibilities include:

- **Security:** Making certain that juveniles remain safe and secure until legally released

- **Safety:** Making certain that the staff, juveniles and visitors are not subjected to physical, emotional, or psychological abuse while in the facility

- **Service:** Providing more than minimum program opportunities in areas such as academic education, recreation, visiting, counseling and treatment, medical attention, and proper nutrition (Farbstein and Miller 1981).

How the mission statement defines security, safety, and service and their importance to the overall mission of the facility will vary from community to community and even from one type of residential setting to another. For example, a juvenile residential facility serving a delinquent population will vary somewhat in its mission statement from one serving non-criminal youths or status offenders. The security status of the facility can also affect its overall mission. A maximum-security juvenile correctional facility has different emphases in security than would a minimum-security juvenile facility.

Similarly, a coeducational facility, serving both female and male residents, has somewhat different emphases in aspects of its mission statement than would a unisex facility. When defining the terms of security, safety, and service, the American Correctional Association's *Performance-Based Standards for Juvenile Correctional Facilities* (2009) and the American Correctional Association's *Standards for Juvenile Detention Facilities*, 3rd edition (updated by the 2010 *Standards Supplement*) are invaluable resources for determining minimum program responsibilities.

Another way of conceptualizing security, safety, and service is that a well run, successful facility has a mission statement which includes the following elements:

- Provides for the satisfaction of stakeholders

- Provides for public safety by assuring custody and effecting proper behaviors of committed youth

- Provides for staff safety by structuring a safe, humane, living environment

- Provides for youth safety by structuring a safe, humane, living environment

- Provides treatment programming which directly addresses committed youths' social and psychological problems linked to illegal behaviors

PROVIDES FOR THE SATISFACTION OF STAKEHOLDERS

Juvenile residential correctional facility administrators must know their objective concerning the youth who are committed to the facility. Does the institution exist to restore the youth committed to law-abiding behavior? Does the institution exist to punish the youth? Is the primary purpose of the institution to stabilize behavior of disruptive youth? Is the sole purpose to keep the youth away from society? Is the institution expected to treat mental health conditions? What about the youth's educational needs? Must chemical abuse and dependency services be provided? Should resources be devoted to making or keeping connections with the youth's family or community?

Some community activists purport that all that is needed is to provide vocational development so that these youth can obtain employment. Some would advocate that just getting some religion in their life would solve their problems. All of these purposes can be legitimate and may have support from powerful stakeholders/constituents.

Administrators of both private and public facilities will be dealing with all of these and other, sometimes conflicting, expectations and demands. Without a clearly understood and accepted mission, these facility leaders become more vulnerable to the whims of all stakeholders, who have the political clout, the purse strings, or both to impose their priorities.

The stakeholders who do get involved and want a "say" in the type of care and services of delinquents in institutions is staggering. A partial list would include: correctional administrators (sometimes at the state level, sometimes at the local or county level), politicians (sometimes state and federal as well as local), victim advocate groups, religious groups, school districts, facility neighbors, parents, law enforcement officials, attorneys (both defense and prosecution), facility staff (possibly employee unions), state licensing agencies and, in the case of private facilities, stockholders, corporate board members, and the corporate chain of command.

Each of these groups can and do have different motivations, philosophies, directives, and "answers" for the leaders of juvenile residential correctional facilities. Attempting to satisfy each and every concerned, interested stakeholder is simply impossible. This is why having a mission statement that clearly states the overall purpose of the facility is critical to the success of the facility.

A mission statement, which is understood and accepted by stakeholders, can become the compass for the leader. It will help to sort through the seemingly endless and sometimes conflicting demands from stakeholders to set priorities, which are consistent with the purpose of the facility's existence. Whether it is implementing cost-saving measures or determining staffing or training needs, a well thought out mission will help leaders to ensure that their resources stay focused on what is important to their success.

There are many stakeholders in juvenile services today because the clients are children and adolescents (see Glick and Sturgeon 1998; 2001). Youth committed to facilities are as young as ten in some states and as old as twenty-six in other states. The stakeholders' interests are varied for many reasons, which include the seriousness of the crimes juveniles are committing and the debate surrounding adolescents' culpability. These stakeholders include staff, residents, the facility neighbors, victim advocacy groups, parents/guardians, public defenders, prosecutors, politicians, and the religious community. Stakeholders, therefore, can be at polar extremes in their expectation of facility administrators' responses to the challenges and rewards in working with delinquent youth.

It is not possible for an administrator to attend to and please every stakeholder. Yet, the administrator must decide who will get his/her direct attention and know how to prioritize responses to these demands. Unfortunately, administrators may be distracted with other very important priorities. Everyday life in a juvenile facility is not necessarily as neat and sequential as planned.

Priorities, as well as the attention that administrators give them, will vary depending on the stakeholders and their issues. What needs to be constant is the method the facility administrators take to prioritize, make decisions, and how they train their staff in ways to carry out their duties to achieve their institutional mission.

Finally, administrators should not expect that all the stakeholders will support their vision and mission. They should not expect that all of their stakeholders will add value or be involved, but they are important. Administrators must know that their vision and mission is the facility's compass for making daily operating decisions and a way to receive the majority of stakeholders' support even in hard times.

PROVIDES FOR PUBLIC SAFETY

If a juvenile residential facility is going to be viable, public safety has to be the number one priority. Public safety is achieved primarily through assuring custody of committed youth. Nothing will ensure loss of public support and funding as quickly as a high number of escapes. (Some facilities term escapes as "runs" or "absent without leave" or "failure to return.") Even one youth who eludes custody and commits a high profile crime in the community can have dire consequences for a facility.

A well known, successful private nonprofit facility in a large midwestern city was shut down due to public outcry over one resident running from the facility and assaulting a woman. In that case, although the program had well qualified and trained staff and utilized accepted and successful intervention/treatment strategies, it operated with only minimal attention paid to security. The doors to the facility were unlocked. There were no fences. Taking "headcounts" to ensure all residents were accounted for was not a routine practice. This was a facility that had extremely low recidivism rates for its program graduates and was referred to in national publications as a "model program."

This one escape incident, however, was enough to motivate concerned neighbors to organize and protest the very existence of the facility. The program's lack of security to assure public safety was highlighted by the news media. Within weeks, this program went from a model of humane, effective treatment to being labeled a public menace. Within two months of the incident, the facility was closed by local authorities over some technicality.

How this goal of public safety is achieved is just as important to success as the fact that it is a priority. Many facilities have been closed, sued, or come under federal control because they worked to achieve public safety while ignoring staff safety, youth safety, and youth rehabilitation. These are programs that have attempted to assure custody primarily through the use of authoritarian controls and "hardware" (security fences, cameras, mechanical restraints) without adequate attention paid to the other three components of a good mission.

A facility in a large eastern city was recently closed because of overemphasizing security while ignoring sound rehabilitation principles. This was a long-term (more than a two-year average commitment) program located in a secure juvenile detention center. Residents of the program had very little freedom, as nearly every minute of their day was dictated by a staff-generated, individualized daily schedule. After operating for more than two years, their first resident completed the program's requirements and was ready to graduate. This youth was the "star" of their program. He followed all of the rules and was utilized as "junior staff," with duties such as orientating new admissions to the program and helping other residents with assignments. He was spotlighted as a role model for successfully completing the program.

One week after discharge to his home community, he was arrested for, and later convicted of, a serious felony assault. The local corrections and criminal justice officials, who were founders of the program, were concerned enough to request assistance from the U.S. Office of Juvenile Justice and Delinquency Prevention. The subsequent investigation concluded, among other things, that so much emphasis was placed on security and compliance to rules that staff virtually ignored signs that this youth was still very dangerous. In fact, rehabilitation of the youth in the facility was not being accomplished. This investigation concluded that ignoring rehabilitation will, in the long run, compromise public safety.

The fact is that when facilities focus only on authoritarian control and compliance to rules and do not allow residents an opportunity to make decisions on their own, youth are robbed of a chance to learn from their mistakes. They are robbed of a chance to practice more socially acceptable behaviors. Internal change, including rehabilitation, does not occur.

Facilities that are experiencing a problem with escapes could learn from a large midwestern institution that reduced escapes from 130 a year to 5 a year. The reduction was attributed as much to enriching programming and emphasizing the importance of staff role modeling as it was to enhancing security procedures. Solid rehabilitative efforts enhance security and thus public safety.

PROVIDES FOR STAFF SAFETY

Staff safety is important to the success of any juvenile facility. It would be difficult, if not impossible, to find a juvenile facility administrator who would not include staff safety as a critical goal of the facility. Most facilities, therefore, include staff safety as a part of their mission. Administrators need to know that this goal can be met without compromising the other elements of the facility's mission statement (public safety, youth safety, and youth rehabilitation). Administrators should be aware that achieving staff safety while maintaining rehabilitation goals is critical to the facility's ultimate success.

Even with this knowledge, achieving staff safety has become more difficult in recent years partly because of the nature of the youth entering the facilities. Youth, as related in the profile of Chapter 2, tend to be more impulsive and prone to violence. They have histories of abuse at home and react to authority and authority figures with anger, intimidation, and violence. Other factors—such as chemical abuse, mental illness, and gang involvement—all increase the risk of staff being harmed.

Nearly all juvenile facilities have, therefore, developed policies, procedures, and safety training to minimize staff injuries. Most have designed their physical plant to support this goal. Motion detectors, alarms, cameras, "time out" rooms or segregation rooms, and locked doors are some of the physical tools employed. They have armed their staff with "hardware," such as radios, pepper spray, mechanical restraints, body-fluid protection gear (masks, gloves, spit hoods) and even "riot" gear. Even with the tools of a supportive physical plant, safety policies, and safety training, many facilities are still dangerous and frightening.

In 2001, at a large for profit juvenile correctional facility in the eastern United States, the director brought all of his supervisory staff together for an "emergency meeting" due to the increasingly numerous and serious staff injuries. This was a newly built facility with a capacity of more than 200 residents. Millions of dollars had been invested in the latest, most sophisticated security systems. Before admitting their first delinquent, months were spent recruiting and training a well educated professional staff that in turn spent months designing what was to be the "state of the art" program for chronic, serious juvenile offenders. Now, just months after opening, the program felt like a powder keg. Fights among residents were occurring daily and both staff and residents were being hurt. Ambulance runs to the local hospital were becoming a common occurrence and during one week, staff injuries were so serious that three were admitted to the hospital.

At the supervisors' meeting, the director delivered an impassioned speech regarding what would be done to "take back the facility." He was not interested in any type of discussion or any ideas from his management team. He believed that the problem with the facility was that too much "treatment" was going on and that staff were being too "soft" with the juveniles living there. He, therefore, would be imposing some new rules that everyone would be expected to follow. Staff would support and enforce these new rules or leave the facility. There would be no questions. He likened the upcoming days in the facility as going into battle. He did not want any of his "generals" (the management team) directly involved with the residents because he would not take the chance of their being injured. The "troops" would be the sole enforcers of the new rules which were to be put into effect immediately.

A partial list of these rules was as follows: Residents were to always walk against the right side of any hallway when going anywhere. There would be absolutely no talking in any hallway. There would be no privileges or any type of recreation for any youth who questioned staff. Supervisors were to instruct their staff to "take kids down" (meaning physically restrain them) quickly when there was even the slightest sign of disagreement or agitation. Consequences were to be given with no discussion. Treatment groups were to be cancelled indefinitely because youth were using them to manipulate staff.

In the name of staff safety, there were other, equally draconian, rules implemented. Important treatment issues and even basic tenets of caring for youth respectfully were relegated to the scrap heap. This facility experienced the opposite of what the director intended as staff injuries increased rather than decreased. Youth, too, began experiencing more injuries. Within the next few months, as the state licensing agency began taking steps to close the facility, the corporate office made the decision to close the doors to new admissions and make arrangements with referral sources to place the remaining residents in alternate institutions.

Staff safety will not occur in a vacuum. Staff will not be working in a facility that is safe if they ignore the profile of the youth they are there to serve. On their own, youth being served by residential correctional facilities will not make the connection between their behavior and the consequences being imposed. In fact, most youth will grow more resistant to staff requests, if treated this way. These youth will be more likely to act out violently if they are scared, if they believe that staff do not care for them, or if they believe that they are being disrespected.

Current research into effective programs clearly indicates that staff who work to identify and build relationships with youth are going to achieve greater success in establishing an environment that is safe for both staff and residents. Institutions where staff are role modeling prosocial behavior and utilizing rewards, in conjunction with consequences, are less likely to experience the facility going out of control as the previous example demonstrated.

Successful institutions where staff are not only physically safe but feel safe are ones that frame staff safety in the context of rehabilitation, public safety, and youth safety. The goal of these facilities is not to just ensure that youth living there comply with the rules. The goal is to provide tools and motivation to youth so they will choose to behave in socially acceptable manners. Following the rules of the institution becomes a choice and following the rules of society upon release will be a decision that they will have practiced and found useful. As discussed in future chapters, the policies, procedures, hardware, and training provided to address staff safety need to be developed in the context of the overall mission.

PROVIDES FOR YOUTH SAFETY

Youth are hurt physically and emotionally in juvenile residential facilities. They are hurt by staff who lose their temper and overreact to threatening behavior or disrespectful language; staff who are not trained to respond appropriately to depression and suicidal ideation; and staff who simply wish to exploit them for their own gratification. Some staff sexually seduce youth, rape youth, beat youth, and kill youth (most times unintentionally).

There is also wide documentation that youths are hurt by other youth (see Chapter 2). These studies, as well as the experiences of those who work in juvenile facilities, offer the following lessons:

- Nearly all juveniles who are sent to institutions are victimized by peers in one way or another. Some youths are victimized part of the time in small ways; some youths are victimized part of the time in major ways, and some youths are chronic victims.

- Some youths find it difficult to protect themselves against stronger peers and may find themselves in situations in which they succumb to sexual exploitation.

- Chronic victims are more likely to be younger, white, from non-urban settings, and from less criminal backgrounds.

- Staff must do everything possible to avoid an exploitation matrix from developing in the institution where the strong victimize the weak. Part of this avoidance of an exploitation culture is the development of sufficient consequence to those who victimize others.

- Staff must also be expected to be aware and responsive to those who are likely to be victimized. Such norms as—"a man will take care of himself"—are totally unacceptable to a youth who has already made the decision that he cannot protect himself. Congress enacted The Prison Rape Elimination Act (PREA) to address the problem of sexual abuse of persons in custody of U.S. correctional institutions (including juvenile facilities). PREA mandates that staff do everything possible to protect the vulnerable.

- Placement in a dormitory makes a youth who feels defenseless even more vulnerable to victimization.

- Chronic victims must be observed carefully so that they do not attempt to hurt or kill themselves.

- Some staff can be remarkable treatment agents. They are dedicated to the task of providing a safe environment for residents. Even though exploitation is often a serious problem in the institution in which they work, these staff are almost uncanny in their ability to spot the residents who are likely targets for exploitation and to know what is needed to support these youths as they serve their time (Bartollas, Miller, and Dinitz 1976).

A facility will not be safe for youth until and unless facility administrators make youth safety a priority that will not be compromised. There should never be a reason for staff members to hurt one of the youth in their care. The youth's behavior or attitude, ignorance of the youth's mental health issues, or failure to know best practices cannot be an excuse for youth to come to harm. The first principle in working with these youth needs to be—if you as staff do nothing else, do no harm to the youth in your care.

While no institution can absolutely guarantee that youth will not be harmed, leaders of safe facilities have developed staff training, policies, and procedures which minimize harmful incidents. These leaders have scrutinized the physical plant and made necessary modifications to support resident safety. Table 5.1 summarizes some sound safety practices when supervising delinquent youth in a residential setting.

Table 5.1 Sound Safety and Poor Safety Practices

Sound Safety Practices

1. Complete formal risk assessments of all new admissions to ensure low- and high-risk admits are housed separately

2. Complete formal needs assessments to ensure suicidal admits are immediately programmed for safety and properly supervised

3. Staff authority is based on prosocial relationships with residents

4. Program uses a behavior management system rich in rewards to gain compliance

5. Staff are respectful in their interactions and interventions with residents

6. Staff are trained to recognize and immediately address any gang-related behavior

7. Isolation/room confinement is used very sparingly as a discipline

8. Staff use physical force only as a last resort to gain behavioral compliance

9. An ambitious program schedule is adhered to. Cancellation only occurs if there is an immediate safety issue

10. Residents who have complaints are listened to and healthy outlets are provided for formal resident grievances

Poor Safety Practices

1. Risk assessments either not completed or if completed are not used for housing/programming decisions

2. Need assessments are not completed, not completed in timely manner, or not used to address suicidal admits

3. Staff authority is based on power, intimidation, and force

4. Program uses punishment and consequences as their behavior management system

5. Staff interactions are usually demanding and demeaning

6. Staff ignore gang-related behavior either because they are afraid or they do not recognize it

7. Isolation from the other residents and staff is a major behavior management tool

8. Physical force and intimidation are the foundation of behavior compliance

9. Program cancellation is used routinely to punish and/or discipline residents who violate rules

10. Resident complaints are ignored or even punished as they are thought to reflect lack of respect for the staff

YOUTH REHABILITATION IS THE GOAL

Safety is the foundation of rehabilitation. If a facility is not safe and secure, no rehabilitation will occur. For rehabilitation to take place, administrators and the staff they hire must believe that the youth who have been admitted to the facility have the capacity to change. Successful facilities across the United States commonly employ the following components, always keeping in mind the profile of the youth they are serving: education; individual, group and family therapy; life skills training; physical health; work programs; recreational programs; and spiritual programs. We will discuss aftercare programming, a critical part of the mission of youth rehabilitation, in Chapter 6.

Educational/Academic Programming

It is widely known that youth who are released from long-term care and have not mastered the basic skills of reading, writing, and doing math, and have no vocational training are at greater risk to recidivate. Facilities that look at the academic school's curriculum, the teacher and teaching styles, along with class size and classroom behavior, are successful at accelerating student learning. Facilities that pay special attention to the communication and relationship between the academic school staff and the care and treatment staff form the base of a real learning environment.

Teachers with a license in a primary area—such as English, mathematics, and science—along with a special education license (dual licensure) will be kept prepared for teaching in residential settings. Youth in the facilities often have an identified educational handicap or mental health diagnosis. Selecting those teachers with a portfolio of teaching ideas and styles that match youth learning styles, and promote learning will minimize classroom behavior problems.

Curriculum should be broad and classes that challenge students should be available. Curriculum should also offer intense special education services in basic skills for youth that have been underserved for years. Many facilities focus only on vocational training and GED preparation, which places delinquent youth on a one-way track, sometimes limiting transition back to mainstream school. Facilities need to provide the educational services to "catch up," receive a GED, be exposed to vocational skill building but also to provide classes requiring rigor to challenge and make graduation and higher learning an option.

Limiting the class size ratio of teacher to youth to one to eight or no more than one to twelve is necessary for serving the profile of the youth in facilities. A less costly method of reducing the ratio of students to teachers is by adding teaching assistants to the classroom. Computer-assisted instruction, when used appropriately, could replace, enhance, and add choice to selective course work in facilities.

The academic school staff is a part of the facility's multidisciplinary team. Care and treatment staff should be engaged in the school each day. It should not be unusual to see these staff in classrooms, in the halls, and routinely sharing information. The reverse is also true; teachers should be expected to attend care and treatment team meetings in the facility's living units.

Life Skills

These classes ensure that upon release the youth are more likely to possess pro-social problem solving skills. Youth in good facilities are responsible for keeping their living areas clean, washing, ironing, providing food service, and doing outside yard work. Many maintenance skills are taught in practical arts and by matching youth with facility maintenance staff.

Youth develop capacities for job-seeking skills and learn general employment skills necessary to maintain a job. Life skills classes should include role-play, followed by practice either within the facility or in a work-release capacity to really build new life skills. Edward Latessa from the University of Cincinnati says: "What curriculums bring to a program is structure; it allows facilities to structure the interventions and activities around target behaviors, teach and model new skills, allowing the youth to practice with graduated difficulty, and reinforce the behavior" (Latessa's interview 2006).

One such curriculum in wide use across the United States is *Thinking for a Change.* It was developed for the National Institute of Corrections and can be obtained by contacting them at their web site, www.NICIC.org.

Individual and Group Work

Individual and group-work interventions are sometimes helpful to address criminal behaviors, chemical health, and mental health. Ideally these therapy components are delivered by facility staff, rather than through a contract with an outside agency. The content, timing, coordination, and communication between staff are always extremely difficult but even more so when needing to deal with an outside agency whose staff does not report to the facility administrator. It is also easier to get the right staff with the right education and experience when the recruitment and hiring is done by the facility itself. This component will be more thoroughly discussed in Chapter 6 on treatment.

Family Counseling and or Family Therapy

These interventions help build capacities for treatment both within the youth's institutional stay and for family systems upon the youth's release. There are many difficulties and barriers to prevent this from being done consistently, such as transportation and family members who themselves have mental health issues, chemical dependencies, and criminal lifestyles. An administrator must understand the critical importance of this component to long-term success and insist on seeing it implemented. See also Lemieux, *Offenders and Substance Abuse: Bringing the Family into Focus* (2009).

Physical Health

Nutrition and fitness, as well as health care such as immunizations, physicals, and dental examinations, hearing, and sight assessments, are all needed. Residential correctional facilities struggle to consistently provide these services because of high costs and the fact that these costs are not offset in any way by state or federal Medicare reimbursements. Federal and state laws disqualify "correctional" clients who are placed in a correctional facility from these payments.

Work Programs

Another way to enrich the youth's experiences is through real work experiences. These work experiences entail getting to work on time, being dressed appropriately, and developing social skills. These programs can also provide the opportunity to earn money to pay restitution to victims or symbolic restitution in the form of community service. Most youth now arrive at institutional placements with conditions from the court that include restitution.

Recreational/Leisure

Recreational activities expose youth to prosocial fun and excitement and must be a part of the daily program schedule. Not only do these programs promote good physical health, but they also are a great place to practice problem solving and team play. They also provide an opportunity to constructively burn off excess energy. Many residents have never gone swimming, fishing, boating, skiing, biking, hiking, or camping. They have not played tennis or golf or horseshoes or croquet. They have not been to a play or a museum, a zoo, or an art gallery. They have never attended a concert or a professional sports event.

Spiritual/Religious Programming/Counseling

Spiritual programs and religious counseling is best carried out by a staff chaplain, not volunteers or contract employees. These youth have multiple grieving issues. Many have parents in jail or family members who have died young due to drugs, neglect, or murder. Most have experienced and/or witnessed ongoing violence. They need someone to confide in who is not an authority figure and is a person they can trust. Chaplains can help youths in adjusting to the facility, can identify objectives for residents, and set up support systems within the community, and can intervene during times of crisis and tragedy in youths' lives. A chaplain on staff also serves the important mission of recruiting and screening leaders of other faiths. It is further the chaplain's job to make sure the youth are not exploited by religious zealots or worse (see Drum 2007).

CONCLUSIONS

Mission is an important concept for juvenile correctional leadership to focus on because it helps set priorities, and guide appropriate training on policies and procedures. It includes public safety, staff safety, youth safety, and rehabilitation. It emphasizes public safety by assuring custody and effecting proper control of committed youth. Mission also provides for staff and committed youths' safety by structuring a safe, humane, living environment, and provides treatment programming, which directly addresses committed youths' illegal behaviors to minimize or eliminate repetition of these behaviors.

REFERENCES

Altschuler, David M., Troy L. Armstrong, and Doris Layton MacKenzie. 1999. "Reintegration, Supervision, Release, and Intensive Aftercare. *Juvenile Justice Bulletin*. Washington, DC: Office of Juvenile Justice and Delinquency Prevention.

American Correctional Association. 2009. *Performance-Based Standards for Juvenile Correctional Facilities*, 4th ed. Alexandria, Virginia:. American Correctional Association.

___. 1994. *Standards for Juvenile Detention Facilities, 3rd ed*. Alexandria, Virginia: American Correctional Association.

___. *2010 Standards Supplement*. Alexandria, Virginia: American Correctional Association.

Bartollas, Clemens, Stuart J. Miller, and Simon Dinitz. 1976. *Juvenile Victimization: The Institutional Paradox*. New York: Halsted Press.

Drum, Vance L. 2007. "Professional Correctional Chaplains: Fact and Fiction." In *2007 State of Corrections*. Alexandria, Virginia: American Correctional Association.

Farbstein, J. and William G. Miller. 1981. *Correctional Planning Handbook*. Sacramento, California: State of California, Youth and Adult Correctional Agency, Board of Corrections.

Glick, Barry and William Sturgeon. 1998. *No Time to Play: Youthful Offenders in Adult Correctional Systems*. Lanham, Maryland: American Correctional Association.

___. 2001. *Recess is Over: A Handbook for Managing Youthful Offenders in Adult Systems*. Lanham, Maryland: American Correctional Association.

Edward Latessa Interview. 2001.

Lemieux, Catherine M. 2009. *Families and Substance Abuse: Bringing the Family into Focus*. Alexandria, Virginia: American Correctional Association.

Sullivan, Patrick M. 2010. *Creating Treatment Environments for Troubled Youth: Evidence-Based Design*. Alexandria, Virginia: American Correctional Association.

CHAPTER 5

HOW INSTITUTIONAL MANAGEMENT FULFILLS THE MISSION—ADMINISTRATOR'S DUTIES

The primary task of juvenile correctional residential administrators is to marshal the necessary resources to develop, maintain, and support quality operations. Leaders of facilities need good boundaries, healthy personal support systems, energy, commitment, and passion for working with troubled youth. Boundaries are needed because the demands of residential operations can drain an administrator of passion and commitment. Good administrators fulfill the institution mission by "getting dirty," by responding to the "all calls," but also by recognizing that they are not "one person bandwagons: running the facility all by themselves." Good administrators know that there are not enough hours in the day for them to maintain a thriving facility without a good team, sound policy, and internal and external support.

CONCRETE DUTIES OF ADMINISTRATORS

The successful leader works to fulfill the mission of public safety, staff and youth safety, and rehabilitation through the following concrete duties:

1. Gathering public and community support
2. Designing and or modifying the physical facility to ensure it supports the mission
3. Recruiting, hiring, and training staff committed to the mission
4. Developing program components to meet the needs of the youth they serve that fulfill the institution's mission

Gathering Public and Community Support

Some juvenile institutions have little or no buffer to their residential or commercial neighbors. The facility operations are both visible to the public and appear secretive. Visibility without explanation encourages the neighborhood to develop and maintain its attitude about the facility based on little glimpses. The media has depicted juvenile offenders as violent, conscienceless, gang members leaving the public only with this image of delinquency. The fact is that sometimes, youth escape and run through neighborhoods, or theft occurs locally.

Allowing neighbors to tour the facility and to understand its mission is important. Administrators must lead the way to demystify juvenile correctional programming. Strong external support increases when the leadership sees community interests as an opportunity rather than a nuisance. Intentionally recruiting neighbors and community agencies to participate first hand, rather than gaining all their understanding through newspaper accounts and external observations, gets the residential setting in front of problems.

Relationship building in the neighborhood is vital. Administrators who become members of local service organizations or are receptive to speaking invitations from the larger community contribute to public support. Relationship building at its best is a means to find resources for the facility. The development of strong public and community relationships help a leader to be able to quickly marshal support for things that are needed.

Public facilities, even more than private ones, must work with their committing authorities to assure that they know which youths are best served. Without a marketing plan, both public and private facilities can become underfunded, overcrowded, or underutilized. They also can be a "dumping ground" for any youth the court does not know how to handle. This results in youth of all risk levels, ages, and mental health diagnoses grouped together without having their needs met.

In addition to neighbors, probation officers, judges, and vendors have interchanges with staff on a daily basis. Instilling in staff the importance of marketing helps them maintain formal and informal networks. Facility tours often become richer when parts of the tour are led by someone other than the administrator.

Standard marketing efforts include issuing annual reports, developing a website, having regular media access, and building ongoing relationships internally and externally. Another marketing effort includes formal presentations to your own juvenile system, courts, probation, county attorneys, and public defenders. Standardized fact sheets that all staff have access to can simplify requests for information. Other suggestions include the following:

- Provide annual reports/displays that have more pictures than narratives and statistics

- Showcase the good work of youth whenever possible by completing restorative justice projects (empathy building). Get positive quotes from your supporters, especially committing authorities

- Hold celebrations and open houses for new programming or after operating a pilot program. Celebrate graduations and all other facility benchmarks

- Invite everyone in the juvenile justice system, especially your funding authority. Invite them to events even when they decline attendance for years

- Involve the youth

- Be engaged professionally. Join juvenile professional associations and those in areas related to juvenile services. Join service agencies and encourage your staff to join also

- Use training and conference sessions as opportunities to network and build support

- Recognize the importance of the community—establish good working relationships with the local police, mayor, and council. Encourage service clubs to be involved in the facility. Involve churches and social service agencies, remembering to involve seniors

- Recognize the importance of the family. Involve family and community in the facility and in individualized treatment of the youth. Establish large blocks of time for visiting

- Hold special family events

- Establish program advisory boards. Do this before the facility has community relationship problems. Be specific about the board's responsibilities

- Evaluate the outcomes of your marketing efforts annually. Periodically hold focus groups with juvenile probation, the juvenile bench, the public defender's office, and the county attorney's office, families, and released residents

Designing and or Modifying the Physical Plant to Ensure it Supports the Mission

Buildings are not just buildings in the business of residential care for delinquent adolescents. As Gerald Schields, Director of Facilities, Hillcrest Training School, puts it: "The physical plant needs to reflect the mission, order, safety, predictability, responsibility and hominess of the facility and our ideals" (Schields 2006). Feature 5.1 discusses key design requirements for a secure juvenile residential facility.

Feature 5.1 Key Design Requirements

A secure residential facility should:

1. Provide an environment that promotes staff effectiveness and enthusiasm

2. Facilitate the interaction and the exchange of ideas and information among all staff members.

3. Provide an appropriate transition from one space to another and from outside to inside. Movement should be easy, natural, clearly defined—and easily observable.

4. Provide separate, non-isolated residential units. Each residential unit can be a therapeutic community. There should be a definite group feeling among the residents and the assigned staff—counselors, therapists, teachers, and cottage staff who need to function as a team.

5. Provide non-obtrusive security. Non-threatening but definite barriers are desirable. These boundaries should involve a sense of personal security rather than confinement. Youth offenders want to know what their limits are; thus, they must be clearly defined.

6. Provide behavioral cues. Certain spaces, colors, and decorations indicate and encourage behavior that is appropriate for those environments.

7. Maximize opportunities for recreation. Provide adequate outdoor areas for large-muscle activities, such as basketball, volleyball, and jogging.

Continued on page 62

Key Design Requirements, *continued*

8. Make allowances for growth and change within the environment, but avoid making the environment so flexible that it becomes ambiguous

9. Use the outdoors as an extension of the indoors (in climates that allow it). In addition to recreation, the outdoor environment can be used for many activities that take place indoors, such as therapy, learning, privacy, socializing, and group activities.

10. Avoid over-stimulating environments. If color, activity, patterns, and noise become too stimulating, they can be a source of distress (but this does not imply that spaces should be bland or uninteresting).

11. Avoid corridors as they tend to be ambiguous, disorienting, and, above all, institutional. If they cannot be avoided, try to incorporate natural light, view, and spatial variations.

12. Avoid large, unbroken spaces. These tend to be threatening, inhumane, and ambiguous.

13. Avoid establishing staff territories. Resist having therapy take place only in the "therapy room" and education only in the "classroom," Keep staff close to the juveniles.

14. Avoid the "fish bowl" effect. Nobody wants to be watched all the time, not even staff.

15. Provide for staff privacy. Staff need a place to be away from the youth, to sit and talk together, and to revitalize their energies during the working day.

16. Provide for sensory experiences other than visual. Architecture should take into account stimulation of tactile, audio, olfactory, and kinesthetic senses. At some facilities, the kitchen is intentionally located adjacent to intake so arriving youth smell food as they enter and get the message that they will be fed and cared for. Food is an important part of the program, and youth at intake are always hungry.

17. Provide furnishings that are flexible (moveable) and comfortable. Tables, chairs, and accessories should reflect the ergonomics of the designated activity (for example, study, board games, TV watching, group therapy, or visiting). At the same time, they must not be able to be used as a projectile or weapon.

Source: Patrick M. Sullivan, 2010. *Creating Treatment Environments for Troubled Youth: Evidence-Based Design.* Alexandria, Virginia: American Correctional Association.

The physical plant is an integral part of how institutional management fulfills its mission.

Facility Physical Support for Public Safety. The immediate public safety portion of the facility mission statement is accomplished by ensuring custody of the court-committed youth. Anyone can build a secure jail cell to keep youth in custody. It takes an administrator who also understands the entire juvenile mission to know that a secure jail cell will inhibit rehabilitation. It is known, yet sometimes ignored, that youth in secure confinement without rehabilitation services can ultimately be more of a threat to public safety upon release. Custody is best accomplished in residential care through personal relationships and personal interactions. Residents are far less likely to attempt escape if they have begun to trust that there are staff in the facility who respect and care about them. They are far less likely to escape if they have an adult they can talk to and if they see hope for a change.

This "people security" can be enhanced by the design of the physical facility. The design goal should be to make the facility "homey" with a good balance between physical plant security and a feeling of openness. This is an art but an art that many institutions have mastered. A security fence on the perimeter is not an absolute necessity when facility administrators employ this balance. Movement outside of locked buildings needs to be closely monitored and supervised. Some facilities, for example, employ staff to patrol the perimeter when large numbers of youth are outside, such as going to school.

Physical Facility Support for Youth Safety: Suicide Prevention. Suicide rates for adolescents in correctional facilities are four times higher than for youth in the general population. Although suicide prevention at correctional facilities for youth is (and should be) generally focused on positive human interaction and mandatory staff training, a well-designed physical plant will be a tremendous aide to preventing suicides (Hayes 2006).

When your physical plant is designed or upgraded, eliminating objects to hang from greatly reduces the risk of suicide. Because it is impossible to remove or modify all objects that could be used for hanging, facilities focus on "suicide proofing" areas where youth spend most time and/or are alone—sleeping rooms and bathrooms. Juveniles are much more creative than adults are. Unfortunately, juveniles are able to take the "proof" out of suicide-proof physical plants. Administrators must, however, continue to learn from attempts and make the necessary changes to aging facilities.

Testing mechanisms that claim to break at certain weights, such as sprinkler heads and hooks, may result in the need for unexpected modification. The same tests are necessary on the mattress that will not rip. Isolation cells without cameras that are used for any time other than sleeping are highly inappropriate for suicidal youth.

Obviously, the answer to addressing the needs for a safe physical plant does not lie in adopting a single, simple strategy. What is necessary is developing a multifaceted approach by taking a look at the institution as a whole and incorporating elements regarding architecture, training, policies, procedure, staff attitude/vigilance, and treatment. Figure 5.2 on the following page presents some effective, widely used design features to help prevent youth suicides.

Figure 5.2 Design Features to Help Prevent Youth Suicides

Sleeping Rooms

- All view ports in the doors should be of a significant size to allow staff to see into the room

- All inside door handles should be recessed hand pulls instead of regular door handles.

- If there are shelves in rooms, they should not be high and should be plastic.

- The pins in all inside door hinges need to be beveled downward to prevent hanging attempts.

- Drapes should be attached by Velcro instead of curtain rods and hooks

- Only light plastic clothes hangers should be permitted (if any) and any bar to hang the clothes on should be hollow plastic. (Bins with residents folding clothes are a better idea).

- Suicide-resistant beds, shelves, desks, and stools in all rooms should be "normal room equipment."

- Overhead light fixtures. There are many security and safety lighting manufacturers. When new lights are installed, be sure they are tight to the ceiling and there is no space between the fixture and the ceiling.

- Fire safety alarms and sprinklers must be either recessed or preferably breakaway at 15-20 pounds.

- Inside electrical outlets and switches need to be eliminated or controlled by a central switch.

- Radiator covers on the floor should be welded.

- Crank handle holes in security screens should be plugged and cranks should be contraband—used only by staff.

Youth Bathrooms

- All showers and toilets must provide for both having privacy for the youth and viewing by staff.

- Install half walls or half doors where youth's feet and heads can be observed.

- Shower heads must be suicide-resistant.

- Shower faucet handles should be suicide-resistant (like buttons) or remote staff-operated.

- Toilets should flush automatically.

- Steel toilet paper dispensers and soap dishes can be replaced with a simple recess in the wall.

- The plumbing under sinks should be enclosed in a vanity or sealed off in some way. If sinks are replaced, the faucet handles should be replaced with push-buttons or automatic timers.

- Exhaust fans should be sealed off in some fashion so that the mesh protecting them is too fine for a rope to be strung.

Source: Patrick M. Sullivan. 2010. *Creating Treatment Environments for Troubled Youth: Evidence-Based Design.* Alexandria, Virginia: American Correctional Association.

This list is not exhaustive. Facilities should stay current since there are always new products placed on the market and products once installed as state of the art may not be today. Use your network of juvenile facility administrators to gather information and to test your physical plant. All superintendents must develop a suicide hazard checklist specific to their institution and establish policy for its administration.

All equipment must be routinely checked to ensure it is in place and working properly. When checks or reports indicate otherwise, the administration must be extremely responsive in addressing physical plant suicide concerns and act immediately.

Physical Facility Support for Reducing Youth-on-Youth Violence. The staff area needs to be in a central location to allow for visual monitoring of all areas of the living units. Facilities that have the ability to provide individual sleeping quarters should do so. If that is not possible, great care should be given to not mixing high- and low-risk youth within sleeping units. Even if this classification is accomplished, youth who are sleeping together must be constantly monitored to prevent violence and sexual misconduct.

Individual sleeping rooms must be secured at night to inhibit predatory youth from entering others' rooms. Institutions that have "wet rooms," that is rooms with a toilet and sink, allow for flexibility. Some allow youth to have keys with staff override. Some are staff locked depending on licensure. In all cases, staff must frequently check on youth. Facilities that have individual rooms with no toilet need to make other modifications to ensure safety. One such method used at one juvenile residential setting has electronic doors that youth can open by pushing a button that releases the door automatically after a five-second delay and a staff-alert system.

Physical Facility Support for Rehabilitation. The final element of mission that can be enhanced by a good physical plant is youth rehabilitation. Rehabilitation takes place twenty-four hours a day, seven days a week. It is accomplished through staff relationships and good programming. Effective facilities have physical plants that support all the programming. For example, traditional therapies such as chemical-dependency treatment, mental health therapy, and family therapy must have space available where interruptions are minimized, yet are still safe spaces. Good facilities have therapy rooms where windows allow for observation and monitoring but the rooms remain quiet. These rooms also are equipped with alarm buttons in case back-up is needed.

Physical Design Can also Undermine the Effectiveness of Programming. We have been in facilities where therapy sessions are held in open, common areas. Maintenance staff, visitors, and administrators walked in and out. The phones were ringing; the walkie-talkies were continually heard. These are not institutions where much progress was being made by youth in their therapy. Even vocational programming can suffer from a poor physical plant. One facility had very expensive tool and die equipment but no room to set it up, and one tiny gym, not much larger than a classroom, for 120 youth. As a result, good recreational programming rarely occurred.

In short, buildings are not just buildings. The physical plant must support its mission—public safety, staff and youth safety, and youth rehabilitation.

Recruiting and Hiring Staff Committed to the Mission

There are a number of staff positions in a residential facility, usually including:

- Administrative staff
- Clerical staff
- Cottage staff

- Cottage supervisory staff

- Social workers

- Social worker supervisor

- Principal, teachers, vocational, and recreational staff

- Business office

- Part-time physician and dentist and part-time or full-time nurse

- Part-time psychiatrist and other psychological staff

- Support staff including laundry, kitchen, janitorial, and grounds-keeping personnel

- Volunteers and interns

Staffing plans are required for American Correctional Association (ACA) accreditation and usually are required for state or county funding requests.

As stated throughout this book, juvenile correctional residential treatment is all about people. The staff who administrators recruit, hire, train, and supervise make the difference in the overall quality of care for youth. The candidate pool can be narrowed based on education and experience but discovering attitude, belief in change, and passion for working with youth is more difficult. The candidate pool includes people who want to save juveniles, with no understanding or belief that they may be dangerous too and may contain perpetrators wanting to abuse residents.

In juvenile residential correctional treatment, more than in any other business, it is the attitudes, values, and beliefs that staff model every day that make the difference in the success or failure of the program. Bad attitudes, a belief that the youth need to be punished to protect the public, are characteristics of staff that may not show up until persons are employed. How the staff operate under pressure, respond to training, recover from setbacks, and develop relationships with the youth all take time to evaluate. In this field, establishing a long probationary period for the direct-care work classifications is essential. Training, supervising, observing, and assuring that staff pass probation is the first defense for resident and staff safety.

Juvenile correctional staff have control of the smallest details of everyday life for the youth. This makes selection and supervision critical. Even when you compare the "power" staff have over residents in everyday life to that of a teacher, probation officer, or any other human service field, the weight is greater in residential care.

Recruiting. The following points are recommendations for the recruiting process:

- *Posting of title and right qualifications.* This always begins with developing the proper position classification. In juvenile corrections the titles of the positions have hardened over the years, corresponding with the attitude that juveniles are merely little adults and should be locked up. The name changed to juvenile correctional workers and changed again to juvenile correctional officers. This attracted people who wanted to be police or jailers. Subsequently, a name was often selected to more closely match the position's responsibilities, "residential youth workers." Just the change in the name alone produced a different candidate pool. The staff should be well qualified with experience in helping professions and/or holding a bachelor's degree. Clinical staff would ideally hold master's degrees. A part of the posting should describe the qualifications for the ideal candidate, including temperament and desire to work with troubled youth.

- *Right length of time posted.* Since turnover in juvenile residential correctional facilities is often high, the need for qualified candidates may be constant. However, if a posting is up too long, good candidates are lost. The same effect can take place if postings are up constantly. Attention needs to be paid to the job market at the time to determine how long to take applications in the current environment. Successful facilities can work with their personnel departments to allow for this flexibility in postings. Begin with a complete plan that includes timelines for posting, interviewing, hiring, and orientating to the new position.

- *Comprehensive, ongoing recruitment.* Where the position is advertised can make a tremendous difference in the candidate pool. Include advertising in publications, radio, and job fairs directed to communities of color. Successful recruitment can be accomplished by word of mouth through the network of community providers and by targeting key colleges and universities using facility alumni.

Hiring. The interviewing process is a critical aspect of hiring good candidates.

Interview Board and What to Look For

Who is hired is just as critical as programming. It is difficult to measure a potential candidate's ability to form positive, meaningful relationships with the youth who are committed to our institutions. Select the right people to conduct the interviews on behalf of the facility. Assign staff who have the ability to look for personal qualities, such as empathy, flexibility, firmness, and life experiences. It is our experience that too much attention is placed on academics and criminal justice/security experience and not enough on the ability to interact positively with youth.

Develop questions that will reveal candidates' attitude about youth. Do they have some elementary understanding of delinquency? Do they have some empathy? Ask open-ended questions that require storytelling. Do they have strength, trust, and love of people?

It is wise to do a complete background check that includes prior work history from at least three sources, two of which should be a former supervisor. Do not appoint people when the employer can give you only dates of employment. Do not accept letters of reference in lieu of answers to your questions. Do not accept personal and co-worker references without supporting references from more unbiased sources. Complete all required criminal record checks (use your own systems, if they are available), including driving checks and drug testing.

Hiring the right staff is a critical dimension of building the quality of staff culture. Hiring the right staff makes the program and overall facility operation stronger. Hiring the right staff is cost effective.

Developing Program Components to Meet the Needs of the Youth Served

Administrators who understand the complexities of youth and the needs that must be addressed to successfully complete their mission (public, staff, youth safety and rehabilitation) have the responsibility of ensuring that their program's structure and the facility's program components will be sufficient to address the identified needs of youth they serve.

In this era of tax reductions and budget accountability, programs are always at risk of losing support and funding. Institutions everywhere are being asked to trim budgets, to cut the "fat" from the budget. The "fat" is usually defined by funding sources, not facility administrators. It is therefore incumbent upon a good leader to be prepared to answer, support, and defend the critical program components. The administrator needs to know what each component is and why it is necessary for success. Why is each one needed and how is each one related to the mission of safety or rehabilitation?

Some components are easy to defend and frequently are not challenged or put on the chopping block. Work programs, restitution, and educational programming (academic and problem solving/life skills) usually have public and stakeholder/funded support and therefore have little risk of being cut. On the other hand, components such as recreation are usually the first to be attacked. Many times they are labeled as "fluff" or "frosting on the cake" and these critical components are cut from the facility's budget.

ENSURING STAFF DELIVER COMPONENTS: SOME CHALLENGES

Administrators who have been successful in obtaining the following components for their facility: (education, life skills, and cognitive-behavioral classes, individual and group work, family counseling, physical health, work programs, recreational/leisure, spiritual counseling, specialty groups) have, as a next step, the challenge of making sure that their staff consistently and properly deliver the components. It is a difficult job due to the number and complexities of the components and the factors working against providing them consistently are numerous.

1. **Staff working at cross purposes.** An example would be a chemical health counselor assuring a youth that stopping drinking is the only thing he really has to do to get healthy and stay out of jail, while an hour earlier a therapist encouraged him to deal with the difficult issue of his childhood abuse.

2. **Staff refusing to share "confidential" information with other staff.** An example would be a youth learning in a family session that his mother has left town and never wants to see him again. The distraught youth returns to his living unit to be supervised by a paraprofessional who knows nothing of the horrible news. This youth attempts suicide by hanging himself.

3. **Scarcity of resources leading some facilities to use under-qualified, untrained staff, or volunteers to conduct some of the components.** An example would be a teacher taking on the task of therapist and asking the twenty youth in her class how many have been sexually abused. This triggers several youth to act out. They get restrained and are disciplined. They also never deal with the abuse issues.

4. **Some facilities allow first-line staff to cancel any scheduled component for almost any reason.** An example would be a youth at a critical point in her group therapy. Anxious about talking about abuse she suffered from family members, she swears at a line staffer just prior to her therapy session, so the line staffer cancels her participation. The consequences imposed for this misbehavior were far easier than to talk in therapy.

5. **Many facilities hire contract providers to conduct some of the components with no provisions for the contractor to establish relationships with the youth or to communicate with other professionals working with the youth.** An example would be contracting with agencies to take the youth off grounds to do community service or paid work. The institutional staff has just determined that a youth is at risk to escape. The contract staff does not check with the living unit staff and the youth escapes at the work site.

6. **Some facilities and/or facility staff will minimize mental or physical health problems for budgetary or personnel reasons.** An example would be a youth continually struggling in all of his classes in the school program because of untreated hearing problems. The facility nurse improperly assessed the issue and no one challenged her for weeks. When finally questioned, she said it was too expensive to diagnose and treat all of the youth's health issues and, furthermore, they did not deserve to get better care than poor kids who did not commit crimes.

Because of these barriers to successful implementation, it is no surprise that many institutions flounder. The administrator of a good facility is a leader who can help bring focus, common purpose, and accountability to implementing these components. A good leader need not be an expert in these various disciplines but must have a clear picture of what is needed. An effective administrator takes on the role of an expert conductor: a person who accepts the role of bringing together various stakeholders, staff and professional disciplines for a common purpose.

It is the heart of the administrator's job to make sure that these services fit together. The administrator must ensure that all people working with a youth are communicating with each other and providing critical information regarding their work with the youth. It is also the administrator's job to make sure staff, volunteers, student interns, and private providers respect each other and work together as a team.

MANAGEMENT TOOLS PROVIDE COMPLETENESS, CONSISTENCY, AND QUALITY

The good leader employs management tools to ensure the completeness, consistency, and quality of the services which the facility provides.

Completeness

Administrators must know the profile of the youth served and what the expected process and outcomes from all interactions and interventions will be. They must also work to get the resources needed to address both the risks and needs of the youth. This is best accomplished by the following:

1. **Complete, objective needs assessments** of youth entering the facility and at identified intervals (usually monthly) during their stay

2. **Complete histories in the areas of delinquency, school, family, and prior placements.** It is helpful to work to obtain prior testing in these areas.

3. **Observations and opinions must be reviewed from all sources who know and/or have an investment in this youth.** This includes the court, the probation officer, the family, and extended family, school officials, and the facility staff.

4. **Individual treatment plans must be developed using the assessment information, the history, and observations.** These treatment plans will help to develop a focus for the youth, their family, facility staff, and other partners who will be working with the youth.

5. **Setting content and timetable for various reports.** Administrators must develop a simple and direct means of finding out if the program components are being consistently carried out. Administrators can achieve this by expecting reports from their staff that document fidelity to the scheduled activities. If an activity is cancelled or a youth is excused from a scheduled activity, "exception" reports must be written and regularly reviewed and responded to by the administrator.

Consistency

Without consistency in the application of the program components, the program will fail to accomplish its mission. Ensuring consistency involves a comprehensive program schedule to accommodate all of the demands. It also requires training and policies and procedures to support the implementation of the program schedule.

1. **Developing a schedule to accommodate all of the individual treatment plans and program components is difficult and time consuming, but good facilities spend the resources and the time to complete one that will work and be used.**

2. **Formal policies are needed to support the consistent deployment of the schedule.** They include:

- **Coordination of team work:** A formal policy is needed stressing the importance that staff who work with the youth also work with each other. An administrator needs to ensure that staff will not only communicate what each is doing but also coordinate their efforts.

- **Communication among team members that is structured and regular.** Some institutions accomplish this through weekly team meetings attended by all team members. Other structures such as monthly "staffings" are attended by all team members, youth, and parents/guardians to formally review progress and update treatment plans. It is common in good facilities for staff to keep a daily journal or log of significant issues regarding the program as a whole and individual youth issues (suicide risk, escape risk, gang-related behavior such as showing colors or signs) as a means to communicate with each other as they "hand-off" the supervision of youth between shifts or between programs.

- **Establishment of limits of authority.** If a schedule is to be followed consistently, there need to be some clear policies regarding who has the authority and under what circumstances the decision can be made to cancel a scheduled activity or excuse a specific youth from an activity.

- **Assurance of confidentiality.** Professional codes of conduct, state licensing boards, federal regulations such as the Health Insurance Portability and Accountability Act (HIPAA), state laws, and training in the fields of social work, education, chemical dependency, law, medicine, psychiatry, theology, and the judiciary all have high expectations regarding protecting the information of youth with whom they work. Every fatal incident, rapes, or serious assaults that one of the coauthors investigated at facilities around the United States could have been either prevented or minimized if communication between team members who were working with the youth had occurred. In every case, they cited "confidentiality" as the reason for not sharing appropriate information. Facility policies, therefore, must insist upon professionals, volunteers and first line staff talking with each other and communicating significant issues regarding the youth with whom they are working.

- **Proper credentials for staff.** Successful implementation of the facility's program components also relies on the abilities of staff assigned to deliver the individual components.

- **Rules and norms for youth.** Youth need to know that it is everyone's expectation that they positively participate in all scheduled activities. Failure to do so requires an appropriate staff response and successful participation must have its rewards. The appendix contains some very effective examples of rules and norms for youth.

Quality

Is what we are doing effective? Is it meeting our mission? Are the staff safe? Are the public any safer? Are the youth safe and are they making the needed changes to be good citizens? That is, are they becoming productive members of society—persons meeting their needs and wants through legal means? What are the outcomes of all of the work being done? Leaders of juvenile correctional institutions need to be able to answer these questions.

Good facilities stay that way because they are continually examining the effectiveness of their programming. Administrators will use outcome reports to change, adapt, enhance, or even cancel program components that are having negative results. A good administrator will also find that positive outcomes not only serve the public and the youth well but also will be a powerful ally in obtaining future support and resources.

CONCLUSIONS

A well-run juvenile facility needs strong effective program components. It is the administrator's role to ensure that these components meet identified needs of the youth they are serving. It is this leader's role to ensure that these components are delivered consistently by caring, committed staff. It is also the administrator's role to ensure that the programming remains effective. Keeping the programming complete, consistent, and of quality is a major undertaking and appears somewhat overwhelming. Good leaders and potential administrators succeed.

Perhaps, Dr. Martin Luther King provides an apt conclusion to this chapter:

> I have the audacity to believe that people everywhere can have three meals a day for their bodies, education and culture for their minds and dignity, equality, and freedom for their spirits. I believe what self-centered people have torn down, other-centered people can build up (King 1964).

We also have the audacity to believe that these very things must and can be provided to incarcerated youth. These things will help restore our youth to health and law-abiding behavior. Nutrition, education, culture, dignity, and equality need to be delivered through the application of a facility's program components.

REFERENCES

Booth, Weldon L. 1989. *Managers Guide to Alternative Work Schedules*, 2nd ed. Jacksonville: Institute of Police Technology, University of Northern Florida.

Bryan Griffith. 2006 interview.

Hayes, Lindsay. 2006. *Juvenile Suicide in Confinement: A National Perspective*. Mansfield, Massachusetts: National Center on Institutions and Alternatives.

Kelly, John. 2006. "Detention Centers." *Youth Today*. March.

King, Martin Luther, Jr. 1964. Acceptance Speech, on the occasion of the Award of the Nobel Peace Prize in Oslo, December 10.

Edward Latessa. 2006. Interview.

New York State Department of Correctional Services. 2003. *Harlem Accountability and Reentry Project (HARP)*. New York: The Division of Criminal Justices Services, the State Division of Parole, the State Office of Mental Health, the New York City Mayor's Office, and the Center for Court Innovation.

Nissen, Laura Burney, Jeffrey A. Butts, Daniel Merrigan, and Katherine Kraft. 2006. "The RWJF Reclaiming Futures Initiative: Improving Substance Abuse Interventions for Justice Involved Youths" *Juvenile and Family Court Journal* 57: 39.

Gerald Schields. 2006 interview.

Sullivan, Patrick M. 2010. *Creating Treatment Environments for Troubled Youth: Evidence-Based Design*. Alexandria, Virginia: American Correctional Association.

CHAPTER 6

THE ADMINISTRATOR'S ROLE IN TREATMENT

By establishing goals for juveniles and staff, the administrator can help ensure that these treatment goals are met.

This chapter discusses the administrator's role in supporting treatment outcomes. It is not necessary that administrators be clinicians themselves, but it is important to have enough knowledge about both the needs of adolescent delinquents and effective treatment interventions to ask the right questions to gauge the overall delivery of treatment. Administrators should consider outside independent reviews or audits of their programs every five years. Administrators also need to know what their programs are doing and why they are doing it in order to present that information to stakeholders for support of continued programming.

Effective models of treatment, first of all, help youth discover the positive strengths that they possess. This is a difficult task. In spite of some of their exterior bravado, most of these youth see themselves as failures and outcasts. They have failed at school, probation, and other programs. They have been to court many times and have been told that society must be protected from them. They have gotten the message loud and clear that they are no good. They learn to embrace an outcast persona for their ego maintenance.

Most youth entering facilities have learned to survive hostile environments and meet their needs through the basic survival instinct of flight or fight. These youth do not need to learn excuses in treatment for not changing. They need to learn that there is a better way of meeting their needs. Many do not believe that they have the capacity to change. These young offenders need to know that they are strong enough and smart enough to learn new legal behaviors to get their needs met. They need to know that they do not have to be violent or run to solve problems and achieve a happy life.

The models that do work in youthful facilities are models that focus "treatment" efforts on working in a partnership with youth, their families, and their communities. These programs know that traditional psychotherapy and/or punishment will be ineffective interventions. Most of these youth take punishment in stride and wear it as a badge of honor. "No one is going to change me" is his or her initial attitude. And, they are right. No one is going to change them. They know how to survive in their environment.

Effective programs are respectful of these survival skills and of where these youth are from. They know that any change that will come will be from them. The program's job, therefore, is to be the catalyst for change. Effective programs must have staff who understand and are sensitive to the cultural and racial barriers that are real reasons for residents to distrust facility staff. Through patience, care, and consistency, staff first must develop enough trust that youth will begin to listen and hear that there might be a better way for them to succeed. They must begin to believe that there is hope for them. Good programs look to teach new skills and to help residents discover their talents and strengths so they can use these skills in real life situations.

One of the most enlightening exercises that one of the coauthors used to conduct with residents was to ask them to think about what was good about them. We would give them a whole day to think about it, to talk to others, and to write down or dictate (for those who could not write) two minutes worth of the good things. When all twenty-four youth in the cottage had completed this, we asked each of them to video record their writings. Without exception, they all struggled with this assignment. They could talk for hours about all the bad or illegal stuff but struggled mightily to talk for two minutes about what was good about themselves.

Treatment must include helping these kids truly understand that they are not stupid and that they are not horrible. They have talents that they can use to make positive changes in their lives. They need to understand that their past experiences and behavior do not need to continue to define who they are and what they do. With a few more tools and some trust in others for support, they need to believe that they can succeed in life without resorting to illegal means. Feature 6.1 on future choices helps adolescents discover who they are, what they are good at, and what they want from their futures.

Treatment, then, is getting to know the youth well enough so that they will begin to trust what it is that staff are teaching. Before kids will listen to what is being taught, before they will be in a position to learn, they must first let down their "guard" (the defensiveness they honed so well on the streets). Current evidence-based practice literature terms this "responsivity." The evidence-based practice research tells us that social learning theory and cognitive-behavioral therapies that focus on criminogenic factors (factors that research has identified as significant to reoffending) have the best chance of achieving positive treatment outcomes (Skowyra and Cocozza 2006).

Administrators need to be cognizant that successful implementation of these proven interventions is difficult. Every facility faces enormous barriers to consistently provide these services. There is always something or someone that becomes a barrier to treatment. Administrators will hear a steady refrain of excuses about why effective treatment is not occurring. A favorite is to blame the young residents. "The kids are too mentally ill." "Their families are all criminals and they support illegal lifestyles." "The youth's loyalties are to their gang." "There is inadequate funding to hire qualified staff." "There is no time in the day." "These kids just need more discipline." "Treatment makes the place unsafe."

Feature 6.1 Future Choices

"YOU MAKE THE CHOICES FOR YOUR OWN FUTURE"

You have the power to make your future happen. Becoming an adult means having the ability to take charge of your own life. How can you do this?

You can do it by being prepared and making choices for your future.

Whatever happens to you in your life, always try to be prepared. Making the right decisions about your life will help you make a great future happen.

To be prepared for your future you should:

- Discover who you are and what you want

- Research different options

- Make a plan for your future

1. WHO ARE YOU?

The following exercises will help you think about your future. There are many options, many ways you can go. It is up to YOU!

What classes do you enjoy? What do you like to do in your spare time? What books do you like to read? What movies do you like to watch? When you are on the Internet, what do you look up? What are your interests? What do you think about? What do you like to do? What are you good at—math, science, building things, cooking, telling stories, art…?

1.	6.
2.	7.
3.	8.
4.	9.
5.	10.

Now, cross off anything on the list above that you think you would not like to do ten years from now. Sometimes, other people can help us understand who we are. Ask a friend, a teacher, and a family member to name some activities they think you are good at doing.

Future Choices, Who Are You?, *continued*

My friend thinks I am good at:

1.	3.
2.	4.

My family member thinks I am good at:

1.	3.
2.	4.

My teacher thinks I am good at:

1.	3.
2.	4.

2. WHAT VALUES ARE IMPORTANT TO YOU?

There are things you like to do, and there are things you value. You might enjoy rollerblading or drawing. But you might value things like traveling, or making a lot of money. In the space below, write five things that you value now. Then, write five things you think you might value when you are an adult. There are some key words listed below that will help you.

Things I value now:	Things I might value as an adult:
1.	1.
2.	2.
3.	3.
4.	4.
5.	5.

Key Words: Travel, money, family, the outdoors, health and exercise, helping others, living in different areas of the country, meeting all kinds of people, marriage, home, adventure, art, spirituality, working in the community, education

Future Choices, *continued*

3. IN WHAT DIRECTION WILL YOU GO?

What types of career paths could your interests lead to? What kinds of jobs/career paths fit with your values and talents?

Using the resources section of this insert [not included in this book], look up some careers that relate to your interests, your values, and your talents. Choose three different careers. Then, under those careers, write why you think you might enjoy the career, how much money the average person in that career makes, and what the outlook (the growth and number of jobs open) for the career is in your state.

Example:

Career # 1: Cook
Why I might enjoy it: I like to cook. I like helping people. I like being creative.
Average salary: $17,000 - $26,000 (half the cooks in Minnesota earn more than $8.20 an hour)
How available are the jobs? Very available. Growth in this career is good.

Career #1: _____

Why I might enjoy it: _____

How available are the jobs?: _____

Career #2: _____

Why I might enjoy it: _____

How available are the jobs?: _____

Career #3: _____

Why I might enjoy it: _____

How available are the jobs?: _____

Future Choices, *continued*

4. WHAT PATH WILL YOU TAKE TO GET THERE?

Most jobs require some skill or education level.

All jobs require basic reading, writing, math, and analytical skills, as well as the ability to speak and listen effectively. Thinking about your interests and your values:

- Choose two of the careers you are interested in.

- Using the resources on the next page, find two higher education institutions in the state that offer programs for that career. Then, find out how much each program costs a year, the e-mail and phone number of the school.

You may also choose other programs to research such as branches of the military, job training programs, or paid volunteer programs.

Example:

I would like to explore this career: Cook or chef
School and location: Northwest Technical College in Moorhead, MN
Program: Chef training
Program cost: $7,286 for two years includes tuition, class supplies, class meals, and fees.
Phone number for school: (800) 426-5603

1. I would like to explore this career: _____

First school and location: _____

Program cost: _____

Phone number for school: _____

E-mail: _____ Web site: _____

Second school and location: _____

Program cost: _____

Phone number for school: _____

E-mail: _____ Web site: _____

Future Choices, *continued*

2. I would like to explore this career: _____

First school and location: _____
Program cost: _____
Phone number for school: _____
E-mail: _____ Web site: _____

Second school and location: _____
Program cost: _____
Phone number for school: _____
E-mail: _____ Web site: _____

5. WHO WILL HELP YOU?

You don't have to go down these paths alone. You can ask many different people you know, or even call people you do not know who work in these careers and ask them questions. In the spaces below, write five different people or places where you can get information on the career you have chosen.

Example:

Name: Dan Sperling
Job title: counselor at Northwest Technical College
Phone number: (800) 426-5603   E-mail: _____

I could call the following people to ask questions about a career or school option:

Name: _____
Job title: _____
Phone number: _____
E-mail: _____

Name: _____
Job title: _____
Phone number: _____
E-mail: _____

Future Choices, *continued*

Name: _____

Job title: _____

Phone number: _____
E-mail: _____

Name: _____

Job title: _____

Phone number: _____
E-mail: _____

Examples of people to call: Consider people or places for financial aid, admissions, tutoring, volunteering, scholarships or extra-curricular activities. Or, consider people who work in the career you have chosen, people in your community, mentors, or teachers.

6. WHAT CAN YOU DO NOW?

Here are six suggestions for activities you can do today to get you prepared for you future. Do three of these activities, write your answers on a separate sheet of paper, and check the box after you have accomplished it.

- ☐ Ask your school guidance counselor or a teacher for the best advice he or she has been given about preparing for the future.

- ☐ Call a person in one of the career fields you have chosen and ask that person the best and hardest part of his or her job.

- ☐ Call a professor or instructor and ask that person what you need to do in high school to prepare for your higher education at that school.

- ☐ Using the resources section of this insert, look up two scholarships that match your chosen paths and write them down. Include phone numbers.

- ☐ Using the resources section of this insert, look up two people in your state who are experts in the paths that you have chosen.

- ☐ Call a financial aid administrator at one of the schools you are interested in and ask that person what you and your parents can do now to help you get ready financially for your higher education.

LEADERS REMOVE BARRIERS

Successful programs have leaders who understand their role is not only to identify resources and effective intervention strategies, but also to identify and remove the barriers that inhibit implementing good programming. Major barriers commonly confronting administrators of juvenile correctional facilities include:

- Lack of clear agreement upon mission

- Lack of funding to provide professional treatment for chemical dependency and mental health

- Little credibility or attention paid to the issue of "responsivity" (ability of the youth to hear and learn)

- Lack of coordinated team work

- Lack of integrated aftercare

- Lack of outcome information to know what is working and what is not in order to make program and/or staff adjustments

TREATMENT AND ADMINISTRATORS

Providing for the safety of staff, youth, and the public is, in and of itself, an enormous task and, if done right, takes skill and resources. When you add to that the facility's responsibility to provide for the rehabilitation of these youth, the task for the administrator begins to feel overwhelming. The array of services that must be provided to address the identified needs of youth entering correctional facilities appears to be staggering. Educating; socializing; providing new skills; attending to their physical, mental and spiritual health; working with the family and the community for aftercare are all part of this rehabilitation responsibility. Providing all of these services comes with an enormous cost. Programs, both public and private, that consistently succeed at providing these services do not rely on just one funding source. Administrators face a major challenge to find the money and the people to meet these requirements and demands.

Lack of Funding

Administrators who succeed at this challenge are persistent in their message that lack of funding from their primary funding source cannot be an excuse to address some needs and not others. An inadequate budget is a fact of life for the administration of these facilities: "Do more with less" and "be more efficient" have come to be a common mantra across the United States. Some, who view this fact as an insurmountable barrier, fail with their mission of rehabilitation. No facility will succeed if lack of funding results in delivering some services but ignoring others.

Creative and persistent administrators find that there are people in the surrounding community who have a stake in the welfare of these youth. They find out who has services that can meet youth needs and engage these people and systems. Local schools, colleges, or universities can all be great sources for volunteers and interns. One institution sought out and found retired businesspeople who provided research to support taxpayers' investment in this institution. Technicians, bankers, homemakers, or a handyperson can assist in training residents with daily living skills such as cooking, grooming, job-seeking, and budgeting. Scholarships for college or technical school can be established with donated funds from retired staff, current staff, and community service organizations such as Rotary clubs, Optimist clubs, Lions, Veterans for Foreign Wars, churches, and mosques.

By partnering with private vendors and other public institutions, staff could trade computer training for presenting safety and security training to another agency, school district, or business. Leaders of residential facilities can get something for the residents out of their collaboration with public health agencies, hospitals, and universities that benefit both agencies.

Responsivity: Youth and the Learning Process

"Responsivity" is all about removing the unique, individual barriers that prevent youth from learning. These barriers include everything from distrust of adults or people of different races or cultures to chemical abuse, poor physical health, and overwhelming traumas such as homelessness, violence, abuse, and neglect.

One residential facility planned to do something special and challenging for ten of the young men who were progressing well in treatment—a week long trip to the three million acre wilderness in Northern Minnesota known as the Boundary Waters Canoe area. It was named as such because the only means of transportation was traversing lakes and rivers in a canoe. Staff began preparing the youth for the trip several weeks in advance to teach them about safety and survival.

It was believed all of the youth should learn orienteering. This is the art of navigating with a compass and map. An expert woodsman—who also taught orienteering to high school students—volunteered to spend an afternoon with the ten chosen young men to teach them orienteering. He came very well prepared. He had a map and a compass for each youth. He had a detailed lesson plan dividing the afternoon up into a classroom session and some practical application. He had taken the time to set out prizes at various locations throughout adjoining small woods and had orienteering directions detailed for each location.

The superintendent decided to stop in the classroom about halfway through the class session. Mr. G. was following his curriculum. He was going through each portion point by point: how to read the compass, what degrees were, how to align the compass with a map to plot direction, and so forth. He looked around the room, and it appeared no one was paying any attention. Some youth were obviously daydreaming; some were visiting with each other, and some were looking out the window. When it came time for the practicum, none of the youth could find any of the prizes.

Mr. G. was upset and befuddled. He had given these youth the same course he had given to hundreds of high schoolers who had demonstrated they could use the skills. He asked the superintendent what was wrong with these kids. Were they so stupid that they could not understand simple things? He wondered how anyone would not be interested and have such a short attention span. Later, the kids told the superintendent that they did not trust him. He was boring, and he did not seem to care whether they were listening. They could not understand what he was trying to teach.

Over the years, all administrators have met or heard from "Mr. G.s" in residential correctional programs. Some were well educated therapists, some master level teachers, and some supervisors and administrators. All forgot about who they were trying to teach. Having an excellent curriculum for teaching facility residents new skills is important. Working with the youth to ensure that they are in a position to listen and learn is the precursor often overlooked or minimized by those doing the teaching. Evidence-based practice literature calls this "responsivity."

One element of helping youth be ready to learn involves healing. The healing of the past wounds and trauma needs to be in the context of not forgetting, in fact focusing on, accountability for their delinquent behaviors. They are looking at the past only for the purpose of learning that they do not need to be controlled by their past. They need to heal to put their past behind them so they will be open to new information. Their past traumas can no longer be an excuse for acting out. Albert Ellis one of the founders of cognitive-behavioral therapies said it this way, "Forget 'god-awful' pasts, face fears and change actions" (*Time* magazine obituary 2007).

Treatment should focus on antisocial behaviors. The clinical practices must be research driven with the theoretical foundation of cognitive behavior. The programs should always strive to provide therapeutic guidance for a juvenile population that is ethnically and culturally diverse. All programs need to focus on the broader mental health needs of youth from a developmental perspective and address a broad spectrum of psychiatric and psychological issues. Most adolescents who find their way into the juvenile justice system have had significant exposure to difficult family and social conditions.

Responsivity: Staff Relationships

First and foremost, the administrator of a residential correctional facility must be certain that his/her staff are role modeling positive behavior. "Responsivity" or openness to treatment has its beginnings in caring staff who reach out to these youth through work, play, and daily activities.

Youth who enter the facility need to know that there are people who care about them and that they can get help. With this "groundwork" in place, newly arriving juveniles begin the process of being "responsive" to what is being said and what is being taught through classes, therapy, and staff role modeling.

Treatment, in this sense, occurs each and every time one of the staff or volunteers interacts with one of the youth. Treatment occurs each and every time that youth witnesses staff having interactions with each other. Role modeling is a powerful treatment tool. How are these adults solving problems as they arise? How are they dealing with conflict and stress? What do they do when they are angry? How are they treating my peers and me?

We know that youth entering juvenile correctional facilities have not had consistent opportunities to witness, learn, and emulate healthy interactions. Most come from highly dysfunctional families and neighborhoods. Most have developed fairly straightforward but somewhat primitive ways of meeting their needs. The human instinct of reacting impulsively by fight or flight is their most common defense. Many have a history of assaults, running from home, school, and other placements.

To begin considering doing any changing, they have to see for themselves that there are other ways of taking care of business—better and, in the long run, easier ways of meeting their needs without having to hurt someone or puting themselves at risk of harm. This is why it is an administrator's job to ensure that staff at the facility are role-modeling acceptable behavior to the youth, as well as acting as professionals. They need to be aware that their everyday actions and relationships with the residents are extremely powerful tools in helping youth through the change process.

Administrators need to gauge the quality of staff/resident relationships through supervision of their clinical directors also. They need to ask questions such as: Do relationships exist? How do you know? Are these healthy non-exploitive relationships? Does the relationship appear too close, too personal? Is the staff in question sharing information or acting differently?

Leaders of these facilities cannot hide or ignore the fact that unhealthy relationships without boundaries between staff and youth can and often times do become criminal acts in residential settings. Administrators must be aware of these potential and often real problems that are inherent in residential care. Supervisors must be trained to look for signs, such as one staff member spending too much time with one resident or treating one resident with special favors. It is not easy to accomplish both the need for strong relationships and the need to make sure that relationships stay professional and positive. Some facilities decide to address the issue by banning staff from developing caring relationships with youth.

Other facilities turn "a blind eye" to relationships between staff and residents, either through neglect or ignorance resulting in youth being exploited and victimized. Facility administrators who do not proactively address this critical issue end up with incidents occurring between staff and residents that not only harm youth and destroy careers but ultimately destroy their program. It is only through healthy relationships that real internal change begins to occur with youth.

Responsivity: Clinical Family Work

Engaging families can be extremely difficult because they have been in the "system" for years and have grown to distrust the courts and distrust the social workers. Many have family members who have been in jail or prison; many have had their children taken away at various times. Inviting them to come to the facility to be a part of goal setting meetings or just to visit is not enough to start building bridges of trust between the institution and the family. Facility staff and administrators

---

Feature 6.2 Family Night

Family involvement can be a real challenge due to conflicts with parents'/custodians' work schedules, difficulties getting daycare for their other children, solving transportation problems, and anger at being identified as the problem by the system.

Social workers at one institution had an innovative idea to begin a "Family Night" where families could bring up to five family members, including siblings as long as they were on an approved list. The facility helped with transportation, when necessary, and the activity occurred at the dinner hour and the facility provided dinner. Each quarter there was a program presentation theme, such as academic school open house, transitional living, mental health diagnosis and interventions, and community reentry.

In this facility, there had always been a portion of the population identified as gang members. Days before an event, rumors spread that there was going to be a big gang fight at family night. Immediately, the staff began to polarize between cancelling family night because of security or going forward with the event and dismissing the information at hand.

The superintendent, using the mission as a guide, knew both of these responses were wrong. To protect the public, youth, staff, and parents, staff were directed to get more information from residents and not allow those involved or their families to attend. A call to "all staff" in juvenile services was made. This brought the chief probation officer, other probation officers, and administrative staff in the central office to attend and support the event. Local law enforcement was asked to be present, along with a county sheriff. All families were screened through a metal detector. The result was a safe evening that did not have to be cancelled, yet paid attention to safety and potential risk.

need to start with the philosophy of respect for the family, not blaming them for the behavior of their children. Most families are struggling with survival issues themselves, such as mental health, chemical health, poverty, and homelessness. A family night can be one approach to involving reticent or reluctant families (see Feature 6.2).

Partnering with community agencies to help address family issues has also met with some success in helping families develop the capacity for better parenting. One such curriculum was offered by a local social service agency where parents were given free classes on topics such as how to effectively communicate with school staff, how the special education system works, why certain behaviors may be a sign of behavior problems, and how to access community resources such as help with heating bills.

Responsivity: Teamwork

The success of residential programs in treatment is directly related to the coordination of the efforts and unique skills of a variety of disciplines, staff personalities, and staff roles. Most facilities talk about the importance of staff professionals working together for the best outcomes for youth with whom they are working.

The first and most common challenge for administrators is the debate that takes place between "custody" staff and "clinical" staff. Generally, the custody staff are required to have less education and are paid less; yet, they have the responsibility of supervising the youth for the entire day. Good line staff take great pride in their ability to keep the youth under control and compliant with facility rules. It is a tough skill to learn. Too often, however, they view clinical staff as interfering with their job. Clinical staff, on the other hand, often view custody staff as interfering with their treatment efforts. Both develop a tendency to distrust each other and to discount each other as unknowledgeable.

The job of the administrator is to break up these natural tendencies and to insist they listen to each other as they work together as a team. The administrator must structure and demand communication between the two "camps:" and must provide training to educate both to the importance of the other with the understanding that they will both fail if they refuse to listen, talk, and respect each other's viewpoints. The administrator is ultimately attempting to communicate that there needs to be a united front to work successfully with kids and their families.

Youth will find ways to discount any and all therapeutic interventions to maintain their view of the world. They will be unresponsive to cognitive-behavior therapies if they can find support from even one team member to validate their defiance. This can happen through ignorance—staff unaware of what the others are doing—or through overt or covert intentional undermining of what other staff do or say.

In a residential setting, these youth speak and act differently with different staff. Thus, the residents' behavior in the living unit or school might be angelic, but they are making no progress in their therapy. The result is that every staffer sees the youth differently. The youth will then use this to "play" staff against each other much like a child in a divorce custody battle.

For example, the youth might act abusive around men but not around women. They might act out after revealing a secret in therapy, but first-line staff who are not cognizant of what was talked about react in a way that is not supportive of the work It is easy for youth to manipulate and not make needed changes if staff are not working together as a team. Without staff working as a team, treatment progress is stifled.

The multidisciplinary treatment team—which is usually headed by a program director—is one example of unified teamwork in action. The program director has the final authority on all team decisions. Team members include the individual living unit staff, the unit supervisor, the social worker, the probation/parole officer, consulting psychiatrists, teachers, nurses, volunteers, interns, and all adults who are involved with each youth. Facilities must encourage input from families or any other people significant in the life of the adolescent that will broaden the scope of both understanding and guiding the youth.

The goal of the multidisciplinary treatment team is to provide the best possible service to youth and their families by ensuring no single influence will be detrimental. Furthermore, the positive synergy of many creative insights and ideas assures quality of care. Team members become acquainted with the broader array of treatment philosophies and orientations. They are encouraged to incorporate this knowledge into their own individual clinical philosophy and the broad programmatic philosophy of cognitive-behavioral therapy.

Team members are further encouraged to develop a role definition for themselves, which allows maximum use of their unique skills, knowledge, and expertise. Learning the strengths, roles and responsibilities of other team members and respecting those are also critical. Team members are expected to participate in all facets of planning and decision-making by sharing their observations regarding resident or group functioning as well as staff functioning.

Team members become knowledgeable about both the broad and individualized treatment goals and strategies for residents assigned to the treatment team. Active support of treatment team decisions and implementation of the objectives of the treatment team is the goal of each team member. The leader must consistently encourage participation in the creation of a safe and confidential treatment-team environment that fosters processing issues relative to both transference and counter-transference. Recognizing signs of severe stress or burnout among staff members and offering support is a benevolent act.

The leader must monitor staff's workload to assure each staffer carries a fair and reasonable share. If a group or youth's issue cannot be resolved within the workday, staff need to provide a full briefing and documentation to the team members with subsequent responsibility. Constructive feedback to fellow treatment team members on their efforts is critical. Equally important is to openly recognize and appreciate others skills and creativity. By doing this consistently, staff are contributing to the raising of standards of service to the youth and their families through a coordinated and consistent treatment team effort.

The administrator must also ensure that there is a schedule that can accommodate all of the demands being placed on the facility. There are licensing requirements including a set number of hours for school and a set number of hours for recreation and physical exercise. There must be time for family visiting and time for spiritual activities. There must be time to take care of personnel hygiene and housekeeping of the living units. There are treatment needs (both individual and group), and there are demands from the various professionals and stakeholders (probation/parole officers, attorneys, courts, and therapists) that must be accommodated. Without a schedule and policies that support consistently adhering to it, facilities will be too overwhelmed to provide needed services.

Teamwork in Action. Staff reports, which generally occur quarterly, reflect treatment goals and progressive changes in programming and treatment goals, and are signed off by the resident. This quarterly reporting occurs in a timely fashion, and the following individuals are invited to attend:

- Parents
- Psychiatric Social Worker
- Probation Officers/Parole Officers

- Family Therapist
- School Teachers
- County Social Workers

The family therapist, psychiatric social worker, and cottage supervisor present some of their individual perspectives. As the resident's progress is reviewed and documented, the treatment goals are adjusted accordingly. Having this many people present with a variety of viewpoints allows the resident a diverse audience and a lot of creative input from many perspectives relative to future programming and goal setting. It is also important to communicate with foster care review boards and placement review boards. The representative teacher from the facility school prepares formal Individualized Education Plans (IEP's) for each resident, which become part of progressive goal setting.

Team Meeting: The program director offers supervision to all staff including line staff, psychiatric social workers, living unit supervisors, recreational therapists, and other adjunct staff who may be involved in the treatment process at that given time, or with certain individual residents. This should occur on a weekly basis and can involve as many as four hours of "process supervision" on a wide variety of programmatic issues including specific treatment plans.

Unfortunately, it is all too common that team work takes a back seat to professional egos and ignorance of its importance. Administrators must ensure that staff not only know that team work is critical but that they are consistently practicing it. The following incident illustrates team work's importance.

A well-trained line staffer attended a unit team meeting where one social worker revealed that she was allowing a youth to write in his journal in Spanish. This staffer was concerned that the social worker, who was fluent in Spanish, refused to translate the journaling for the rest of the team. She cited "client confidentiality" as the reason. This concerned line staff came to talk to the superintendent of the facility. After hearing the report, the superintendent responded: "For heaven's sakes, there is a social worker in this institution who is allowing a child to write in Spanish in his journal and the only one who reads Spanish in that particular cottage is that social worker. This means the assigned line worker is not aware of the journaling content. The probation officer is not getting the information. The teachers do not know what this youth is writing. This must change immediately."

He then recalled a story about how he had been summoned by the chairman of the board of directors of a twenty-five bed facility for serious, violent delinquents in Pennsylvania to request that a program audit be done. The situation, as the board chair explained it, was that they had been operating for two years and had just released the first youth to complete the program. The youth was only in the community for one week when he was arrested for the rape and murder of a fifteen-year old girl. The chairman hoped to get some answers about how this could have happened, since the youth was a model resident and had spent two years in the facility. He wanted to know if this could have been prevented. He wanted to know if there was something inherently wrong with the program's structure and services.

The audit revealed that this program had well trained and well qualified professionals as staff. The program had excellent assessments and services for the youth committed there. The program structure, safety, and security were top notch. There were very few assaults, and no one had ever escaped. What the program lacked was any consistent team work. Staff were not communicating with each other about the youths with whom they were meeting. This was best illustrated by the staff's failure to share with each other the circumstances concerning the recently released youth arrested for this horrendous crime.

This youth had been writing a journal every day at the request of his social worker. In the course of two years, he had filled up more than thirty notebooks with his journaling. When the auditor asked what was in the stack of journals, no one really knew. Periodically, the social worker read the journals, but she did not share the contents with other team members. The auditor took the time to read all of them. The journals revealed the portrait of a youth overwhelmed with anger toward most everyone in his life, including program staff. In the last six months of his stay, his journaling grew quite candid about the fact that he was scared about reoffending because he had done no changing. He spoke of how he could tell staff what they wanted to hear but that he did not believe any of this psychology that they were preaching. The social worker knew some of this and did not tell anyone else. No one else read the entries. The youth was asking for help the only way he knew how. He was expecting staff to respond to his confessions and no one did. Since he had completed the program as they had defined it, they released him. A tragedy!

Integrated Aftercare

Collaborating with local and metropolitan community organizations is important. Community connections helps to normalize the daily living environment for youth and aid them in the transition back to the community.

Pre-Transition/Reintegration. Aftercare must begin when a youth is first committed to the facility and remain a focus throughout the youth's stay. The National Council of Juvenile and Family Court Judges Association in a paper entitled "*Reconnecting: The Role of the Juvenile Court in Reentry*" states: "Planning for the transition back into their communities should begin immediately upon arrival at the correctional facility or other residential placement, if not sooner" (National Council of Juvenile and Family Court Judges 2005).

Procedures and interagency agreements need to be established to ensure timely transfer of youth records between the releasing and the receiving programs (both education and treatment) so that preplacement decisions can be based on previous program and evaluation information (see the transitional living cottage workbook and timeline in the appendix). This area of work with youth is known to be critical, yet historically one where there is system breakdown and finger pointing. Residential facilities need an assigned case manager with the authority to speak with the public school to assure a smooth transition and the responsibility to check in daily or weekly with the public school for six weeks depending on the level of structure the youth needs.

All involved agencies must be aware of the youth's needs and the services that the various agencies involved with the youth provide. Communication of this information can take place through interagency administrators' meetings, interagency in-service training, and agency site prerelease staffings occurring for each resident leaving the institution.

This includes family, outside counselor—if appropriate, facility school representatives, chemical-dependency treatment counselor—if appropriate, transition case manager, probation officer, and primary therapist. A release staffing also needs to be held to evaluate the resident's progress in gradual transition. This staffing can be facilitated by the case manager and must include the assigned probation officer and representatives working with the youth in the community.

The various agencies (for example, education, mental health, correctional) should assign all transitioning youth to one point of contact (a counselor, social worker, or case manager) who can serve as an advocate for the youth, ensure parent involvement, and maintain communication among the various agencies and people involved with the youth. This would be the transition case manager.

The search for service providers should not wait until after the juvenile has been released from secure confinement or other out-of-home placement. Even short delays or gaps in the delivery of services increase the chance that any gains made while in the institution will be eroded. Services should include mental health treatment, vocational training, job placement, secondary and post-secondary education, individual and family counseling, mentoring, recreational programming, health services, social skills development, culturally competent and gender-specific programs, intensive supervision and monitoring, transitional housing services, transportation, spiritual counseling, and family support, where desired and appropriate.

The Office of Juvenile Justice and Delinquency Prevention (OJJDP) 1999 publication *Developing a Comprehensive and Community Wide Approach to Serious Violent and Chronic Juvenile Offenders* states:

> Contact should be encouraged between the youth, family and others in the neighborhood. The planning and involvement of community institutions such as schools, parents, churches, neighbors and peers should begin when the youth enters a residential program. Coping mechanisms, including school and job training, self-esteem, and self-reliance skills and establishing productive peer groups are essential components of a reintegration program (Office of Juvenile Justice and Delinquency Prevention 1999).

CONCLUSIONS

The previous chapters have laid the groundwork for treatment to occur. This background includes understanding the profile of youth served and the clear mission of the facility. Add to this, the role of the stakeholders and the need to provide safety for the public, staff, and youths. Combine this with the resources needed to fulfill the mission to develop a safe and nurturing facility culture.

The enlightened administrator knows that any change will come from youths themselves. The program's job, therefore, is to be the catalyst for change. There must be staff who understand and are sensitive to the cultural and racial barriers that are real reasons for these youth to distrust facility staff. Staff must develop enough trust with the youth so that the youth will begin to listen and hear that there might be a better way for them to succeed. Youth must begin to believe that there is hope for them. Good programs look to teach new skills and to help youth discover their talents and strengths so they can use these skills in real life situations.

This chapter examined the administrator's role in treatment, which includes:

- Developing an adequate funding base

- Making certain that staff are modeling positive behaviors to youths

- Equipping staff to deal with problems, such as gangs in the facility

- Adapting both traditional and nontraditional treatment methods in the facility

- Extending treatment to families of youths

- Emphasizing the importance of teamwork with staff

- Collaborating with community organizations to create an integrated system of aftercare for youths released to the community

REFERENCES

Lubow, Bart and Barry Krisberg. 2006. American Youth Policy Forum address, *Juvenile Offenders and Victims: 2006 National Report.*

Moore, Solomon. 2007. "Gangs Grow, but Hard Line Stirs Doubts." *New York Times*, September 13.

National Council of Juvenile and Family Court Judges. 2005. *Reconnecting: The Role of the Juvenile Court in Reentry*. Reno, Nevada. Author.

Nissen, Laura Burney, Jeffrey A. Butts, Daniel Merrigan, and Katherine Kraft. 2006. "The RWJF Reclaiming Futures Initiative: Improving Substance Abuse Interventions for Justice Involved Youths." *Juvenile and Family Court Journal* 57:39.

Office of Juvenile Justice and Delinquency Prevention. 1999. *Developing a Comprehensive and Community Wide Approach to Serious, Violent and Chronic Juvenile Offenders*. Washington, DC: U.S. Government Printing Office.

Skowyra, Kathleen and Joseph J. Cocozza. 2006. *A Blueprint for Change: Improving the System Response to Youth with Mental Health Needs with the Juvenile Justice System*. Washington, DC: National Center for Mental Health and Juvenile Justice.

Time. 2007. Obituary of Albert Ellis. www.timesonline.co.uk/tol/comment/obituaries/article2147957.ece. Accessed August 12, 2009.

CHAPTER 7

THE ADMINISTRATOR'S ROLE IN BUILDING POSITIVE CULTURE

Authors Joseph Heinz and Theresa Wise demonstrate positive culture by rewarding Hennepin County Home School graduates with a carnation.

The effective treatment of youth will not occur unless the facility has developed and maintained a positive prosocial culture—a culture that is safe, supportive, and nurturing. It is a difficult goal to achieve but administrators must make it a priority. Building a positive culture is about leadership having the persistence and courage to communicate often, what their facility stands for, and what is and is not acceptable behavior.

PAST EFFORTS AT BUILDING POSITIVE CULTURES

In the 1960s and 1970s, the concept of positive peer culture generated considerable excitement in juvenile corrections. Developed by Harry Vorrath and associates as an outgrowth of Guided Group Interaction, positive peer culture was implemented in all of the juvenile state institutions in West Virginia, Michigan, and Missouri. Vorath believed that Positive Peer Culture "is a total system of building positive youth subcultures" (Vorrath and Brendtro 1974).

Vorrath acknowledges the pervasiveness of peer influence and feels that winning over its subculture is necessary if its influence is to be positively rechanneled. Young people, according to Vorrath, can become experts in dealing with the problems of other young people. However, the group meetings sponsored by Positive Peer Culture must break through the antisocial values of young offenders if such meetings are to be positive. Certain problems are implicit in the use of Positive Peer Culture, which contributed largely to its waning popularity by the end of the 1970s. First, where does Positive Peer Culture expect to find these "ideal" leaders? Bartollas and colleagues' studies of juvenile institutions found relatively few staff in juvenile corrections who come anywhere near filling these high expectations. Also, Vorrath seems to underestimate the ingenuity and resourcefulness of peer subcultures.

BUILDING POSITIVE CULTURES IN THE PRESENT

The fact that very little is presently being written about positive peer culture in residential facilities makes it appear to new facility administrators that it is of little importance. Formal education, such as criminal justice or social work curriculums, are sparse if not void in the area of 'building positive culture' in residential institutions. Concentrating on building positive culture has actually taken a "back seat" to evidence-based practices, which uses such terminology as "Motivational Interviewing," "staff morale," and "targeted interventions." Administrators have learned to use phrases such as "return to law-abiding behaviors," "responsivity," and "skill building" instead of "rehabilitation and positive culture." Secure, quiet, clean, well run, and respectful replaced the overarching term of "therapeutic culture."

Current descriptions of prosocial, positive facility culture have become more of a random collection of these evidence-based terms than a complete picture of positive facility culture. As the authors reflect on this concept of positive culture, it has become apparent to us that the reason little is written about building positive culture is because it is such a difficult subject to capture in writing, or, for that matter, to teach. Developing a positive culture seems to be more of an art form than an objectively attained goal.

This is one of those critical pieces of residential care that is best taught by role modeling, but it is so critical to success that we should attempt to discuss, frame, and recommend direction for building positive culture. Although much has been written about identified successful programs, they are difficult to replicate. We believe that implementing all of the individual elements of evidence-based practice without proper attention to the overall culture has contributed to this difficulty.

Many programs that wanted to replicate successful ones have simply failed. At times, security and safety were forgotten about, and incidents of new criminal acts, violence, drugs, and escapes defined and ultimately doomed many of these programs. Other times, rehabilitation or treatment was ignored or minimized leading to abuse and physically injured youth. These failures were highly publicized in Texas (Springer 2007) and Maryland (Green 2005). Combined with highly publicized youth violence, they helped to highlight the fact that incarceration and punishment without rehabilitation will lead to failure.

We believe that the overall success of a program will occur only if the facility has developed and maintained a positive prosocial facility culture. The prosocial culture is not designed to replace the cultural experiences or identity of any individual, but simply to make special meaning out of the placement and create a sense of belonging within the residential setting. The resident's individualized cultural experiences must be recognized and respected. The prosocial culture established within the facility will help a diverse population of youth connect with each other and lay the foundation for individual change.

An institution's prosocial positive culture is formed through the everyday interactions of staff and residents. It is formed from all the values and beliefs of the people who enter, live, and pass through the facility. These facilities are much like an isolated small town. Just as in a small town, there is a feel that is apparent when you enter it. Is it inviting and warm? Is it sterile and tense? Is it out of control and scary? A seasoned administrator could tell you within minutes of entering if this were a safe place where youth could learn new ways of behaving. In all residential centers, there is a feel that is developed, a certain type of energy, a sense of how things are done. This is what the culture will reflect.

LEADERSHIP AND POSITIVE CULTURE

In the best of facilities, positive, dynamic leadership is an essential and potent ingredient in the development and maintenance of the facility's prosocial culture. In these facilities, prosocial culture has been nurtured through leadership. If asked, staff should be able to say, "This administration does not tolerate residents being locked in their rooms for long periods of time, programming being cancelled, and recreation being seen as a luxury." Unfortunately, in too many cases, staff will respond to this question with statements such as: "I have no idea what the administrator thinks" or "I have no idea what the director thinks or believes." Building positive prosocial culture starts with the awareness of the importance of the director's role in building culture.

The administrator must be an intentional leader. "I am doing this today so that others will know where I stand" and then going forward with the decision making that supports this spirit. Administrators can build positive culture by knowing that their actions and, for that matter their inactions, will set the direction for the type of culture that develops.

As the leader of the facility, administrators have the authority to decide:

- Who works at the facility

- What training staff should receive

- What schedules staff will work

- How and when staff and residents are rewarded or disciplined

The decisions and actions that the facility administrator makes in these four areas will determine the culture of the facility. The training staff should receive will be examined in the next chapter, but we discuss the other three elements here.

Who Works at the Facility?

Ensuring that the right staff are recruited and hired, as well as promoted, is a vital responsibility of administrators. Since role-modeling is a powerful influence with youth during their adolescence, staff who are hired should be people with whom youth can relate and can form positive relationships.

One of the important traits of effective staff is that their ethnicity, race, and gender need to reflect the population of youth who are entering the programs. In almost all states, there is an overrepresentation of youth from minority groups being committed to residential correctional institutions.

Although most leaders in this field would agree with this premise, it frequently is an extremely difficult task to recruit and hire a well qualified diverse staff at all levels (support services, professional health workers, direct service workers, supervisors, and administrators) of the facility. Many facilities are located in rural areas where it is difficult to recruit staff of color. Often institutions have a reputation in their referral areas as being unwelcoming to staff of color. Too many administrators let these facts become absolute barriers to the goal of having a diverse staff and simply give up trying. This is a major mistake.

It takes some work and a lot of energy but the successful facilities succeed in recruiting well-qualified minority staff. These facilities target their recruitment efforts and creatively get their message out to communities of color that this facility is a place where people can make a real difference in the lives of youth.

Some ideas are to do the following:

- Advertise on minority radio stations

- Send staff to area colleges and universities to speak to students in the social sciences

- Hold job fairs

- Attend neighborhood meetings and find out who the community leaders are and invite them to the institution

- Hold open houses at the facility for the public to come and experience the positive nature of the work

- Contact local private agencies with roots in the communities that these youth come from and let folks there know of the opportunities available

- Provide some incentives such as transportation options or help in finding housing, if relocation is necessary

Other important traits of effective staff is that they love and respect children, that they believe that these adjudicated delinquents have the will and the capacity to become productive citizens, and that they have skills in working with this population. Staff must establish and maintain the norms and values to create a positive environment where social learning theory and cognitive-behavioral interventions will be effective. Residents observe and mimic staff actions. Residents shape their behaviors through their interactions with staff. This is one of the issues highlighted in the *Blue Ribbon Task Force Report: Transforming Juvenile Justice in Texas* (2007). The Task Force recommends that staff are appropriately educated and that "they are youth focused and strength based in their approaches. This is a critical issue that requires sustained attention."

A third important trait is that those staff who are promoted are the most appropriate to supervise other staff and residents. Thus, administrators need to be thoughtful and careful about whom they select for promotions. Some administrators think that they can promote people who have mastered some technical correctional skills such as disciplining youth or writing good reports. However, staff who do not connect with the youth or form appropriate relationships with them are a problem. If they become supervisors, they are a much bigger problem. They become an impediment to developing the type of environment necessary for success.

What Schedules Will Staff Work?

Staff schedules must not be solely for the convenience of staff. If a facility's prosocial culture is to be maintained, it is important to have seasoned staff (both direct services staff and supervisors) working when the youth and their families are available. Since most residential programs have the youth in school Monday through Friday during the day, experienced staff and supervisors need to be available evenings and weekends.

Staying at the facility at "off hours" must be part of the job. Building and maintaining positive culture is a continuous process. Leadership's physical presence is important.

Administrators must establish work schedules for themselves, their management, their supervisors, and their professional staff to work some nontraditional hours. This supervisory presence and positive role modeling will support direct service staff and lead to a caring culture, where staff respect each other and work as a team.

Supervisors must understand and have their behavior support positive role modeling. It is counterproductive if supervisors are present during these non-school hours but are complaining the entire time about being at the facility. The administrator's role is to not let these all too common negative attitudes go unchallenged. The administrator must respond quickly to these attitudes to stop them from becoming entrenched or affecting the quality of care. Institutions that have not addressed these issues in a timely manner have found that, much like a disease, these negative attitudes can spread quickly and infect the entire facility's culture.

How and When are Staff and Residents Rewarded or Disciplined?

Historically, institutions for correctional youth maintained an orderly facility by establishing clear rules, by making sure that staff and residents understood the rules, and by consistently enforcing those rules. Having a facility that appeared safe and orderly seemed to be sensible and effective. Yet, the problem with this type of order is that it was not conducive to youth rehabilitation. It tended to have staff acting more as guards than as change agents. The staffs' job was defined by keeping order and was spent catching residents doing something wrong and then correcting and/or disciplining them. This one-way communication stimulated by wrongdoing did not lead to the type of helping relationships that were conducive to change.

Although some youth benefited from this arrangement, learning from their mistakes, most never internalized the changes. Youth learned to respond appropriately when staff were physically present but returned to their old habitual behaviors when staff were not. Worse—high recidivism rates were the norm for youth after discharge from almost all of these institutions confirming the lack of internalized positive change.

By contrast, administrators of successful facilities have learned that one ingredient of creating a positive culture is to look for and reward the positive behaviors of both staff and residents. This is not to say that rules are ignored, it simply means more time, energy, and training go into reinforcing staff and residents' positive behaviors. Experts now understand and research supports the idea that a ratio of four compliments/rewards for positive behavior to every one correction/consequence for negative behavior is a formula that will help build positive culture or even turn around a facility that is struggling (Salisbury 2003).

This is accomplished by establishing policies and procedures that clearly expect staff interactions with each other and with residents to be consistent with this ratio of four positive interactions to each negative one. This positive method of supervising and interacting with youth in a correctional facility runs counter to years of correctional tradition, institutional history, occupational expectations, and even formal education which all emphasized finding out what was wrong and fixing it. The focus was constantly on negative behaviors. However, to now expect, because research demonstrates better results with positive reinforcements, that seasoned correctional institutional staff will simply embrace this "new" focus is naive.

Many institutions have attempted to change their focus but have had little success. Staff feared loss of control. They believed that if they kept complimenting them, youth would take advantage of the staff and see them as "soft." Those facilities that have succeeded in this paradigm shift from the negative to the positive had one thing in common: strong, assertive, and involved leadership.

In both new facilities and existing ones, for positive recognition to be the norm and a natural part of everyday life in the facility, the administrator and his/her supervisory team must be directly involved. This leadership team needs to have direct and indirect, formal and informal, methods of assessing the positive and negative health of the culture. They need to respond in a timely manner to the results of these assessments. They need to role model administering the recognition and rewards (both formal and informal) to both staff and residents. Staff need to see first hand that the facility will not become unsafe because of all the positive recognition. On the contrary, facilities that have implemented the four to one positives have experienced a reduction in residents' behavior problems.

ASSESSING THE FACILITY CULTURE

For administrators to know what is going on in their institution, there is no better way than by walking around and interacting with staff and youth. Effective leaders get out of their office and have a "hands on" philosophy. This does not mean they believe in micromanaging, but understand it is a good way to show that they care and a good way to get a quick assessment of how things are going with programming, with the kids, with the staff, and with the overall culture.

Important questions include: Are staff and residents treating each other with respect? Are staff talking with the youth they are supervising? Is there an overall sense of safety or does the facility feel out of control? Are the staff interacting with residents or are they preoccupied with their computers or newspapers? Are staff being helpful in their interactions with youth or is there much yelling and/or demands? Are the youth interacting with each other respectfully? What are the attitudes of staff and residents? Are they happy? How is the hygiene and clothing of the staff and youth? What does the physical facility look like? Is it clean and in order? Are youth rooms appropriately decorated?

There are other informal methods for administration to obtain current information regarding the health of the facility:

- Eat lunch every day in the dining rooms with the youth. Talk with the youngsters as much as possible and ask your staff: "What are the kids talking about?"

- Be involved in special events with the youth. Good facilities have lots of "special" events during the course of the year—everything from holidays, to carnivals, to sporting events. Attend them. Participate in them. Both staff and residents will appreciate your involvement and you will get a sense of how things are going.

- Volunteer to fill in as a "hearing officer" or attend disciplinary hearings periodically. When youth get in trouble, they usually have an opportunity to be heard in the facility before they are given a consequence that limits their movement. There is nothing better than filling in as the hearing officer for the day to get a sense of where the facility culture is at. Be that person that hears the case as to what is going on (violation of the rules) and what discipline is being administered (how severe or lenient).

- Be available to go and talk to youth when they are in a difficult situation. This can build positive culture for the residents and the staff. Staff see that the superintendent will go where "the tire meets the road" and that this is not just a one-time occurrence. Sometimes line staff are having a difficult time with a youth, and the administrator's authority alone can deal with the problem.

- Require daily briefings from supervisors on duty. This will assure that administrators are briefed, not just on the negative events of the day but the positive ones as well.

Types of Rewards for Staff and Residents

Knowing which staff are consistently practicing the four to one favorable interactions is the first step in ensuring the establishment of positive culture. Staff who are doing their job within the spirit of the mission and not just going through the motions need to be recognized. Administrators need to make sharing the supportive work of staff a topic of discussion with managers and supervisors and a standing agenda item.

Informal Recognition of Staff. Do not wait to recognize staff annually. Recognition should be daily, with something as small as saying, "good job." Administrators, who recognize the importance of positive culture, look to everyday activity as the first way to build and support it.

Ongoing support needs to be a part of the daily dialog. In some sense, this daily recognition is far more important than organized recognition events because it is the foundation for positive staff culture. Formal and informal ways of noticing and acknowledging good work become the culture. Administrators can make it a point to end staff's day on a supportive note and begin other staff's day with a supportive note.

Staff should know that the administration cares about the daily work they are involved in with residents. Follow-up directly with staff who have been involved in situations where someone has been hurt. Staff will truly believe that caring is not just empty rhetoric when they experience first-hand the director's support and care. Directors build positive culture by role modeling and interacting with staff the way staff are expected to interact with residents. Hold them accountable but support, nurture, and reward behavior that supports a safe and caring environment.

Formal Recognition Events for Staff. Hold quarterly events and annual recognitions. These recommendations for staff recognition should have a special filter. Administrators need to choose staff who consistently perform well and may have a single positive event that raises the acknowledgement to the level of an award. Nothing is wrong with saying "good job" even to someone with a history of poor performance.

Formal Recognition of Residents. In addition to the recognition of staff, residents also need recognition for positive efforts and behaviors. It is important to allow residents who have been released from the program and have been successful in aftercare to come back and be keynote speakers at events, such as at graduation. There is nothing better than peer role modeling, and these residents always acknowledge care and treatment staff, along with teachers.

An event such as this not only excites the graduates but also creates a favorable impression to staff and improves resident culture in the facility for weeks. It sweeps through the place, especially when teachers are asked to take the time to recognize other students in the student body at graduation. These recognitions can be for "best improved," "positive behavior," "excellence in math," and so forth. Something simple but meaningful can be done for the students, such as giving them a certificate and a rose.

One advantage of making a big deal out of graduation is that stakeholders, (even the media) politicians, central administration, probation, parents, and local service clubs can be invited, and one or more of the key stakeholders can have an honored role in the event. This is another way to normalize the facility to a community-celebration standard. Residents, staff, parents and key stakeholders see the successes, become inspired, begin to believe in their value, and gain the energy to continue their hard work.

CONCLUSIONS

Today, administrators of juvenile residential correctional treatment facilities need to pay special attention to building a prosocial therapeutic culture. This is a culture that has positive norms, caring values, clear and fair rules, and expectations, which support safety, nurturing, and accountability. Only in this type of environment can residents respond to role modeling and be attentive to learning so they can achieve the positive internalized change necessary to thrive in life without resorting to criminal behaviors. Administrators have the responsibility to develop and maintain this culture by:

- Hiring and promoting staff who have a passion for working with youth. This is staff who have the capability of forming positive relationships with the youth who are committed to the facility

- Training the staff to recognize their power as change agents and their influence as role models

- Ensuring staff (all staff) are working and available evenings and weekends when youth are not in their school programming

- Ensuring that formal and informal rewards for positive behaviors outweigh correcting negative ones.

REFERENCES

Bartollas, Clemens, Stuart J. Miller, and Simon Dinitz. 1976. *Juvenile Victimization: The Institutional Paradox*. New York: Halsted Press.

Green, Andrew A. 2005. "Hickey School to be Closed." *Baltimore Sun*, July 1.

Salsbury, Robert. 2003 "Incentive Programming Principles and Applications." Training Session Hennepin County Home School.

Springer, David W. *Transforming Juvenile Justice in Texas*. 2007. Austin, Texas: Blue Ribbon Task Force Report.

Vorrath, Harry H. and Larry K. Brendtro. 1974. *Positive Peer Culture*. Chicago: Aldine Publishing Company.

CHAPTER 8

STAFF TRAINING

Staff training can make the difference between a successful program and one that does not make a difference.

Training plays a critical role in the overall safety, security, and quality of care in residential programs for youth. Leaders of these programs are faced with some unique challenges when deciding who should attend the training, what training should be presented, and when the training is to be given. These decisions are affected by the fact that staff from many different disciplines are working at different times on different days—twenty-four hours a day/seven days a week.

Psychologists, teachers, social workers, doctors, nurses, chaplains, maintenance personnel, security staff, direct services staff, and volunteers who work with these youth have training needs both unique to their profession and generic to their facility. Work being performed twenty-four hours a day, in different buildings, with different populations, and on different days and shifts add timing, delivery, and location problems to any facility's training plan. Training is also more costly with residential staff since direct service staff either must be replaced or paid overtime to attend any "live" training. The variety and scope of training topics available make it challenging for facility administrators to sort through all of them and make decisions on what their facility needs and does not need. For instance, some training is required by licensure/law; some is essential for safety; and some meets unique needs of the institution at the time. The following figure will help guide leaders through this difficult decision-making process.

Figure 8.1

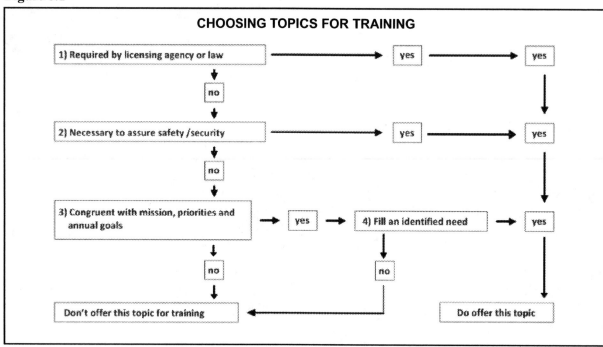

CHOOSING TOPICS FOR TRAINING

1. Training Required By Licensing Agency or Law

An ongoing training curriculum should be established with training standards that comply with the agency's licensing rules and city, state, and federal law or codes, including the American Correctional Association accreditation standards. All residential facilities today are subject to inspection and licensed by a licensing authority whether it is the state department of corrections, health and human services or some combination of these. The licensing authority establishes rules or standards under which facilities operate. The training section provides a list of requirements for custody staff, program staff, and support staff. They include training in such issues as emergency procedures, security procedures, and blood-borne pathogens. These requirements need to be met, but rarely is the list exhaustive or tailored to the population served at a specific facility.

Concurrently, training is often required as directed under city code for facilities that operate their own food service, and fire safety training. For example, local fire marshals, who inspect the buildings for fire safety, may require specific training. This type of training usually is more prescriptive. Often it involves detailed curriculum such as food-borne illness prevention in the handling of food for food service workers.

Federal or state law or statute addresses specialized training such as the Prison Rape Elimination Act (PREA), the medical records requirement of the Health Insurance Portability and Accountability Act (HIPAA), the safety requirements of the Occupational Safety and Health Act (OSHA), and the regulations of the Americans with Disability Act (ADA), and mandatory reporting training. Meeting or exceeding the training directed by these agencies is essential in the delivery of services, shielding facilities from frivolous lawsuits and consent decrees, and providing a foundation for a rehabilitative environment.

2. Training Necessary to Assure Safety and Security

The list of training pertinent to safety and security is a long one. It includes the obvious such as first aid, C.P.R., suicide prevention, and "headcounts," but it also includes the not so obvious, yet important, training necessary to establish and maintain a safe and secure institution. These would include the following:

- Developing a profile of youth in the facility

- Using authority and relationship building

- Understanding staff/client boundaries

- Developing skills in behavior management, de-escalation, and use of force

- Debriefing of physical incidents

- Understanding gangs and dealing with gang members

- Using technology

- Understanding facility culture

- Developing teamwork

Developing a Profile of Youth. Training required for safety and security must be tailored to fit the profile of youth in residence. This means that training on the use of force and gaining compliance to rules needs to be tailored to youth with mental health problems. Lecturing a noncompliant developmentally delayed youth will be ineffective (see Boesky 2010). Modeling and practicing the desired behaviors will have better results. Responding to a noncompliant youth diagnosed with Post Traumatic Stress Disorder with loud orders and demands will likely result in increased acting out. Staff who use their professional relationships to calmly and clearly state their expectations are more likely to succeed in having these youth come into compliance.

Using Authority and Relationship Building. The relationship staff have with youth is a staff-safety issue. When a youth understands, really knows, that a staff member cares, he/she is far less likely to resort to violence and far more likely to respond to a staff request. The youth also is more likely to positively respond to de-escalation techniques. Safe facilities understand that relationships are protective factors for staff. Authority without a relationship foundation often must be supported by intimidation of youth. Authority of this kind is not only short lived but counterproductive to rehabilitation.

Therefore, authority is most effective when used in the context of a solid therapeutic relationship. Dale Hardemenn in an article in *Federal Probation* discussed the importance of relationships when exercising authority:

> the degree to which I can create relationships which facilitate the growth of others
> . . . is a measure of growth I have achieved myself. The exercise of my authority will
> always be executed with empathy and understanding of the offenders total needs as
> a person—a person always worthy of my interest, respect and affection (1960).

His observations are still pertinent today. Feature 8.2, presents a sample policy and is an effective staff-training tool.

Feature 8.2 Sample Policy

This policy provides basic principles for the professional use of authority and the treatment of clients. These principles represent the general treatment philosophy of the institution and the basic treatment knowledge for all work with clients.

DISCUSSION

Juvenile facilities serve youths with specialized needs and risks. Institutional policy requires that all direct supervision staff have a demonstrated knowledge of principles behind the professional use of authority in the process of change.

PROCEDURE

1. PROFESSIONAL PRINCIPLES ON THE USE OF AUTHORITY

1.a.   <u>Whenever I use authority, I will</u>

- Use it openly and honestly

- Never make a referral, recommendation, or report about a client without sharing the knowledge of this with him/her

- First let the resident know from me, if I am required to submit an evaluation, a pre-sentence report, or referral to a psychiatric clinic

1.b   <u>I will be crystal clear in defining my role, know where my authority begins and ends, and I will consistently function within these limits.</u>

- I will avoid using veiled threats, bluffing, or employing any behavior that might be so interpreted, since this could cloud rather than clarify my limits.

- This rule will eliminate a vast amount of testing by the client.

1.c   <u>I will further clarify which decisions are mine to make and which the client must make,</u>

1.d   Once I have made a decision, I will steadfastly resist all client efforts to alter my decision by threats, tantrums, seduction, illness, and so forth.

- I will just as steadfastly defend the residents' rights to make decisions and stand by them.

Continued on the next page

Sample Policy *continued*

- In the same way, if a resident shows me rational evidence that I have made a hasty or unwise decision, I will alter my decision and will tell him or her so.

1.e   <u>Once a client has made a decision, I will insist that he/she assume and face the responsibilities impinging on that decision. I will just as aggressively stand by the responsibility for my decisions.</u>

The worst approach toward correcting this is to lecture a person on accepting responsibility, then hedging to avoid our own. An example would be a parole officer who says: "It is the committee's decision to revoke your parole," when, in fact, it was the parole officer who made the report and recommended that the parole be revoked. At this point, his admonition to the parolee sounds pretty hollow.

1.f   <u>I cannot effectively help a person with a conflict of authority unless I have resolved those conflicts myself.</u>

- If I feel reluctant to use my authority, guilty for having used it, and seek someone else to use it for me, then I had better examine my own motives.

- I can never show a probationer or parolee that authority can be kind and just if I perceive or act in my role in a punitive and/or capricious way.

1.g   <u>The exercise of my authority will always be executed with empathy and understanding of the offender's total needs as a person—a person always worthy of my interest, respect, and affection.</u>

- This implies that my role is re-constructive rather than retributive, helping rather than punishing, friendly rather than hostile.

Understanding Staff/Client Boundaries. A precursor to serious incidents, which compromise facility safety, is often times a staffer becoming involved in a personal rather than professional relationship with a resident.

- The staff becomes involved in a relationship for profit and smuggles contraband such as drugs and weapons.

- The staff becomes involved in a romantic relationship (letters, phone calls, fantasies), which does not involve sexual contact but additionally smuggles gifts and contraband.

- The staff becomes involved in sexual misconduct, defined as anything from touching, or kissing, to raping.

The Prison Rape Elimination Act of 2003 (PREA)—Public Law 108-79—requires the Bureau of Justice Statistics within the U.S. Department of Justice to conduct an annual national survey of residential correctional programs and prisons to report the extent and effect of prison rape. The 2005 survey reported the following:

- That two-thirds of sexual incidents reported were "romantic" or consensual

- That coercion by staff (force, pressure, indecent exposure, unwanted touching) is more common in jail (43 percent) than in residential facilities (26 percent)

- That 47 percent of the facility staff involved in the incidents were more than forty-years of age

- That most substantiated incidents involved correctional officers as perpetrators

These inappropriate relationships are poison to facility safety. Stopping such behavior requires training employees to be fair, firm, and impartial in their relationships with residents. Training needs to focus on how to identify and stop staff from crossing the line between a professional and a personal relationship.

Listed below are some staff behaviors that are indicators or "red flags" that, when witnessed by other staff, need to be addressed and brought out into the open (see Cornelius 2009):

- Isolation from other staff

- Staff granting special requests or showing favoritism

- Staff is too familiar with a resident, nicknames, secrets, and so forth

- Staff spending an unexplainable amount of time with a resident

- Staff in the facility during off hours

- Staff overly concerned about a resident

- Staff working with a resident in a secluded area

- Staff going through a personal crisis

- Staff requesting favorable treatment for a resident

- Conversations between staff and resident that are sexual in nature

- Undue amount of contact with the offender's family

Employing Behavior Management, De-Escalation, and Use of Force. Staff and youth should expect that the first response to negative behavior is always to talk with the youth and to de-escalate the behavior even if, in the end, physical restraint is necessary. This expectation will help to set the tone of a respectful and safe facility culture.

Policies need to emphasize that in most non-life threatening incidents, physical force is the last option for staff to use for maintaining safety. According to the U.S. Department of Justice Civil Rights Division:

> When staff are trained or allowed to resort too quickly to threats and force in the face of non-compliant adolescent behavior, minor incidents get escalated and the risk of harm increases for both the juvenile and the officer (2006).

Policies should reflect a continuum of interventions, beginning with ignoring the behavior, requesting compliance, and employing de-escalating techniques before demanding and restraining the youth. Most facilities also employ a "show of force" when it appears a situation is becoming threatening. Policies direct all available staff to the scene of the altercation. Many times, just the sight of so many staff will motivate the youth to stop misbehaving.

Use of "hardware" such as handcuffs, restraint beds, and pepper spray needs to be limited to youth transport or used as a last resort in gaining behavioral control. To assure appropriate use, administrators must review with staff the use of all physical restraints. Training needs to encourage staff to exercise their de-escalation skills and professional judgment in each situation.

Evidence-based practice tells us that the most effective behavior-management systems include consequences and rewards. Staff are safest when youth are motivated by their own internal values and controls to behave in a socially acceptable manner. Incentives and rewards are the surest and quickest way for youth to learn these new behaviors. Clear rules and norms that are enforced swiftly and consistently when combined with rewards for expected behavior will result in a safer facility.

Safe facilities also have policies that prohibit other youth from being involved in restraints and overall behavior control. Children cannot safely restrain other children without a higher risk of injury. They do not have the maturity, training, or professional boundaries to ensure safe interventions. Unfortunately, there are juvenile correctional facilities that, either because of philosophy or staffing shortages, permit residents under certain circumstances to physically restrain other residents.

In 2007, a large private juvenile correctional institution in Maryland experienced the tragedy of the death of one of its residents because other youth were involved in the youth's restraint. Although it was a tragic accident, Maryland authorities believed it possibly could have been avoided if properly trained professional staff had been the ones intervening.

Understanding the Importance and Method of Debriefing Incidents. Improvements in staff safety happen if each occurrence where staff safety is compromised is thoroughly reviewed by both administrators and staff. Debriefing will also ensure that the follow-up with staff is appropriate and that improvements are made in training and programming. Important questions at this time are the following:

- What happened?

- What could have been done differently leading up to the incident or during it?

- What have we learned?

- What do we need to improve?

- Is it our training?

- Is it our programming?

- Were appropriate physical restraints used?

- Was documentation from staff complete?

- What follow-up plans are needed with the staff or youth who were involved in the incident?

Understanding Gangs and Dealing with Gang Members. Many facilities are faced with the fact that gang members and gang "wannabes" can, and many times do, undermine residents' learning and practicing pro-social behaviors. If left unchecked, gang members will attempt to recreate the environment they originated from and often will look to recruit other youth in the facility.

Gang membership and numbers of youth gangs have decreased slightly in the past decade, but, at the same time, many jurisdictions are reporting increases in gang membership. In Los Angeles for example, "over the last decade, the authorities throughout Los Angeles County have arrested more than 450,000 juveniles, while gang membership doubled" (Moore 2009).

Many juvenile institutions now are faced with increasing numbers of gang members. They need to take a proactive approach, beginning with recognizing that gangs exist. Facilities must have rules that are consistently enforced regarding colors, clothing, hair styles, signs, and the language of gangs. There must be zero tolerance for any gang behavior. There needs to be a response to rule violation, but the response does not have to be locking the youth up in "segregation." Responses that are more effective and build stronger relationships include consequences with cognitive interventions such as "thinking reports."

Some facilities have regularly scheduled meetings with local and state police gang units. These meetings provide an effective means of communicating up-to-date gang awareness information to facility staff. Since signs and symbols change often, this knowledge helps interrupt gang communications and threats in the facility and in the community.

Staff training needs to include the following items:

- Being aware of each resident's gang affiliation

- Making decisions for housing and program assignments that consider gang ties and whether past interactions included violence

- Observing attempts at secret communication and intervention techniques

- Documenting gang activity with photos, whenever possible

- Knowing the confidential list of local gang acronyms

- Employing peer reminders to closely supervise residents when grouping occurs. Take into consideration gang activity and affiliation when making decision for off-campus activities or home visits

- Making clear your expectations about acceptable behavior and providing a clear message with consistent consequences, which can include disciplinary segregation for serious violations

The most effective policy is zero tolerance for any gang activity. Gangs are only as powerful as the facility allows. To support the zero tolerance policy, the staff need to be equipped with the knowledge and the tools to teach, build relationships, and expose the myths that are part of the gangs allure. Youth need to know that they are being exploited in many instances by adult members.

They need to learn that there are alternatives to the gang lifestyle that make it possible to succeed without resorting to drug sales and violence. Lonnie Jackson's *Gangbusters—Strategies for Prevention and Intervention* (1998) is an excellent training curriculum specific to gang intervention.

Employing Technology such as Cameras, Radios, Alarms, and Automatic Door Locks. Employing the right technology for the facility and training the staff in the use of this technology as an aid to safety and security is an important consideration in training. Yet, staff need to remember that these are just tools. Policies need to reflect that these tools are never to be used as a replacement for staff interaction with youth. The fact is that overreliance on technology, as well as not employing technology, can create an environment where staff will be unsafe.

A large private secure institution in the Western United States exemplified this by requiring all staff to wear headsets as a means of communicating facility activity. Staff were pre-occupied with the listening devices, spent very little time talking with committed youth and, therefore, did not develop relationships with them. This, in turn, created an unsafe environment. This facility was closed due to the inordinate number of restraints used, resulting in staff and resident injuries.

Some administrators have made conscious decisions not to employ technology. They do not have magnetic locks on the doors–thus making it unsafe for residents and staff in some situations. They usually do not use cameras but when using cameras they do not record or store any of the images for review during investigations.

Understanding the Facility's Culture. There must be an expectation and training program to ensure cultural competence. This involves the ability to understand others, to accept and use the uniqueness of their problem-solving skills and to recognize that their action-oriented skills vary from one cultural group to another. It is important to recognize, acknowledge, and honor the differences and similarities within varying cultural communities. Whether you are the cook, the psychologist, the teacher, or direct service line staff, every interaction with youth and other staff effects the environment and the culture of the facility. All interactions have a direct impact on the progress of youth on their treatment issues. Staff should understand the power they have over these young lives and how harmful it can be to tolerate negative behavior from their colleagues. A large block of staff training should focus on how each and every member contributes to the overall culture of the facility. All staff need to understand that they truly do make an impact whether it be positive or negative. In effective residential centers, the leaders instill in their staff the importance of each of them in making the facility a success. When staff believe that they can make a difference, the signs of positive facility culture emerge.

Employing Team Work. All personnel, whether they be support, direct service, or professional staff, need to be accountable at all times for the whereabouts of the youth with whom they are working. Many institutions that sustain an inordinate number of staff injuries separate the roles of security and treatment. Treatment staff do the "clinical work" while the role of security (such as transporting youth and completing "head counts") rests solely with security staff. Youth in these unsafe facilities have learned that when they are with professional staff, they can act out or break rules without being held accountable. Training and expectations for clinical staff must include their security responsibilities. Conversely, training and expectations for direct service staff need to include their responsibility to understand and support clinical work.

There must be a facility expectation that all staff operate as a team—communicating with each other, working out their differences in style and philosophy, and agreeing to adapt and follow team decisions even if they personally disagree. This takes time, training, and meetings. This team development is intensive and contributes to the need for a greater number of required training hours for all staff.

Staff must also understand the value of and need to come together and function as a team. This is no easy task considering the formidable barriers: the nature of the residents who are skilled at manipulating, and the differing backgrounds of staff—education, experience, philosophy, and ethnicity. Facility training must emphasize that a group with diverse backgrounds and education simply will not be effective in working with youth in residential care, unless they function as a team. They have to learn to respect each other, and they need to schedule times to ensure that they consult each other.

They should develop formal, structured and informal methods to keep each other informed of their work and interactions with the youth. They must find ways to support each other's work and find some common ground. Appropriate training will help facilitate this effort. Professional staff need to attend security training, and security- and direct-service staff need to learn the basic fundamentals of clinical work.

Kate Anderson and Kimberly Sperber developed an excellent training curriculum for non-clinical staff, *Advancing Skill Sets and Interactions of the Security and Support Team*–"A.S.S.I.S.S.T" (2005). This curriculum provides basic fundamentals of cognitive-behavioral theory and practical cognitive-behavioral intervention techniques. To date they have trained staff in Illinois, Iowa, Indiana, Ohio, Florida, Minnesota, and California.

Ongoing training also needs to ensure that clinical staff (psychiatrists, psychologists, social workers, chemical dependency counselors) see themselves as members of a treatment team and not as clinical experts who work as isolated individual therapists. Many facilities that struggle to develop a positive culture are ones that have allowed various professionals, such as teachers, therapists, or medical personnel, to operate in a vacuum with no responsibility to the rest of the staff team working with the youth. The disregard for the importance of team work leads to lack of support from other staff and lack of progress for the youth being treated.

Professional clinical staff actually can place residents and staff in danger by consciously withholding information from other team members because of their own professional code of confidentiality. Harm can occur when clinical staff do not communicate vital information from their youth therapy sessions to direct services staff. If safety concerns and vital resident information is not communicated clearly and in a timely manner, along with a plan for structure and support at the living unit, behavior problems and tragedy are oftentimes the result.

In one institution, after a serious assault against a staff member, the follow-up investigation revealed that during an individual therapy session, the perpetrator of the assault shared that he was extremely angry with that staff member and had fantasies of beating him up. The therapist testified that because of confidentiality, he could not warn the staffer who was the object of the resident's anger. However, if a facility is to be safe, team work and all of its aspects must be included in the training curriculum.

3. Training Must Be Congruent with Mission, Priorities, and Goals

When the facility administrator has decided what training topics are required by law and licensing and what is needed to maintain safety, he or she must then decide what other training should be offered. What other needs have been identified that training will help meet?

In terms of the mission, what is left is treatment. Recent research shows what types of interventions and treatment strategies work best with specific populations. New research helps staff to understand adolescent learning styles. Effective family interventions such as structural family therapy and multi-systemic family therapy (MST) are being successfully used with juvenile delinquent populations. Evidence-based practices with cognitive-behavioral interventions embedded in anger management, chemical dependency treatment, and Motivational Interviewing are proving to be effective with adolescents.

Better understanding and clearer diagnosis of fetal alcohol syndrome, post traumatic stress syndrome (PTSD), and reactive attachment disorders have led to some innovative treatment approaches. Sorting through this dizzying array of training possibilities—making decisions about which ones to offer and which ones not to offer—is an important task as resources are limited. Only so much training can be expected or provided, and the administration should select the training that best fits its current facility needs.

Training—Filling an Identified Need. The responsibility of the administrator is to identify ongoing training needs and make decisions about what to provide this month or this year. Larger facilities have found that because of the complexity, scope, and importance of this task, a full-time training director is required.

Here are some ideas to help ensure that a facility training plan is addressing current needs.

a) Review all injuries during the year. One secure facility found that during the previous two years, almost 30 percent of staff injuries occurred when personnel pulled a muscle running to respond to an "all call" (a request for help from other staff). They conducted a brief training session on stretching leg muscles throughout the day. The following year, they saw a significant drop in leg-muscle injuries.

b) Review and de-brief every suicide and suicide attempt. One facility changed all of their in-room water sprinklers after a youth attempted to hang himself and the head of the sprinkler failed to break off at the specified weight.

c) Annually conduct a training survey: include things such as what training was most helpful, what format worked best, and any training that staff attended on their own that would be good for the facility.

d) Annually review the profile of youth entering the facility because changes in that profile will dictate changes in the focus of the clinical training. As an example, there might be an increase in an immigrant population that would make it important for training to focus on that population's unique cultural differences.

e) Develop a training committee representative of all of the job classes and programs in the facility. Developing a comprehensive annual training plan that meets the requirements of law, licensing, and the needs of the staff is the primary task of the training committee. This training committee needs to meet regularly and report on any emerging trends or needs and make recommendations to the administrator for including or excluding specific training topics, curriculums, and schedules. Recommendations from this committee can prove invaluable to the administrators in their task of ensuring that training is meeting the current needs of the staff.

For example, at one facility on the east coast, the night staff training committee representative expressed concerns for the safety of the staffer who worked the overnight shift. Budget reductions had changed staffing patterns to just one staff in each of the twenty-four bed living units. Several "backup" staff were located centrally to respond to problems. Permanently assigning more staff to overnights was not within their budget. Locking the resident rooms was prohibited by licensing because the rooms were not equipped with toilet facilities. Locking the hallway doors that separated the residents from the staff would prohibit staff from important responsibilities such as conducting routine bed checks or responding to the needs of the residents who required medications.

After discussion and debate, the training committee recommended some simple adjustments that included: where and how residents could legitimately interact safely with night staff; completing bed checks only when the central backup staff were present; and communicating with staff working in the other living units if there was a need to interact with residents at other times.

WHEN THE TRAINING IS OFFERED

Now that the list of training topics that address laws, licensing, mission and needs has been compiled, the administrators' role is to determine what should be offered as pre-service or orientation and what needs to be included in the ongoing requirements.

Pre-Employment Training

Some jurisdictions require specific training for direct service staff (California requires completion of a sixteen-week curriculum) or courses in criminal justice (Hennepin County requires forty college credits in the behavioral sciences) before staff can even qualify to apply to their facilities. Other facilities, most notably private for profit ones, require nothing more than a high school diploma.

Pre-Service or Orientation

Some jurisdictions such as Michigan have statewide pre-service academies for newly hired institutional staff but, even then, site-specific orientation training is important. Because new staff originate from a wide variety of backgrounds, experiences, and education, team work will not occur without a comprehensive orientation. We know from our previous discussion how critical teamwork is to the overall success of the facility and that is why we are recommending intensive cohort training for all classifications. Classroom training topics typically include treatment philosophy, mission, safety, security, teamwork, and policies and procedures. A comprehensive orientation also should require forty to eighty hours of on-the-job training (shadowing a veteran staffer) prior to assuming assigned job duties.

Figure 8.3 is an example of an orientation outline that displays suggested content.

Figure 8.3

NEW EMPLOYEE ORIENTATION TRAINING SCHEDULE

DAY 1

9:00–9:30	Registration and Welcome
9:30–10:30	Facility Tour
10:30–11:00	Break
11:00-12:00	Introduction to Facility and Mission Statement– Superintendent
12:00-12:30	Lunch as a Cohort
12:30–1:00	Personnel Paperwork and Introduction to Supervisors
1:00–2:30	Emergency Procedures
2:30–3:00	TB Test and Break
3:00–4:00	Suicide Prevention—Part I Characteristics of Juvenile Suicide in Confinement (Hayes 2009)
4:00–5:00	Training Materials and Policy Manuals

DAY 2

9:00–9:30	Driver's License Requirements Policy and Sign-up for Defensive Driving
9:30–10:30	Suicide Prevention—Part II Policy Review—Assistant Superintendent
10:30–10:45	Break
10:45 –12:15	Diversity Policy and Diversity Icebreaker
12:15–1:00	Lunch
1:00–1:30	Suicide Prevention—Part III Demographics of Adolescent Suicide—Medical Director
1:30–2:30	Introduction to Medical Unit and Medical Services—Nursing Supervisor
2:30–2:45	Break
2:45–4:15	Medications Administration—Nursing Supervisor
4:15–5:00	Sexual Harassment Awareness Video

DAY 3

9:00–10:00	Code of Ethics Policy–Superintendent or Assistant Superintendent
10:00–10:15	Break
10:15–12:15	Introduction to Incentive Programming
12:15–1:00	Lunch
1:00–1:45	Report Writing—Operations Coordinator
1:45– 3:45	Introduction to Rewards and Consequences
3:45--4:15	TB Check and Break
4:15–5:00	Wrap Up

Continued on page 114

NEW EMPLOYEE ORIENTATION TRAINING SCHEDULE, *continued*

DAY 4

8:30–9:00	Processing of Training to Date—Program Manager
9:00–11:00	Program Tour (specific to unit)—Program Manager(s)
11:00–12:00	Time Cards/Payroll Information
12:00–12:30	Lunch
12:30–4:30	Security Procedures Training Operations

Presenting portions of this orientation training is an opportune time for the facility administrator to meet new staff and directly communicate with them his/her philosophy and priorities. This will not only begin to build relationships with the new staff but will underscore the importance of the training being provided.

On-the-Job Training

After completion of preservice classroom training, many residential centers require new direct service staff to a "field training officer" (veteran direct service staff who volunteer to help train new hires) who assures that their first days on the job are spent learning the best ways of responding to and intervening with residents. These field training officers are usually specifically selected because they are proven role models and outstanding performers. They themselves receive special training so they will be more effective with the new hires. Special recognition and/or additional compensation help to recruit and retain these on-the-job trainers.

WHO ATTENDS TRAINING?

Deciding who should or who must attend a particular training session and who should not has both fiscal and programmatic implications. The decision matrix of Table 8.1 will help guide those decisions.

Table 8.1 Who Should Be Required To Attend Training?

1. Everyone in facility needs	yes	no
2. Needed to fulfill duties of a specific job class	yes	no
3. Need to fulfill duties of a specific shift	yes	no
4. Needed to fulfill duties of a specific team	yes	no
5. For fulfillment of individualized development plan	yes	no

Oftentimes, administrators overlook the need to include contract staff, volunteers, and interns in their training. When using the decision matrix, it is important to include these personnel. We will now examine each of the elements of Table 8.1.

1. <u>Training required for everyone in the facility</u>

   Since safety and security is everyone's responsibility, topics such as emergency procedures, restraint training, security and key control, suicide prevention, OSHA regulations, and the right to know need to be mandatory training.

2. <u>Training needed to fulfill duties of a particular job class</u>

   This training is sometimes referred to as professional training with topics such as adolescent development for all staff who work directly with residents. One method of ensuring that the appropriate training is presented to the right staff is by offering training according to the five most common job categories: clerical, support, professional, direct service staff, and administration/ management.

3. <u>Training needed to fulfill duties of a specific shift</u>

   In a residential facility, some training is needed only during certain days or on certain shifts. For example, during school days and the hours the school is in session, direct service staff on duty need to have training on how to provide behavior management in the classroom with a set of rewards and consequences.

4. <u>Training needed to fulfill duties of a specific team</u>

   When a facility serves both genders, training needs to be gender specific for the staff working with girls.

5. <u>Training for fulfillment of Individualized Development Plan</u> (see pages 116-118)

   Staff should be encouraged to have an Individualized Development Plan (IDP) that includes new training or new experiences. A well developed IDP will not only aid the professional development of the individual staffer but will contribute to the overall positive culture of the facility. It is, therefore, important for the facility administrator to approve specific training for staff who have completed their IDP but have not met identified needs listed in the criteria discussed in items 1-4. Motivators to encourage staff to develop IDP's include: approving of tuition reimbursement, providing special assignments, and approving attendance at professional conferences. Table 8.2 on the following page is an example of what one jurisdiction implemented as an Individual Development Plan for its staff.

Table 8.2 Staff Individualized Development Plan

Name:	Date:

DEVELOPMENT OBJECTIVES:

(*For Directors, Managers, and Supervisors*):
What critical business results do I need to achieve in the next 6-18 months?

_____

_____

What are my development goals?

_____

_____

What competency or two will I focus my efforts on in the next 12 months?

_____

_____

OBSERVABLE BEHAVIORAL CHANGES

How will I know that I have accomplished my goals? What will be different?

_____

_____

DEVELOPMENT ACTIONS OR METHODS

What mix of development actions or methods do I intend to use?

_____

_____

FEEDBACK METHODOLOGY AND FREQUENCY

How will I receive feedback (from my manager, peers, stakeholders, and others) on my progress and how often?

_____

_____

SUPPORT

My manager can support my development by:

Send a copy of the completed plan to your manager within one week of your development discussion for review and approval.

Your signature _____ Date _____

Your manager's signature _____ Date _____

Individualized Development Plan Instructions

An Individualized Development Plan is a self-assessment instrument that should be completed annually by all staff. Its purposes are to (1) support employee development; (2) systematically collect information to guide training efforts and allocation of resources; and (3) foster a culture of learning. The components of an IDP are the following five:

1. Development Objectives

The first step is to clarify your developmental objectives. These differ depending upon the purpose for preparing an IDP. There are five different reasons for preparing an IDP.

Purpose for Completing IDP	Objective
IDP for Leadership Development	What critical business results do I need to achieve in the next six to eighteen months?
IDP for Self-Development (Assumes you are meeting "fully capable" standards in all aspects of your current job).	In what ways do I want to be more effective on the job? What skills do I want to enhance?
IDP for a Career Move	Where do I want to be in the next six to twenty-four months? What competencies or skills do I want/need to develop to achieve that goal?
IDP for Performance Improvement	What gaps need to be filled? To what level do I need to enhance these areas?
IDP for Team Development	What business results do we want/need to achieve in the next six to eighteen months? Do we want/need to become a stronger team? In what ways do we want/need to become that?

Next, you need to identify the competence or competencies on which to focus.

1. What are the competencies for which I am responsible?

2. How many competencies should I focus development efforts on?

3. How do I know what competency to focus on?

4. Should I have my boss use the self-assessment form in evaluating my relative strengths and weaknesses?

5. How should I use the results of this assessment?

6. Should I focus on my strengths or weaker areas?

2. Observable Behavioral Changes

Realistically, skill/job/career development time is limited by needing to meet pressing demands of daily work. However, for each employee to continue to be a strong contributor to the organization's mission, ongoing development is vital and must be viewed as an essential job requirement.

To balance ongoing work demands with development activities, it often helps to select one or two competency areas for attention. These should be areas of knowledge or skill that, if acquired or improved, would make big positive differences in your work outcomes, your job satisfaction and/or career opportunities.

Examples of development areas are the following:

- Meeting facilitation skills
- Improving interviewing skills
- Gaining proficiency in specific computer programs
- Improving presentation skills
- Learning delegation skills
- Improving time management
- Enhancing listening skills
- Asking good questions
- Developing team leadership skills
- Learning team member skills
- Increasing specific clinical or technical knowledge and skills

3. Development Actions or Methods

Learning can occur in a variety of ways. So, be creative and flexible when developing your own plan for development. Resources to help you reach your development goals may include:

- Health care training/workshops
- Tuition reimbursement for college courses
- Workshops offered by private vendors
- "Expanded" work assignments, in other words, doing something you have not done before to learn a new skill
- Job shadowing
- Reading, self-study

- 360 degree feedback
- Cross functional and/or cross-departmental assignments
- Mentors/coaches
- Regular time set aside to reflect on your work, accomplishments, and performance
- Supervisory and collegial moral support for practicing new skills
- Informational interviewing with other staff

4. Feedback Methodology and Frequency

For development to take place in a visible way, it is necessary to get feedback on progress being made in the specific competencies where development is being focused. To best accomplish this, there needs to be some understanding of how and how often this feedback will occur. A discussion of this between the supervisior and the employee completing the IDP helps answer this question on the IDP, which sets out how the parties will hold each other accountable.

5. Support

Identifying up front the methods or actions (see item 3) to be taken in developing a particular competency helps you anticipate and articulate the support that will be needed to ensure this development occurs. Some of this support involves financial support, but much development can and does occur through being afforded new learning opportunities and receiving effective feedback on the job from a number of sources.

CONCLUSIONS

Training staff working in residential institutions is essential to the overall safety and effectiveness of the facility and its programs. Careful planning by the administrator is required to insure that the training offered meets the mandates of law, what is necessary to assure safety and security, that it is congruent with the mission, priorities, and goals of the institution, and training that fills an identified need, such as dealing with staff injuries during the year, and residents' suicide attempts. The administrator then must determine what should be offered as pre-service or orientation and what needs to be included in the ongoing requirements. The chapter further considered who should attend the training and concluded with a staff individualized development plan.

REFERENCES

Anderson, Kate and Kimberly Sperber. 2005. *Advancing Skill Sets and Interactions of the Security and Support Team (ASSISST)*. Self-published. Information available at www.assisst.net

Boesky, Lisa. 2010. *Juvenile Offenders with Mental Health Disorders: Who are They and What Do We Do with Them, 2nd ed*. Alexandria, Virginia: American Correctional Association.

Hardemenn, Dale. 1960. "Function of the Probation Officer." *Federal Probation 24-25: September: 3-14.*

Hayes, Lindsay. 2009. "Characteristics of Juvenile Suicide in Confinement," *Juvenile Justice Bulletin*. U.S. Department of Justice, Juvenile Justice and Delinquency Prevention, Office of Justice Programs.

Jackson, Lonnie. 1998. *Gangbusters: Strategies for Prevention and Intervention*. Lanham, Maryland: American Correctional Association.

Moore, Solomon. 2009. "Gangs Grow, but Hard Line Stirs Doubt," *The New York Times*. January 9.

Prison Rape Elimination Act (PREA). 2003. Public Law 108-79.

U.S. Department of Justice, Civil Rights Division. 2006. *www.usdoj.gov/crt/activity.php*

CHAPTER 9

MODELS OF INSTITUTIONAL CARE

Celebrating a positive occasion is important. Two of the authors, Theresa Wise and Joseph Heinz, award a Hennepin County Home School graduate a diploma.

This chapter provides a brief description of three facilities selected as model juvenile correctional treatment facilities. The three facilities are the Hillcrest Training School in Cincinnati, Ohio; Hennepin County Home School in Minnetonka, Minnesota; and Hogan Street Regional Youth Center in St. Louis, Missouri.

At the conclusion of the descriptions is our analysis of the common elements that make them special. Our understanding of Hennepin County Home School comes from direct experience, as two of the authors were former superintendents of the facility. We asked juvenile expert Edward Latessa to recommend a juvenile residential facility that he was familiar with and believed was a model facility. He recommended Hillcrest, and we made an onsite visit with access to all staff and residents. Our onsite visit to Hillcrest also included in-depth interviews as well as visits to all parts of the facility and its offsite vocational programming. We used our professional networks, making calls to Carl Wicklund, executive director of the American Probation and Parole Association, and this led us to Missouri, specifically Hogan Street Youth Center. Although we made attempts to visit The Hogan Street Regional Youth Center in St. Louis, it was not possible within the framework of this publication's deadlines. We have included Hogan Street because it has been cited by many states for its positive outcomes and treatment of youth.

Hillcrest Training School

Hillcrest in Cincinnati, Ohio, operates 118 treatment beds for adjudicated male delinquent youth placed by the Hamilton County Juvenile Court. There are also twelve assessment beds for girls and twelve assessment beds for boys. Aftercare services are provided for boys and girls who have completed the program.

The program primarily serves youth who have committed felony offenses. The age of youth in residence ranges between twelve and eighteen. Hillcrest has dual accreditation by the American Correctional Association by meeting both the "Training School" Standards and "Aftercare Services" Standards. The Ohio Department of Mental Health has certified the facility's psychological services. The facility is handicapped accessible and meets all American Disability Act (ADA) standards. In addition, Hillcrest maintains National Commission on Correctional Health Care Services accreditation. The American Association of Suicidology also certifies Hillcrest. All clinical and educational staff are licensed. Many other staff have state certifications in specialized services.

In addition to the two assessment units, ten cottage units have a capacity of twelve youth in each and two cottage units have a capacity of eleven youth. The average length of stay for the general population is seven months (youth who are assigned to the sex-offender program average between fourteen and eighteen months in residence). Youth assigned to the Multidimensional Assessment Programs are in residence an average of twelve days. Services provided include individual counseling, group counseling, and many developmental activities. Parental participation includes weekend visitation, parent nights, home visits by social service staff, family counseling, and education and support groups.

Education. The education program is a "Special Needs Independent Charter School." Students have their educational needs met through a challenging, multidisciplinary curriculum designed to consider current credit needs, academic skill deficiencies, vocational interests, and cognitive self-management strategies for the classroom. The educational program supports each student's return to his or her community school. College scholarship funds are available for deserving students.

Cognitive-Behavioral Treatment. The Hillcrest Training School treatment program consists of three tracks:

- Youthful offenders who have sexually abused others

- Youthful offenders who have abused alcohol and other drugs

- Youthful offenders who have disruptive behavior disorders

The campus is divided by these three program tracks. Cottage assignments are based upon security and treatment needs. The majority of the treatment programming is cognitive-behavioral. The programs' focus is on changing thoughts, beliefs, values, and attitudes that will, in turn, impact behavior. The treatment programs are empirically based and have been evaluated and sanctioned by outside experts.

Hennepin County Home School (County Home School)

Hennepin County Home School is a Minnesota state-licensed residential treatment center for juveniles ages thirteen to nineteen, with an average age of sixteen years. Eighty-six percent of its residents are male, and 81 percent represent minority ethnic groups. Sixty percent reside in Minneapolis, 34 percent reside in Hennepin County suburbs, and 6 percent are from other counties and states on a fee-for-service basis. The court commits most of the juveniles for assault, robbery, and sexual offenses. Lengths of stay range from two-and-one-half weeks to eighteen months.

The County Home School provides a safe, secure, healthy environment on a 167-acre site in Minnetonka, ten miles west of Minneapolis. The grounds include seven stand-alone twenty-four-bed residential cottages, a transitional living unit, a school with gymnasium, an administrative and services building, a horse barn, and recreational areas. The County Home School offers a comprehensive range of medical and health services, available twenty-four hours a day, and either onsite or at Hennepin County Medical Center. In addition to committing a crime, most of the juveniles have significant behavioral problems, mental illness, and chemical dependency issues.

Youths are committed by the juvenile court to these treatment and intervention programs:

- Adolescent Male Treatment Program

- Adolescent Female Treatment Program

- Adolescent Female Community Service Program

- Juvenile Sex Offender Program (male)

- Transition Living Center (community reentry for all treatment programs)

The Intensive Aftercare Program has six phases. The first two are assessment and case planning. After a comprehensive assessment the resident and parent or guardian, together with significant County Home School, probation, and education staff, help the teens develop plans to take responsibility for their actions, address delinquent behavior, and understand the impact of their offenses on victims. The third phase of primary treatment lasts six-to-nine months. County Home School uses learning approaches that change antisocial beliefs, attitudes, and feelings. The centerpiece of treatment employed is social learning (role modeling), along with cognitive-behavioral interventions (*Thinking for a Change* curriculum) within the Intensive Aftercare Program model, which is designed to gradually increase residents' responsibility and freedom.

Residents are rewarded for positive changes in behavior. The Pre-Release and Transition Phase is completed in County Home School's on grounds Transitional Living Cottage where the resident prepares detailed plans for his/her community reintegration phase. In the Transitional Living Cottage, each youth has an opportunity to practice his or her plan, and attend school in the community while living at the County Home School. The County Home School provides transportation to school and work, shifting responsibilities to the youth and his/her family with continued guidance. The last two weeks of the Transitional Living Cottage begin the last phase, community reintegration, where the youths live at home and County Home School staff and an assigned probation officer monitor their progress in getting to school, aftercare group, and AA.

Hogan Street Regional Treatment Center

The Missouri Division of Youth Services won the 2008 Annie E. Casey Innovations Award in Children and Family System Reform. Hogan Street Regional Treatment Center is a Missouri Division of Services facility that serves some of the most serious offenders who are committed to youth services. Located in St. Louis, Missouri, Hogan Street Regional Treatment Center is a secure residential treatment center for serious juvenile offenders with a capacity of thirty-five youth. It is designed exclusively for boys between fourteen and sixteen. The average length of stay is one year.

The facility is designed to be a welcoming place with a family atmosphere decorated much like a college dorm. As with the other thirty-two Missouri sites, Hogan House is committed to maintaining ties to the family. Youths, whenever possible, are within fifty miles of home. Youth are placed in treatment groups of ten-to-twelve. They receive educational services, vocational guidance, and a variety of counseling services. It is designed as an open-dorm model with a limited number of individual rooms for pre-release students and youth not functioning well in the group setting.

Although we attempted to tour the facility in 2007, it was apparent that they had experienced many inquires as to their successful programs and services and were unable to accommodate us. Our conversations with the facility, and the fact that they say "no" to visits, speaks volumes to the assertion that they follow their mission, acting in the best interest of youth. We were told that it is an expectation that staff develop prosocial relationships with the residents, treat them with respect, and use the best practices approach of "social learning," role-modeling, to promote positive change. This model of small facilities for rehabilitation of youth is becoming known as "the Missouri Model."

WHAT MAKES THESE MODEL FACILITIES?

A number of features distinguish these model facilities:

Strong Leadership

Our overall impression of the three facilities was that staff administrators who demonstrated strong leadership led them. Their peers saw them as leaders in the field. They always represented their facilities with a sense of pride in what they were doing (rehabilitation not punishment). Their staff are role models, passionate for youth justice.

Open to Outside Reviews

These facilities are open to all outside reviews. This approach to openness to outside review allows the residents privacy but not at the expense of input, observation, and critique.

Organized within a Framework that Small Is Better

Missouri has designed all of its thirty-three programs across the state with no more than thirty-five residents. The physical plant and approaches are homey, making it easier to provide for classification and separation of more vulnerable youth. This model is preferred but can and is replicated in larger capacity facilities through a "cottage system." This cottage system is the configuration of both Hillcrest and County Home School. The cottages are semi-independent from the larger institution. Each has a cottage director and staff dedicated to that individual program. Housing capacity is no larger than twenty-four. This smallness allows for individual attention and a stronger ability to form pro-social relationships with residents that is lost in the large dormitory systems. Smallness and consistency of staff lead to residents identifying with and building trust quicker with staff. The bottom line is that these facilities end up being safer, and safety is the foundation for rehabilitation.

Facilities are Safe

These models institutions make safety their first priority. They train to prevent accidents. Any allegation of abuse or use of force is dealt with in a timely way. They use strong staff relationships to keep informed in terms of peer relationships.

Staff are Dedicated

Staff at all levels have demonstrated a commitment to this field of rehabilitation. Direct care staff view their employment as more than just a job. Staff actually like residents, and they want to see them succeed. They are dedicated, and educated (formally and informally) in the principles of adolescent development.

Staff lead with positive role modeling and relationship building. However, because correcting youth misbehaviors becomes an opportunity to teach problem-solving skills, it is not seen as an opportunity for staff to punish. The facility management understands the importance of investing in staff through rewards such as specialized training, words of encouragement, merit increases, special assignments, and of course, a salary that is a living wage.

Staffing is at an Adequate Level and Competent

Both the ratio of staff to residents and professional competencies are important. For the population that these facilities serve, this means no more than a one-to-eight staff ratio and professional disciplines that include psychologists, social workers, licensed special education teachers, and traditional diverse youth care staff.

Administrators and Staff Have Strong Pro-Youth Philosophy

These facilities have a philosophy, shared by the administration and the staff, that no matter how serious the presenting crimes are, the youth who enter their facilities have the capacity to change. Youth are self-empowered; they are taught that they have strengths and are given tools to meet their needs legally. Facility rules are fair and enforced with rehabilitation and learning, not punishment, as the goal. The philosophy is a belief exemplified in practice that treatment, if done right, can and will succeed.

Programming Meets Youths' Needs

Programming is designed in these three model facilities to meet identified youth needs. All three have strong educational, vocational, life skills, family involvement, health, psychological services, and transition. A high percentage of youth successfully complete these programs. Their model of treatment is cognitive-behavioral social learning, which is consistent with evidence-based programming.

Family Connections are Built or Strengthened

These facilities recognize the power and influence families have in the success or failure of the youth committed. Therefore, they make working and partnering with family a priority. They engage, re-engage, and create nonthreatening ways to build trust with families/extended families. These facilities recognize the everyday difficulties of the resident's families and help break down the barriers to involvement by such things as allowing siblings to visit and helping with transportation.

Community Involvement is Stressed

All three of these facilities place a high value on not isolating youth from the communities from which they came. For all three, this means bringing community agencies and advocates into the facilities and creating opportunities for youth to practice learned skills in their community (at school and work and in recreation).

REPLICATING THESE PROGRAMS IN OTHER PLACES

Building on a foundation of safety and security is important, but as we discussed in the chapter on mission, relying solely on mechanical/hardware and fences is not a foundation. One of the most important principles of attempting to replicate these programs is not to use one component of the models and ignore the others. Good solid evidence-based programming will fail without good staff. Good staff will fail without a good facility. Treatment without safety will fail. A good philosophy without a strong leader will mean nothing. This is why replicating programs that work is so terribly difficult.

Administrators of good programs, such as our three models, understand that it is the workings of the whole that support quality juvenile correctional treatment. Our experience shows that the integration of treatment, quality programming, and safety are the key components in successful facilities. If we have one piece of advice to take away from this book, it would be that it is vitally important to hire a strong, committed, dynamic leader.

APPENDIX

The appendix contains hands-on selections that readers might find useful and replicate for their own setting. They include a model daily schedule; information for staff and residents on the behavioral management system—norms and responses to norm violations including slow down and closed cottage. The next section contains rules and expectations for residents. After residents complete the cottage program, they are eligible for the transition cottage, and this section prepares them for that.

The following section contains questionnaires to see how effective your program is and what people have learned from it. These questionnaires are for the referring agency, parents, and residents. Again, these should be modified to fit your own program. However, this evaluation section allows the agency to prove the value of its program for its intended audience

What follows is an outline for skill content to help residents prepare for release. This section includes suggestions for training on time management and transportation, job skills, education and leisure, health and safety, housing, and money management. This section needs to be modified to fit the laws, regulations, and customs of your state and locality.

Model Daily Schedule

Sunday	Monday	Tuesday	Wednesday	Thursday	Friday	Saturday
	Wake Up 6:30	Wake Up 6:30	Wake Up 6:30	Wake Up 6:30	Wake Up 6:30	
	Breakfast 7:00 - 7:25	Breakfast 7:00 - 7:25	Breakfast 7:00 - 7:25	Breakfast 7:00 - 7:25	Breakfast 7:00 - 7:25	
	Charges 7:25 - 7:40	Charges 7:25 - 7:40	Charges 7:25 - 7:40	Charges 7:25 - 7:40	Charges 7:25 - 7:40	
	Hygiene 7:40 - 7:50	Hygiene 7:40 - 7:50	Hygiene 7:40 - 7:50	Hygiene 7:40 - 7:50	Hygiene 7:40 - 7:50	
	Movement 7:55	Movement 7:55	Movement 7:55	Movement 7:55	Movement 7:55	
Kitchen Crew 8:00 - 8:30						Kitchen Crew 8:00 - 8:30
Breakfast 8:30 - 9:30						Breakfast 8:30 - 9:00
Weekend Recreation 10:00 - 11:00	SCHOOL TIME 8:00am - 2:00pm					Super Clean 9:00 - 11:00
Brunch 11:00 - 12:00	Lunch 11:35	Lunch 11:35	Lunch 11:35	Lunch 11:35	Lunch 11:35	T4 A Change 11:00 - 12:00
Charges 12:00 - 12:30						Lunch 12:00 - 1:00
Super Clean Rooms 1:30 - 3:00	Staff Meeting 12:30 - 3:30					Leisure and Board Time 1:00 - 2:00
Church 1:30 - 2:30	Odyssey CD Group 2:00 - 4:00 Every Other Monday	Arts & Crafts 2:30 - 4:00	Sex Education 2:00 - 3:00	R Therapy Gym (JW) 2:00 - 3:00	R Therapy Gym (JW) 2:00 - 3:00	Weekend Recreation 2:00 - 4:00
Leisure 2:00 - 3:00			After School Group 3:00 - 3:30	Leisure		
Hygiene/Showers 3:00 - 4:00	Large Group 4:00 - 5:30	Community Service Work 2:30 - 4:30	Small Group 3:30 - 5:00	Small Group 3:30 - 5:30	Empathy Group 3:00 - 4:00	Showers and Open Time
Visiting 4:00 - 6:00		Odyssey Individual 2:00 - 4:30	Small Group Wrap-up 5:00 - 5:30	Small Group Wrap-up 5:00 - 5:30	Renew Group 3:00 - 4:00	4:00 - 5:30
		R Therapy (JW) Gym 4:30 - 5:30	Aftercare Group 4:00 - 5:30		Hygiene/Showers 4:00 - 5:30	
Dinner and Family Group 6:00 - 7:00	Dinner 5:30 - 6:00	Dinner 5:30 - 6:00	Dinner 5:30 - 6:00	Dinner 5:30 - 6:00	Dinner 5:30 - 6:00	State of the State & Treatment Hour 6:00 - 8:00
	R Therapy (JW) Gym 6:00 - 7:00	Hygiene/Showers 6:00 - 7:00	Leisure 6:00 - 7:30	T4 Change 6:00 - 8:00	Library 6:00 - 7:00	
Charges 7:00 - 8:00	Life Skills / Transition 7:00 - 8:00	T4 A Change 7:00 - 8:30	WC Ride 7:30-8:45 (6-Youth)		After School Group And Leisure Time 7:00 - 9:00	Late Night 8:00 - 9:30
Movie or Treatment Group 7:30 - 9:00	Hygiene/Showers 8:00 - 9:00		R Therapy (Gym) 7:30 - 8:30			
	After School Group 8:00 - 9:00	Hygiene/Leisure 8:30 - 9:00	Hygiene/Showers 8:30 - 9:00	Hygiene/Showers 8:00 - 9:00		
Bedtime 9:00	Bedtime 9:00	Bedtime 9:00	Bedtime 9:00	Bedtime 9:00	Bedtime 9:00	Bedtime 9:00

Charges=Work

WC Ride=Community Service

Odyssey=name of cognitive-behavioral chemical-dependency program

T4 A Change= Thinking for a Change, a cognitive-behavioral curriculum

Information for Staff and Residents on the Behavioral Management System

Norms

Norms are patterns or traits of expected behavior. They establish a pattern of respectful behavior. This allows staff and residents to expect that youth behave in a manner favorable to a learning/treatment environment, which promotes the health and safety of all persons. The norms cover most behavior. However, it is not a complete list of everything that residents cannot do. Two examples under each norm help residents understand the meaning of the norm. Each program needs to look at the norms for its site and provide examples that are meaningful for residents in its particular programs.

Note to residents: If you do not understand the following norms, please ask. If you do not know whether your behavior violates any of the norms, look at what is forbidden and think about your behavior. If you are still not sure, please ask your counselor.

Norm 1: Respect for Laws, Safety, and Security

Residents shall behave in a manner that is law-abiding and is not hazardous to the health and safety of any person.

- No escape or attempted escape
- No leaving class without permission
- No fighting
- No threatening others
- No substance abuse
- No sexual behaviors with other residents

Norm 2: Respect for Self

Residents shall behave in a manner that exhibits respect for their own well being and that of others.

- Clothing worn must meet the County Home School dress code. (Details on pages 141-143)
- Residents are to wear robes and shower flip-flops to and from the showers. When out of their assigned wing, they must wear a shirt and shoes or slippers.

Norm 3: Respect for Others

Residents will show respect for other residents, and all County Home School employees and volunteers. Disrespectful and disruptive behavior including abusive language is a violation of this norm. The following list describes behaviors that are NOT PERMITTED.

- Failing to follow staff directions
- Failing to respect staff and peers
- Bullying
- Making physical contact
- Having sexual contact
- Engaging in or using gang activities, gestures, or symbols

Norm 4: Respect for Property

Residents shall respect property belonging to the County Home School, staff, and other residents. Vandalism, damage to property, theft, or use of property without permission of the owner, extortion, or trespassing violate this norm.

- Going into staff or residents' rooms is prohibited without staff permission
- Loaning or trading of personal property is prohibited

Norm 5: Respect for Work, Education, and the Treatment Process

Residents will comply with and show progress in school, at work, and with their treatment plan when on or off grounds.

- Come to treatment groups prepared and on time
- Arrive at classes on time
- Arrive at work on time and be ready to work
- Attend and participate positively in school
- Attend and participate positively in groups and activities
- Show continuous progress on treatment goals
- Follow the daily schedule

Responses to Behavior

If residents violate norms, they will receive responses to this behavior. This includes logical responses, restorative practices, assignments, loss of privilege, time outs, seclusion, or disciplinary room time. If residents engage in illegal acts, the response could include court intervention. The following chart shows responses to norm violations.

Responses to Norm Violations

County Home School Norms	Minimum Responses	Maximum Responses
Respect for Laws, Safety, and Security	Restorative practice Logical responses Thinking report Timeout/remove from activity	Court intervention 0-5 days disciplinary room—time secure Seclusion
Respect for Others	Restorative practice Logical responses Thinking report Timeout/remove from activity	0-4 days disciplinary room—time secure Seclusion
Respect for Property	Restorative practice Logical responses Thinking report Timeout/remove from activity	0-3 days disciplinary room—time secure Seclusion
Respect for Self	Restorative practice Logical responses Thinking report Timeout/remove from activity	Seclusion
Respect for Treatment Process, Education, and Work	Restorative practice Logical responses Thinking report Timeout/remove from activity	Seclusion

Staff may use any response assigned to each norm. Staff must justify the response used.

Logical Responses

These may be used as a minimum response to any norm violation. Following is a list of possible logical responses that can be tailored to the particular norm violation:

1. Assignment(s)
2. Role play appropriate interaction
3. Work with peer mentor

Restorative Practices—Empathy

Restorative practices may be used as a minimum response to any norm violation and are best delivered by staff with a relationship with the resident. They are designed as an opportunity for a resident to look at his/her behavior and find a way to attempt to repair the harm done to a person, property, or the community. Residents work closely with staff to enhance empathy building through processing the following:

1. Apologize verbally or in writing, as appropriate

2. Make restitution (staff will specify an amount)

3. Participate in a victim-impact group

4. Employ mediation (specify who was involved)

5. Perform community service

6. Make symbolic restitution (do something nice for someone) (specify nature of activity)

7. Other

Staff Checklist: Reintegration from Disciplinary Room

☐ *Assessment: Does this relate to resident's commitment offense?*

If yes, has the resident related the Thinking Report to the commitment offense?
[A "thinking report" is a written cognitive-behavioral tool that assists youth looking at their thoughts, feelings, and beliefs that precipitated their negative behavior. It is also a tool that can be used to conceptualize problem behavior and to explore different ways the issue(s) could have been dealt with in a pro-social manner. Some cognitive-behavioral curriculum includes exercises that counselors can use with youth for this purpose. Thinking reports should be adapted to the cognitive/behavioral curriculum and language that the facility is using. See Boyd Sharp's *Changing Criminal Thinking: A Treatment Program*, 2nd ed. (2006. Alexandria, Virginia: American Correctional Association) for some examples of the use of thinking reports.]

☐ *Secure Unit*

The secure unit is a locked room closely monitored by camera and staff. This is used for residents to regain control of themselves with the goal of returning them to regular programming. It is also used for residents who are at high risk for suicide on the overnight only—to ensure that they do not harm themselves. Board time is work consequences for negative behavior that a resident can work off to get privileges and rewards.

☐ *Case Plan signed by resident*

I, _____ understand that I am responsible for accomplishing the following expectations:

1. _____

2. _____

3. _____

4. _____

5. _____

6. _____

_____   _____
Signature of Resident / Date   Signature of Staff / Date

Facility Rules Shift for Resident Behavior Enforced for Short Period of Time After Major Incidents

Increase in Staff/Administrator Coverage

Provide the following rules to residents in writing and establish a time limit with incentives to move from A/B/C Groups (See Slow Down page 134)

Rules

- No bathroom use at the beginning or ending of school, 1st hour and 6th hour—unless you have a medical pass
- No bathroom use during passing time—unless you have a medical pass
- No going into the school office without permission
- Once you arrive at school, put items in your locker and go to homeroom. Staff will supervise.

Lunchtime during School

<u>Lunch</u>

- Line up in the designated area assigned by your program staff
- Walk to the lunchroom silently
- Those with prescribed medications should stop at the medical unit (staff will monitor)

<u>Lunchroom</u>

- Set books at the table (assigned seating chart is on the clipboard).
- Get all food, silverware, and drinks on the FIRST time through the line

- Ask staff for permission to get up

- NO talking between tables

- Bus at the appropriate time and line up on the ramp in silence, facing forward

- Return to school in silence, stop by the bathroom or your cottage's assigned area

- Use the bathroom in silence

- Wait to be dismissed by staff and go quietly to your classroom

After School

- Line up at your cottage's designated area; staff will monitor your use of lockers.

- Return to the cottage in silence

Staff will hold an after-school community group and determine whether to remove these restrictions for the entire program or move individual residents from C Group to a created B or A Group (with A being regular programming, movement, and privileges).

Slow Down and Closed Cottage

Slow Down

A "*Slow Down*" is an intervention that may be used when the program as a whole is struggling with following some of the basic behavioral norms and individual responses are not effective in changing behavior. A "*Slow Down*" involves just that—slowing down the regular programming and schedule. By "slowing down," the program staff are better able to monitor and regulate residents' behavior.

During a Slow Down, the objective is for the group of residents to focus on the issues or problem behaviors causing the need for a slow down. Staff should identify target behaviors they are seeking from the residents to earn their way back to regular programming.

The staff multidisciplinary team decides when a change from regular programming to a "Slow Down" status should occur. There can be two levels of Slow Down; Level I or Level II. The program director needs to approve a move to either Slow Down Level I or Level II status.

Staff Information on Closed Cottage

Closed cottage is an intervention used for a cottage where the majority of the residents are not following basic behavioral norms and expectations and/or there are major security issues jeopardizing the safety of the residents and staff. When a cottage is placed on closed status, regular programming is essentially shut down and a more correctional response is put into place. The cottage team and its program director must determine when it is appropriate to go to a closed-cottage status and get final approval from the superintendent before moving to this status. Closed cottage usually occurs due to major safety reasons or when other less restrictive interventions, such as a "*slow down*," have failed to achieve the desired results.

The basic objective is to rebuild the cottage culture and program to a functional and safe level. Safety and security are the focus in the early stages of the closed cottage. The goal is to have the majority of the residents following the rules and norms of the program. It is usually a short-term intervention where privileges are gradually earned back through residents demonstrating compliant behavior.

During a closed cottage, the following regular programming is suspended:

- School
- Treatment groups
- Work program
- Specialized groups
- Visiting
- Family counseling
- Staffings
- Off-grounds activities
- Incentive programming
- Response board [A "response board" is a visual tool and reminder of the responsibilities that a resident is obligated to complete or the privileges that he or she has earned. The response board should include both consequences for negative behavior and privileges or rewards for pro-social behavior. Examples of consequences include community service hours or an apology letter that the resident has agreed to write to resolve a conflict with a staff person or resident. Examples of privileges include extra earned phone calls, free time, and computer time.]

Residents are allowed to call attorneys and probation officers, but not their families. Families will be informed by the resident's social worker that the cottage is on closed status and that visiting, family therapy, and phone calls are suspended. Residents may not attend Sunday church services, but if residents would like to meet with the chaplain, staff should ask him/her to come to the cottage to see the individual residents.

The day will be structured with things moving at a slow pace. Residents will eat and do their large muscle activity in small groups so they can be monitored and observed closely. Staff will rotate them in and out of rooms to these activities. Residents will be expected to eat in silence at tables in the dining area. Cleaning projects in the cottage can be done by residents in small numbers. Residents will shower two at a time.

If residents cannot follow the norms while in their small groups, they will be sent to sit on a chair outside their room for a timeout or be sent to their room to finish the activity. The residents will be asked to do group work projects as determined by staff. This may involve carrying wood to the cottage, cleaning the barn, performing landscape projects/yard work, or doing inside cleaning.

Whenever residents are in their rooms, they must be afforded bathroom breaks and well-being checks must take place every thirty minutes at a minimum and should be recorded. Staff should walk the wings to monitor activity and safety of residents intermittently. Residents may not be in their rooms for more than one hour. After one hour, the residents must have time out of their rooms. Staff may want to rotate residents in and out of rooms by wing during closed cottage status. Residents should not eat meals in their rooms.

Staff will observe and record residents' behavior to determine residents' progress. They may use grade sheets on individual residents as a tool for this purpose.

Responses for negative behavior should happen immediately, if possible. Options could include taking a timeout on a chair, going to their own room from an activity, writing the norms from the rule packet, performing a work project, making a woodpile trip, or the staff may "strip" a room of luxury items. The response board should not be used at this time; residents will not have the opportunity to work off the consequence.

As group behavior improves, large groups should re-instituted. The focus of these groups should be the issues that led to the closed cottage.

All staff should participate in all aspects of the closed cottage. This includes social workers, cottage directors, line staff, and recreational therapists. Extra staff may be provided to help facilitate programming, if needed.

The following is for residents.

Rules and Norm Expectations for Residents

1. No escape or attempted escape

2. No use of drugs or alcohol

3. No stealing or breaking property

4. No fighting or threatening others

5. No sexual behaviors with other residents

If you do break these rules or engage in anything illegal, you will be violating a norm. Depending on the norm's seriousness, you can be returned to the court with new charges and/or receive responses/consequences including placement in disciplinary separation from your program.

If staff decide you can stay in the cottage, you will lose your cottage privileges and receive individualized responses/consequences.

General Rules and Expectations

1. Follow all staff directions. This includes directions from staff from other cottages, on-call staff, support staff, and administrative staff. All staff have the responsibility to help guide you and to also reward your behaviors.
2. Attend and participate positively in school
3. Attend and participate positively in groups and activities
4. Show continuous progress on treatment goals

5.   Follow the daily schedule

6.   Follow room standards of cleanliness

7.   Eat at the dining table during meals

8.   Complete work charges on time as a member of the cottage community

9.   Dress according to the dress code

10. Sleep under the sheets of the bed in either sleeping attire or clean underwear (no street clothes and no nudeness)

11. Refrain from using abusive language, name calling, swearing, lying and cheating

12. Do not engage in any sexual contact, tattooing, ear/body piercing, bodily harm, gambling, or trading

13. Wear robes and shower thongs to and from the showers

14. No gang behaviors. This community is a place to get help with your problems. If anyone in the group sees or hears you doing any gang-related behavior, you will be subject to discipline.

15. No smoking

16. Be respectful to staff and peers and expect to be respected

17. Confidentiality. What is said or done in your cottage remains in your cottage. No discussion of treatment or cottage issues in the school or with residents from another cottage.

18. No physical contact with other residents

19. Rooms, letters, and all resident property are subject to search and Inspection by staff at any time. Residents may also be searched (including strip searched) at any time if there are reasons to suspect that safety and/or security are compromised.

20. No sagging pants. Your pants MUST be within two inches of your waist size.

21. No cameras allowed at any time (this protects your confidentiality).

22. The only jewelry you can wear is a watch, posts in your pierced ears, and/or jewelry made in arts and crafts.

23. You must sign up for laundry. No combining clothes with other residents

24. No running in the cottage, main building, or school at any time

25. Masturbation must occur in your room only. You must be under your sheets with the light off when masturbating. Remember your personal hygiene and clean up after yourself.

Items Not Allowed: Contraband

- Hygiene products (these are provided or "purchased" with incentive points) except for deodorant, soap, sanitary products for women, and toothpaste, which is allowed

- Clothing with logos

- Clothing that may be deemed offensive to one's race, culture, religion, gender, and so forth

- Gang-related clothing (staff determine what is and is not gang-related)

- Magazines not pro-social (degrading of gender, race, culture, religion, and so forth)

- Food (from outside or in your room)
- Money, bus tokens/vouchers or "pre-paid" cards of ANY kind
- "Boom boxes" (you may have a small clock radio)
- Drugs, alcohol, tobacco products
- Cell phones, pagers or other technological communication pieces
- Any device that could be considered as a potential weapon (scissors, nail clippers, and so forth)

Items Allowed

- ✓ 7 pairs of pants
- ✓ 5 pairs of shorts
- ✓ 11 shirts (blue or white only)
- ✓ 2 nightshirts/PJs
- ✓ 1 robe
- ✓ 2 pairs of shoes (including 1 pair sandals/casual shoes and tennis shoes)
- ✓ 1 pair of slippers
- ✓ 1 coat
- ✓ 1 "do-rag"
- ✓ 1 watch
- ✓ 1 clock radio (no CD)
- ✓ 1 deodorant
- ✓ 1 bar of soap (in a container)
- ✓ 1 box of tissues
- ✓ 1 brush
- ✓ 1 comb
- ✓ 1 pick
- ✓ 1 toothbrush
- ✓ 1 tube toothpaste
- ✓ 20 hair ties
- ✓ 1 coloring book
- ✓ 3 pens
- ✓ 2 pencils

✓ 1 sketch pad

✓ 2 folders (including this packet)

✓ 2 journals (includes feelings journal)

General Expectations for School

You are ready for school by getting up on time, eating breakfast, and dressing appropriately. You have completed your homework the night before and packed your school bag (including tennis shoes for gym). You bring a positive attitude into this learning environment and you seek out help from your teachers or cottage staff for support.

Small and Large Group Rules

As part of your treatment and daily activities, you will be expected to participate in various groups. Groups are scheduled by staff, at any time. These groups may include, but are not limited to, the following: after-school group, community group, ceremonies performed in a group, helping-table groups, small group therapy, treatment work groups, anger management groups, chemical dependency programs, and Thinking for a Change.

Small and Large Group Expectations

- No talking in lounge
- Raise your hand
- Sit in your assigned seat
- No whispering
- No feet on furniture—keep your feet on the floor
- Respect others' issues
- Participate (no sleeping)
- Respect each other
- No knuckle cracking or other avoidable noises
- No doodling/drawing
- No side comments
- No personal grooming (such as, braiding combing, or otherwise playing with hair)
- No reading during group
- Keep your hands to yourself
- Support each other
- Sit up straight, no slouching
- No leaving without permission

Responses for Behavior

1. No Group Process Privilege:

   You will be allowed to sit on a chair just outside of the group. You will ask permission to speak.

2. Confidentiality:

   Everything that is said in the group and everything that happens in the group is confidential. It all stays here.

3. Listening:

   Listening is encouraged. When one person is speaking, give your full attention. We all learn from each other's experiences and struggles. Empathic listening is encouraged in the group. This means that we "out" ourselves as much as possible and try to understand the experience of another person.

4. Feedback:

   Feedback means recognizing and expressing how you perceive the other person's behavior or experience. We encourage feedback. Feedback is given with permission of the person receiving the feedback. Good feedback is a solid form of validation. It is not critical, nor is it meant to be corrective. Feedback communicates acceptance of the receiving person's being.

5. Right to Pass:

   Everyone has the right to pass: to choose not to say something or to choose not to participate in a group.

6. Request for Time:

   Everyone is encouraged to ask for time from the group to discuss something if there is an issue or a problem that you would like to present to the group. Check-in is a good time to ask for this time, but requests will be heard at any time during the group. If there are many requests for time, we cannot guarantee that everyone will have a chance to discuss his or her concerns, but the facilitators will try to be responsive to your needs.

7. You Receive Consequences for the Following Actions:

   • Breaking confidentiality

   • Any negative behaviors as listed above in small and large group expectations

Dress Code for Males

PANTS: All pants must be <u>blue</u> jeans (denim). Jeans must NOT sag and must NOT be more than 2 inches larger than measured waist size. Both pants legs must be worn at the ankle.

SHIRTS: All shirts must be <u>plain blue</u> (may have white shirt underneath). Clean and unwrinkled shirts can be long sleeved, short sleeved, collared, button-up, sweatshirt, and so forth. Residents may also wear T-shirts given to them by programs such as Summerfest or plain T-shirts. They can only be worn for large muscle activities or for a special event, but not to school or during the regular program day. The blue shirt must be worn at all times in the cottage except for bedtime.

SHORTS: Denim blue jean shorts or large muscle shorts may be worn. In the summer, shorts may be worn. Staff will announce the date that shorts can be worn at school, if at all.

BELTS: Belts can be worn but must be black or brown.

LOGOS: No logos on any clothing.

JACKETS: Residents may wear any color jacket. Jackets must be taken off in buildings and stored in lockers at school or in the boot room in the cottages.

SHOES: Residents may wear any type of shoe that is tied. Shoes must be tied. Shoelaces must be the ones that come with the shoes or replaced with white, black, or brown laces. Shoelaces must look the same in each shoe. There must be only one shoelace in each shoe.

SOCKS: Residents must wear plain white socks with NO logos.

JEWELRY: Residents may wear a single stud earring and a single watch. If a resident makes a necklace or other jewelry item in arts and crafts, he may wear it.

HAIRSTYLES: They must not have any symbols or numbers in them. Rubber bands and/or beads must be black or tan and all one color. Hairstyles must be symmetrical—the same on both sides of the head.

DRESS OUTFIT: Residents may have one dress outfit. It must not be gang related or have any logos. This outfit is for residents to wear for special off-grounds or on-grounds activities—job interview, transition meeting at school, court, and so forth. Residents must make a request through a staff meeting ahead of time if they want to wear their dress outfit.

PAJAMAS: Residents must wear some sort of pajama pants to bed. No sleeping in underwear only. The pajama pants may be any color but cannot have any logos on them. Pajama pants can only be worn to bed and not around the cottage during other times of the day.

HATS: No hat with any logo (no hats worn in ANY buildings). A hat may only be worn in outside activities.

Other Notes:

- **No "do-rags" outside of your room.**
- **Residents may not have any clothing that has a value of more than $150.00.**
- **Residents may not wear any clothing items inside out or use tape to conceal logos.**

Dress Code for Females

SHIRTS: You can wear a shirt in any shade of solid blue. It cannot have any logo on it. You can have any type of shirt (long or short sleeve, button up, sweatshirt, and so forth). You can also wear any shirts given to you by the Summerfest program or a plain T-shirt. These types of shirts can only be worn during large muscle activity, for the special event, or while in the cottage. You must wear the blue shirt any time you leave the cottage. You may wear a white T-shirt underneath your blue shirt. You may also wear a white shirt around the cottage. Any sleeveless tops must have straps 2 inches wide—no exceptions. This includes pajama tops. Shirts need to be long enough, 3 inches past your waist.

PANTS: You may wear any type of blue pants. Logos on pants must be smaller than a credit card. Pants must not sag. Pants must be no more than 2 inches larger than your measured waist size. Both pants legs must be worn down at the ankle. When you can wear shorts in school, Capri pants are acceptable. NO SPANDEX OR LEGGINGS!

BELTS: Belts must be black or brown.

SHORTS: You may wear any type of blue or khaki shorts. All shorts must be no shorter than 2 inches above the knee. Capri's can count as shorts. NO SPANDEX!

LARGE MUSCLE CLOTHING: For large muscle activity, you may wear blue or black athletic shorts or sweatpants. Shorts or sweatpants can have white strips on the sides, but no logos. You may wear these items anytime in the cottage, but not in school. NO SPANDEX OR LEGGINGS!

JACKETS: You may wear any color jacket. Jackets must be taken off in buildings and stored in lockers at school or in the cottages.

SHOES: You may wear any type of shoe. Shoes must be tied. Shoelaces must be white, black or brown. Shoelaces must be the same color in each shoe. Only one lace is permitted in each shoe. Heels must be no higher than 1 inch from the base of the sole.

SOCKS: Residents must wear plain white socks without any logos on them.

HATS: Hats must be a solid color with no logos. Hats may not be worn in buildings and may only be worn for outside activities.

JEWELRY: You may wear earrings if you have pierced ears upon arrival. Earrings may not be larger than your pinkie finger. You may also wear a watch.

HAIR: Hairstyles must not have any symbols or numbers in them and must be symmetrical—the same on both sides of the head. Hair accessories must be solid and can be black, tan, white, or blue. You may only wear one color at a time.

BEDTIME CLOTHING: You must wear some sort of pajama top and bottom to bed. Pajamas can be any color, but cannot have logos on them. They can have flowers, Pooh, and so forth. Pajamas can only be worn on the floor after showers. No exceptions!

DRESS OUTFIT: You may have one dress outfit. It must not be gang related or have any logos on it. This outfit is for residents to wear for special off-grounds activities, such as job interviews, presentations to the judges, and so forth. You must make a request to wear your outfit through a team meeting. Your outfit must be pants—not a skirt. The outfit must also be appropriate for interviews. Therefore, no low cut tops, no belly shirts, no spandex, no shiny metallic outfits, and so forth.

You may not have any clothing that has a value of more than $150.

You may not wear any clothing items inside out or use tape to conceal logos.

Maternity Clothing

Pregnant girls are excluded from the dress code policy. However, there are guidelines.

1. If you chose not to wear maternity clothes, you must follow the dress code policy.

2. Once you reach your fifth month, you must wear maternity pants.

3. Your clothing cannot have logos on it unless it is maternity. Example, the word "Cherokee" is across the front.

4. You cannot wear black with a solid color that staff feel is gang related.

5. You cannot wear sweatpants to school.

Going Home Clothing

The clothes that you leave in must fit all the requirements above. If it cannot be put on your inventory, you cannot leave in it.

Mail Procedures

1. All residents will be provided with writing paper, envelopes, and postage for the purpose of writing to family and friends. Writing beyond these two groups will need special staff approval.

2. Mail can be scanned by staff in the presence of the resident. This is for security purposes. If mail is read, you will be informed in advance and be present when the letter or package is opened. These events will be described in the Cottage Log and reviewed by the Cottage Supervisor.

3. Staff may inspect your mail for contraband (drugs, weapons, tobacco, and so forth) at any time. Again, the letter or package is opened when you are there to watch.

4. Notify program staff of all official correspondence. (This includes court hearing notices medical issues, court summons, notice of new charges, and so forth.)

5. The cottage supervisor, your social worker, or family therapist may, for legitimate reasons, place limits on the amount of mail you receive. This must be done with the proper notification of the individual sending the mail.

Resident's Phone Procedures

Length and Frequency: Residents may make one 10 minute phone call per week. This call is typically to their parents or guardian. If their parents do not live together, they may be able to make a call to each parent. In some cases, the person they may call may be a guardian or grandparent if the parent is not involved.

List of Approved Callers: The list of approved callers for each resident is listed on his or her phone card or phone list in each cottage.

Staff Duties

If a resident asks to make a call, first check to see if he or she has made his or her call already this week. If the individual has not, check his or her phone list to see who is approved. Individuals may try to manipulate making calls to someone who is not on their list. If the person or phone number the resident wants to call is NOT on the list, do NOT make the call. Social workers are responsible for updating the phone list with current numbers.

Making a Call. When placing the call, dial the number and ask for the person the resident is approved to talk to. Inform the person that you are putting through a call from the resident. Then, allow the resident to pick up the phone and talk. After the individual has completed the call, log it on the phone tracking list, which is usually located on a clipboard in the staff area. If the resident goes over his or her allotted time for the call, a typical consequence is monitoring his or her call next week. If the resident does not appear to be talking to the approved person, you may question the individual or randomly pick up the phone to check.

Monitored Calls: Some residents may be on monitored calls, in which case you need to listen to their conversation or monitor it closely. Inform all parties that the call is being monitored.

Extra Phone Calls: Residents may earn one "extra" phone call per week through the incentive program. If they are using this, they may buy a second 10 minute call to someone on their approved calling list.

Special Phone Calls: Residents may have special phone calls to someone other than a parent or guardian. These calls must be facilitated by their social worker. If a resident wants to call someone not on their list, refer them to their social worker.

No Incoming Phone Calls Allowed: Except from resident's attorney or probation officer.

Three-Way Calling Not Allowed. Residents sometimes have family do a "three-way call" for them to talk to girlfriends or friends. If this is the case, end the call immediately and determine consequences.

Visiting in the Cottage

1. Parents/visitors will be picked up at the main building and dropped off at the cottage door.
2. All bags/packages for residents will be given to staff in the main building. The staff will bring packages back after visiting. Items will be checked in sometime within 24 hours (as much as possible).
3. All visitors must sign in the Cottage's Visiting Log.
4. All visitors must visit in the dining room. If it is too crowded, chairs will be brought in from the lounge and visitors can visit in the Recreation area. Visitors cannot go into the lounge to visit; this is for residents without visitors.
5. Coffee is provided for visitors only; residents may not drink coffee.
6. Visitors may not go down the wings without approval by staff.
7. Visitors may use the staff bathroom.
8. No smoking inside or outside the cottage.
9. Visiting should be between the parents/visitors and their child. No other residents should visit with other resident's parents/visitors.

10. Any residents' property that needs to go home will go home with the visitors/parents at the end of visiting. All clothing/shoes must be taken off the inventory before going home. Residents cannot open or go through the bag.

11. If a parent needs to leave early, staff should radio the driver to come to the cottage and pick up the parent. Parents do not have to wait until 5:00 p.m. when visiting is over.

12. Residents without visitors and clean boards should be in the lounge or their room. They cannot be in the dining or recreation area.

13. Visitors should not be in the lounge for any reason. If there is overcrowding, staff can pull the tables in the library into the recreation area.

14. Parents or visitors are not allowed to bring food or beverage of any kind (Food Service Rules).

For Staff: Visiting Procedure for Checking-In Visitors

A version of this should be sent to each parent/guardian and be posted in the main lobby of the facility where all visitors sign in.

1. Each unit has assigned visiting time scheduled. Know what is appropriate for your unit.
2. One staff person from the cottage checks-in visitors at the main building.
3. The approved visitors' list and the handheld metal detector are in the main reception area.
4. All approved visitors must check in at the main building. All visitors must have a picture I.D., a driver's license, a work picture, and so forth. Each must be on the approved social worker/primary therapist's list. If they are not on the list, call the cottage to see if they are listed in the main log. If nothing is logged, they may not visit.
5. All packages must be left in the main building and staff should bring them back after visiting.
6. Parents with infants: Infants may come to the cottage. Diaper bags should be left in the car, if possible. Visitors with infants can bring up a diaper, wipes, a toy, and a bottle.
7. Things not allowed: No purses, candy, pop, phones, cameras, or water, may be brought to the cottage. These items need to be put in the visitor's car or in a locker at the main building.
8. All items must go through the metal detector. This includes coats, bags, hats, and so forth. If the metal detector goes off, staff will use a magnetic wand.
9. If a visitor smells of alcohol or if something does not seem right to the staff person, the visit will not be approved and will not take place.
10. Once at the cottage, the visitors must sign the cottage visitors' log.

Special Visits. Special visits must be approved and supervised by the social worker/primary therapist.

REFERRING AGENCY DISCHARGE QUESTIONNAIRE

(To be completed by supervising Probation Officer)

Name of Client _____

1. What cottage was your client assigned to?   1 2 3 4 5 6 7 Don't know

2. Please rate the following components of the County Home School Program:

RATING:	VERY GOOD	GOOD	AVERAGE	POOR	VERY POOR	NA
Assessment and Treatment Plan	5	4	3	2	1	0
Victim-Impact Group	5	4	3	2	1	0
School	5	4	3	2	1	0
Medical Services	5	4	3	2	1	0
Family Counseling	5	4	3	2	1	0
Cottage Treatment Program	5	4	3	2	1	0
Visiting	5	4	3	2	1	0
Thinking For A Change	5	4	3	2	1	0
Odyssey (Chemical Dependency Treatment)	5	4	3	2	1	0
Youth Employment	5	4	3	2	1	0
Life Skills	5	4	3	2	1	0
Recreation	5	4	3	2	1	0
Spiritual Counseling (Church)	5	4	3	2	1	0
Family Night	5	4	3	2	1	0
Transitional Living Cottage	5	4	3	2	1	0

Note: The Transitional Living Cottage is a reentry cottage. It can be a wing in a program or any area that the facility sets aside for residents who have earned more privileges and are gradually gaining responsibility and freedom.

Continued on the next page

REFERRING AGENCY DISCHARGE QUESTIONNAIRE *Continued*

3. What program components helped your client the most?

_____

4. Please rate the communication between County Home School Staff and you:

RATING:	VERY GOOD	GOOD	AVERAGE	POOR	VERY POOR
Social Workers	5	4	3	2	1
Cottage Staff	5	4	3	2	1
Cottage Director	5	4	3	2	1
School Staff	5	4	3	2	1
Medical Staff	5	4	3	2	1
Transition Case Managers	5	4	3	2	1
Community Specialists	5	4	3	2	1

5. How would you, as a probation officer, rate your overall experience with the County Home School?
   Circle one: 5 (Best)   4   3   2   1 (Worst)

6. Did you feel safe while at the County Home School?
   Circle one: Yes   No

7. Did you feel your client was safe while at the County Home School?
   Circle one: Yes   No

8. Were you treated respectfully by staff?
   Circle one: Yes   No

9. Has your client's behavior improved because of the treatment provided by the County Home School?
   Circle one: Yes   No

10. Did your client improve in school because of his/her stay at the County Home School?
    Circle one: Yes   No

Continued on the next page

REFERRING AGENCY DISCHARGE QUESTIONNAIRE *Continued*

11. Did the County Home School supply you with information early in your client's stay at County Home School?

    Circle one: Yes   No

12. Did you feel your client was prepared to return home at the end of his or her stay at the County Home School?

    Circle one: Yes   No

13. Do you feel the case plan goals were met?

    Circle one: Yes   No

14. What do you feel County Home School staff did to help your client return home?

_____

_____

_____

Staff Only Exit Code: (Computer Code to automate the responses) _____

PARENT/GUARDIAN DISCHARGE QUESTIONNAIRE

[This is handed to the parent or resident to complete prior to the resident's release. Mailing it does not work well]

1. What cottage was your son/daughter assigned to?   1 2 3 4 5 6 7 Don't know

2. Please rate the following components of the County Home School Program:

RATING:	VERY GOOD	GOOD	AVERAGE	POOR	VERY POOR	NA
Assessment and Treatment Plan	5	4	3	2	1	0
Intake	5	4	3	2	1	0
School	5	4	3	2	1	0
Medical Services	5	4	3	2	1	0
Psychiatric Services	5	4	3	2	1	0
Cottage Treatment Program	5	4	3	2	1	0
Visiting	5	4	3	2	1	0
Food (Meals/Snacks)	5	4	3	2	1	0
Odyssey (Chemical Dependency Treatment)	5	4	3	2	1	0
Youth Employment	5	4	3	2	1	0
Life Skills	5	4	3	2	1	0
Recreation	5	4	3	2	1	0
Spiritual Counseling (Church)	5	4	3	2	1	0
Family Night	5	4	3	2	1	0
Thinking For Change	5	4	3	2	1	0
Victim-Impact Group	5	4	3	2	1	0
Transitional Living Cottage	5	4	3	2	1	0

PARENT/GUARDIAN DISCHARGE QUESTIONNAIRE, *Continued*

3. List one program component (from the prior list) that you believe helped your child:

_____

4. Please rate the communication between County Home School Staff and you:

RATING:	VERY GOOD	GOOD	AVERAGE	POOR	VERY POOR	NA
Social Workers	5	4	3	2	1	0
Probation Officers	5	4	3	2	1	0
Cottage Staff	5	4	3	2	1	0
Cottage Director	5	4	3	2	1	0
School Staff	5	4	3	2	1	0
Nurses	5	4	3	2	1	0
Transition Case Managers	5	4	3	2	1	0
Community Specialists	5	4	3	2	1	0

5. How would you rate your overall experience with the County Home School?
   Circle one: 5 (Best)   4   3   2   1 (Worst)

6. How would you rate your experience during visiting?
   Circle one: 5 (Best)   4   3   2   1 (Worst)

7. Did you participate in planning for your child's release?
   Circle one: Yes   No

8. How many times per month did you participate with your child in the following?

Family Counseling	0	1	2	3	4	5
Visiting	0	1	2	3	4	5
Telephone Contact	0	1	2	3	4	5

9. Did you want your child placed locally rather than out-of-state or out-of-town?
   Circle one: Yes   No

10. Did you have problems getting transportation to the County Home School?
    Circle one: Yes   No

Continued on the next page

PARENT/GUARDIAN DISCHARGE QUESTIONNAIRE, *Continued*

11. Did you feel safe while at the County Home School?
    Circle one: Yes   No

12. Did you feel your child was safe while at the County Home School?
    Circle one: Yes   No

13. Were you treated respectfully by staff?
    Circle one: Yes   No

14. Has your child's behavior improved because of the treatment provided by the County Home School?
    Circle one: Yes   No

15. Did your child improve in school because of his/her stay at the County Home School?
    Circle one: Yes   No

16. Did the County Home School supply you with information early in your child's stay at County Home School?
    Circle one: Yes   No

17. Did you feel your child was prepared to return home at the end of his or her stay at the County Home School?
    Circle one: Yes   No

18. Name one thing County Home School staff did to help your child return home:

_____

Staff Only Exit Code _____ Computer code for automation.

RESIDENT'S DISCHARGE QUESTIONNAIRE

Please rate the following components of the County Home School Program:

RATING:	VERY GOOD	GOOD	AVERAGE	POOR	VERY POOR	NA
Assessment and Treatment Plan	5	4	3	2	1	0
Orientation	5	4	3	2	1	0
School	5	4	3	2	1	0
Medical Services	5	4	3	2	1	0
Psychiatric Services	5	4	3	2	1	0
Your Individual Treatment Team	5	4	3	2	1	0
Group Therapy-Small	5	4	3	2	1	0
Group Therapy- /Large	5	4	3	2	1	0
Employment/Restitution	5	4	3	2	1	0
Food (Meals/Snacks)	5	4	3	2	1	0
Odyssey	5	4	3	2	1	0
Meld (Father's Group)	5	4	3	2	1	0
Osiris (Community Agency)	5	4	3	2	1	0
Recreation	5	4	3	2	1	0
Spiritual Counseling (Church)	5	4	3	2	1	0
Family Counseling	5	4	3	2	1	0
Incentive Program	5	4	3	2	1	0
Thinking For A Change	5	4	3	2	1	0
Victim-Impact Group	5	4	3	2	1	0
Special Programs:	5	4	3	2	1	0
Holiday Events	5	4	3	2	1	0
Plays	5	4	3	2	1	0
Carnival	5	4	3	2	1	0
Speakers	5	4	3	2	1	0
Cultural Groups	5	4	3	2	1	0
Visiting	5	4	3	2	1	0
Family Night	5	4	3	2	1	0
Transitional Living Cottage	5	4	3	2	1	0
Community Service	5	4	3	2	1	0
Other _____	5	4	3	2	1	0

Continued on the next page

RESIDENT'S DISCHARGE QUESTIONNAIRE, *Continued*

1. From the items listed above, write the two that were the most helpful:

   _____

   _____

2. From the items listed above, which two would you change?

   _____

   _____

   Please explain why: _____

   _____

3. Please rate the following staff member's relationships and support:

RATING:	VERY GOOD	GOOD	AVERAGE	POOR	VERY POOR	NA
Your Family Counselor	5	4	3	2	1	0
Your Social Worker	5	4	3	2	1	0
Your Probation Officer	5	4	3	2	1	0
Your Individual Treatment Team	5	4	3	2	1	0
Line Staff// juvenile correctional officers	5	4	3	2	1	0
Cottage Director	5	4	3	2	1	0
Cottage Supervisor	5	4	3	2	1	0
Recreation Therapist	5	4	3	2	1	0
Teachers	5	4	3	2	1	0
Doctors	5	4	3	2	1	0
Nurses	5	4	3	2	1	0
Psychiatrists	5	4	3	2	1	0
Chaplain	5	4	3	2	1	0
Volunteers	5	4	3	2	1	0
Transition Case Manager	5	4	3	2	1	0
Community Specialists	5	4	3	2	1	0

Continued on the next page

RESIDENT'S DISCHARGE QUESTIONNAIRE, *Continued*

4. Did you learn things at the County Home School to help you stay out of trouble?

Please explain what:

_____

_____

5. Did you feel safe while you were at the County Home School?   Yes   No

    If not, in what way? _____

6. Did you want to do treatment in the Twin Cities or be sent out-of-state or out-of-town?

    Circle one: Twin Cities   Out-of-State/Out-of-Town

7. Did you feel the consequences were appropriate for bad behavior?   Yes   No

8. Did you feel the rewards for good behavior were effective?   Yes   No

9. Were you ever sent "upstairs" to the Secure Unit as a consequence?   Yes   No

10. Did your stay in the Secure Unit teach you anything?   Yes   No

    If yes, what? _____

11. How much better do you understand your family since you came to the County Home School?

    Circle one: VERY   MODERATELY   NOT AT ALL

12. How prepared were you to return home?

    Circle one: VERY   MODERATELY   NOT AT ALL

13. How can the Transitional Living Cottage Program be improved?

_____

STAFF ONLY: EXIT CODE: _____

TRANSITIONAL LIVING COTTAGE: A COMMUNITY-BASED PROGRAM

The Transitional Living Cottage was created to assist residents who have completed the treatment phase of their County Home School commitment, and are preparing to return to their communities. The program focuses primarily on teaching the resident the necessary basic life skills to allow for a successful transition home. Upon completion of cottage treatment, a resident would then transfer to the Transitional Living Cottage and begin the 10-week program. The resident, his/her family, and staff have worked together to create a plan that will make the transition successful.

Basic Life Skills (Four Weeks)

- Learning job skills–interviewing, resume writing, and so forth
- Using public transportation
- Planning money management
- Learning positive recreation pursuits
- Planning housing

The Basic Life Skills component teaches the resident a variety of life skills. The class is taught using field trips, guest speakers, assignments, and classroom discussion. During these four weeks, the resident will also begin home visits. These home visits will begin with twelve-hour visits, and progress to forty-eight-hours at the completion of the four weeks. Upon successful completion of the basic living skills program, the resident will move to the community wing.

Community Wing (Six Weeks)

- Attending community school
- Preparing for employment
- Participating in community chemical dependency groups
- Taking extended home visits
- Engaging in community recreation
- Accessing continuing education opportunities

During the final six weeks of the program, the residents have many opportunities to practice the skills they have learned at the County Home School. The majority of their time will be spent within their own communities. This includes participating in education, employment, recreation, and time with their families. The residents are required to attend community-based chemical awareness groups, when appropriate; continue family counseling/therapy, and maintain regular contact with their probation officers. Upon successful completion, the resident is released from the County Home School, and achieves furlough status. The resident will then remain 100 percent at home, and is simply required to follow his/her probation requirements.

TRANSITION PROGRAM WORKBOOK

THIS IS <u>NOT</u> HOMEWORK.
THIS IS <u>YOUR</u> LIFE.

This workbook is designed to help you make good aftercare plans so you can build for yourself the kind of life you deserve—a happy, productive, drug-free, and crime free life. The planning you complete in this task will allow you to make the most of your transition program to practice the skills you have learned before returning home.

Work Hard.
Be A Leader.
Get Help When You Need It.
Enjoy Watching Your Plans Become Reality!

Your Name: _____

Your Primary Therapist: _____

Your Community Specialist: _____

Transition Case Manager: _____

Your Probation Officer: _____

Pre-Release Goals/Checklist

The following assignments must be finished prior to entry into the Transition Program. After you have completed each assignment, write in the date that you completed it. In addition, your Primary Therapist, Transition Case Manager, Community Specialist, or Probation Officer will confirm you have completed each assignment by signing the contact box.

Pre-Release Checklist:

Goal/Items	Date	Contact
1. Birth certificate		
2. Social Security card		
3. State ID		
4. Transition badge		
5. Education records		
6. Health insurance/medical records		
7. Transitional Living Cottage contract		
8. Restitution amount		
9. YMCA pass/application		
10. Library card		
11. Medical unit meeting		

Workbook Assignments:

Goal/Items	Date	Contact
1. Relapse Prevention Plan		
2. Re-offense Prevention Plan		
3. Future Plan		

Relapse Prevention Plan

Now that you are getting ready to leave County Home School you need to plan how to use what you have learned. To relapse means to "return to your old negative behaviors." So, to keep yourself on track in your community, you need to develop a good relapse-prevention plan. A relapse prevention plan is your written guide that will help you avoid returning to your old negative behaviors. This relapse prevention plan includes:

- How you will live your daily life

- How you will use your time

- Situations you need to avoid

This relapse prevention plan should take into account your strengths and challenges, as well as your goals, to ensure success. It is important that you create a relapse prevention plan that is honest and sincere.

This section of your workbook will help you put together a good relapse prevention plan.

How will you live your daily life?

To understand your daily life, you need to plan according to your specific needs. This assignment will address your specific needs. In the following pages, you will be asked to develop a plan and goals for different areas of your life. You may be asked to meet with different individuals from the County Home School who will be helpful to you in the development of your plan. Please take this seriously and remember. THIS IS NOT HOMEWORK, THIS IS YOUR LIFE!!!!!

Transition Program Rules

It is very important that you read and understand the following rules. Your success in the program will depend on it. You will be asked to sign a Transitional Living Cottage contract before entering the program. By signing that contract you are saying that you have read and understand these rules. If you do not understand something, please ask!

- **Staff members on duty are in charge.** Residents must follow staff directions and all rules and policies throughout the County Home School program. The residents must follow staff direction at all times: including staff in other programs.

- No physical contact with others is allowed. This includes no horseplay.

- No fighting, fake fighting (shadow boxing) with hands or feet.

- Do not use foul language. No put downs, nicknames, or mimicking of others.

- Rooms, letters, personal property, and person are subject to search or inspection by staff.

- Destruction of county property will result in consequences that could include restitution.

- No cameras or audiovisual equipment is allowed on grounds.

- Do not tattoo, pierce, scar, or mark a body; yours or anyone else's in anyway while on County Home School property.

- No gang-related behavior is allowed at the County Home School. This includes all clothing, verbal, physical (sign) or written forms. The staff on duty will determine what is or is not gang related.

- Residents are not allowed in the staff area, offices, or other resident's sleeping quarters without staff permission. No socializing in another resident's quarters.

- Lights and radios should be turned off before leaving your room. Lights and radios need to be off by 10:00 P.M.

- You may hang pictures on the corkboard in your sleeping area.

- You are required to keep your sleeping area clean. Staff will post expectations and check rooms daily. You and your roommates will receive consequences if expectations are not followed.

- You will be required to complete a work charge daily. Failure to do so may result in consequences.

- All bedding in the unit must be county issued.

- Plastic gloves and hairnets must be worn when handling food.

- Residents are not allowed to sit on counters, heaters, tables, or place shoes upon any furniture.

- Staff MUST first check all property or other items being brought into the cottage.

- You will be issued a key for your personal locker. This key must be checked out through staff. You may not give your key to any other resident.

- The County Home School reserves the right to confiscate any property found to be contraband or offensive to others.

- No candy or food may be brought into the unit. Food is only allowed in the dining area of the Transitional Living Cottage, not in sleeping areas.

- Transitional Living Cottage residents must eat at the assigned Transitional Living Cottage table in the dining area.

- Sunday evening meal will be served in the Transitional Living Cottage unit.

- No personal play stations are allowed in the unit.

- No "R" or "X" rated movies are allowed in the unit.

- No CD players are allowed in the unit, only a Walkman or personal handheld CD players are permitted.

- Any music deemed offensive by any staff member or fellow resident must be turned off. Residents may listen to music on personal headphones in the sleeping area only.

- You may have a personal radio/alarm in your sleeping area.

- No TV/radio is allowed in the morning.

- No TV or video games or radio from 5:00-7:00 P.M. This is quiet time for eating, work charges, and homework (computers may be used at this time for homework-related items).

- You must fill out the off-grounds clothing description form before leaving the unit. Failure to do so will result in a consequence.

- If 18, residents may smoke off grounds. There is no smoking on the grounds of County Home School.

- All Transitional Living Cottage residents must have I.D. in view at all times while on County Home School grounds.

- Driving is permitted while in the Transitional Living Cottage under the provisions of State law. No driving is permitted on County Home School grounds.

- Residents returning or leaving County Home School grounds must use sidewalks or paved road, no cutting through yards, woods, parking lot, and no walking or riding bikes around grounds unsupervised.

- Computer hours are from 9:00 A.M. - 9: 00 P.M.

- The computers are available for your use and are not to be abused. Any misuse may result in a loss of this privilege.

- Incoming and outgoing mail will follow institutional policy.

- No money is allowed in the unit. You must have staff deposit all money in the unit safe.

- Money-request forms need to be filled out on Sunday night.

- If you owe restitution, 90 percent of your paycheck deposited at County Home School will be deducted and paid toward restitution.

- You are to be in your room by 9:30 P.M. and lights need to be out by 10:00 P.M.

- No talking or horseplay in the shower area.

- Hygiene items can be brought in and kept in your living area, except razors. Razors must be kept in the staff area.

Dress Code in the Transitional Living Cottage

- Dress appropriately. You are not expected to wear county-issued uniform.

- No sagging

- No inappropriate logos

- Proper clothing will be worn any time you are out of your room.

- Shoes or socks must cover you feet.

- You must wear a shirt.

- Do rags are allowed in your sleeping area ONLY.

- You must be fully dressed before you leave the sleeping quarters.

- Sleeping in the nude is not permitted.

- The only jewelry allowed in the Transitional Living Cottage is a watch, post earrings, one necklace—no pendant.

- No hats or any other headwear are to be worn in any building at the County Home School.

- Residents are strongly discouraged from bring expensive items into Transition Living Cottage. The County Home School is not responsible for lost, stolen, or damaged property.

- REMEMBER, you have limited space in the Transitional Living Cottage. All your personal items must fit neatly into your wardrobe locker and drawer.

- You will be provided with a laundry pen to mark your personal property. County Home School is not responsible for lost, stolen, or damaged property.

Phone Rules

- Incoming calls are discouraged and staff may verify that a call is an authorized party before connecting the resident to the call.

- You need staff permission to use the phone. On staff's phone, you are only allowed to speak to your parents, probation officer, or lawyer. If you have a special need to talk to anyone else, you need to talk to the staff on duty.

- Use of the telephone is a privilege and not a right. Abuse of this privilege by the use of three-way lines or any other means will result in suspension and/or supervision of your telephone use.

- You may earn extra phone calls as an incentive for successfully completing your goals.

- Phone calls cannot exceed 15 minutes.

- No cell phones or pagers on grounds.

Residents' Rights

All residents' rights as outlined in the institutional operations manual will be observed in the Transitional Living Cottage. Each resident has the opportunity to file a grievance through the grievance policy. Residents may also contact the ombudsperson upon 24 hours request.

Sanctions/Incentives

Consequences are a natural part of choices we make. Residents may receive consequences at any time based on staff's discretion. The goal is to help you make life-enhancing choices that help you achieve success in the community. Some natural consequences are good, some are bad. Examples of good choices may be increased trust and freedom, paychecks, increased self-esteem, and so forth. Examples of bad consequences are loss of privileges, additional chores, and even legal issues. A Transitional Living Cottage staff person will review all rules, incentive programming, and sanctions with you upon intake to the Transitional Living Cottage.

The following is a list of positive and negative consequences you can receive:

- Movie tickets
- Sporting event tickets
- Positive self-esteem
- Trust
- Extra phone privileges
- Food vouchers
- YMCA pass
- Early check in—You need to be back at the County Home School before regular curfew hours.
- Work hours—helping out with special projects, cleaning or putting away supplies
- Loss of phone privileges—no incoming or outgoing personal calls
- Room time—you need to be in your sleeping area. Your radio is shut off
- Grounded on weekend home visits
- Loss of weekend home visit—weekend visit is suspended
- Home electronic monitoring
- Sentence-to-serve hours/Community service work hours
- Community service
- Placement in secure unit—administrative/disciplinary segregation.

Weekend Visit Rules

Weekend visits are designed to rejoin and strengthen family relationships. This is accomplished through clearly defined goals. The weekend visit is one way to have families resolve issues through the process of defining and accomplishing goals during the home visit process.

Consistent participation in family counseling is a pre-requirement for home visits. The goal of family counseling is for family members to identify issues, which need to be worked on between the resident and family members. Preparation for home visits involves the development of written goals and working out issues, which have been identified. Family visit goals are developed, reviewed, and approved with the resident, primary therapist, transitional living cottage case manger, and discussed in family counseling prior to home visits. Resident and parents submit a written summary of each visit and report on how each goal was accomplished and any problems or concerns during the visit.

Transition is a time when healthy decision making and being responsible are very important skills to practice. As part of transition all residents are required to take on these responsibilities. Before a resident leaves on a home visit, he/she must complete a Home Visit form. This form must be signed by his/her parent or guardian and returned to the Transitional Living Cottage upon completion of the visit. (See incentive section).

Weekend Check-in Rules

- Residents will have a curfew of 10:00 P.M. This means you must be at home. No exceptions.

- Residents will be expected to call and check-in on Saturday and Sunday in the A.M. between 8-10 A.M.

- The on-call weekend staff will call residents on Friday and Saturday night sometime after 10:00 P.M. to insure compliance with curfew.

- If a resident is not home in the evening when staff call, a warrant will be issued.

- If a warrant is issued, you will earn an extra week in the Transitional Living Cottage.

- If you are late on your A.M. check-in, you will be given a consequence of sentence-to-serve hours/community service work hours.

- Residents must follow ALL parents' and probation rules.

- Residents are to remain law abiding.

- Residents must not eat, drink, sniff, inject, or smoke any chemicals.

- Residents are required to focus on family therapy goals for unification.

- Resident is required to follow ALL Transitional Living Cottage Rules while on weekend visits.

** All residents must return to the Transitional Living Cottage between 4:00 P.M.-6:00 P.M. on Sunday**

If residents fail to check in or return as expected, negative consequences will be given. I have read and understand the Transitional Living Cottage rules and expectations.

Signature _____ Date _____

Well done! You have completed the County Home School Transition Program. You should be proud of your accomplishments and be ready to take on your new life. The years ahead of you can be wonderful and successful if you use what you have learned and make positive choices for yourself.

You may keep this workbook to refer to when you feel that you may need some help. Just remember that you have learned a great deal here and have grown a lot. You now have the opportunity to try out your new skills and use your knowledge

GOOD LUCK WITH MAKING POSITIVE
CHOICES IN THE FUTURE!

TRANSITION PROGRAM MODULES AND TIMELINE

- Week 1: Time Management and Transportation
- Week 2: Job Skills
- Week 3: Education and Leisure
- Week 4: Health and Safety
- Week 5: Housing
- Week 6: Money Management

Time Management and Transportation

Lessons

- Prioritizing
- Using a checklist
- Scheduling with a daily planner
- Navigating with a map
- Using a bus schedule
- Getting:

  A license

  Car insurance

  Proper registration

Skills

Discussing community resources
Troubleshooting/role playing
Setting goals

Daily Checklist

(To be reviewed before going to sleep and before leaving in the morning)

- ✓ Homework completed and packed
- ✓ Transition work completed
- ✓ Bag lunch planned/made

✓ Clothing cleaned/ironed and set out (including work uniform packed)

✓ Bus schedule and pass reviewed and packed

✓ Daily planner reviewed and packed

✓ Hygiene completed

✓ Alarm set

✓ Books, notebooks, pens, pencils, erasers, and so forth in your book bag

✓ Emergency phone numbers in daily planner

✓ Schedules updated and scheduling needs/changes communicated to staff

Automobiles

If using this material outside of Minnesota, substitute your state's laws and regulations.

Automobiles and Driving

1. Must I have a license to operate any vehicles other than a car (such as a boat, motorcycle, or snowmobile)?

Yes, Minnesota law prohibits a person from driving "any motor vehicle upon any street or highway" unless the person has a valid license for the class of vehicle being driven. The law defines "motor vehicle" to include mopeds, all-terrain vehicles, motorcycles, snowmobiles, and other "self-propelled" land vehicles. The law also requires the driver of any motorcycle, motor scooter, or motor bike on a street or highway to have a valid driver's license with a two-wheeled vehicle (in other words a motorcycle) endorsement. The law also allows a "motorized bicycle" (in other words, a moped) to be operated with either a driver's license or a motorized bicycle permit.

With regard to boats, Minnesota law requires persons between the ages of thirteen and eighteen to hold a valid watercraft operator's permit when operating any motorboat with a twenty-four horsepower motor or more. A permit is also required for operating any "personal watercraft" such as a Jet Ski.

2. Am I required to carry my driver's license with me whenever I am driving?

Yes, Minnesota law requires every driver to have a license in his or her immediate possession at all times when operating a motor vehicle and to display it upon demand by an officer authorized to enforce laws relating to the operation of motor vehicles on public streets.

3. Must I have a license if the vehicle is used on my own or a friend's property?

Minnesota law does not require a driver's license to drive a motor vehicle on private property. If, however, the person's driver's license is suspended, revoked, or canceled, the law forbids operating any motor vehicle anywhere in the state, including on private property.

4. What if I drive after my license has been suspended?

Minnesota law makes driving after suspension, revocation, or cancellation a misdemeanor. Accordingly, the maximum sentence would be ninety days in jail and a fine of $700. In addition, the violation would result in a suspension of driving privileges.

5. Can the law require me to wear a seat belt or a helmet when I operate motor vehicles?

Yes. Minnesota law requires the wearing of a properly fastened and adjusted seat belt by the driver of a passenger vehicle, a passenger in the front seat of the vehicle, or any passenger between the ages of three and eleven in any seat of a passenger vehicle.

The law also requires drivers of "motorized bicycles" to wear protective headgear until the age of eighteen and requires anyone under the age of eighteen to wear protective headgear when operating a motorcycle. All motorcycle operators, regardless of age, must wear protective eye devices unless the motorcycle is equipped with a windscreen.

6. At what age can I own my own car?

In general, a person must be eighteen or older to own a car. Under Minnesota law, persons under the age of eighteen may own a car if;
- That person is seventeen and has completed a driver's training course
- The person is seventeen and a high school graduate
- The person is an employed emancipated minor with a Minnesota driver's license
- The person became a car owner while the resident of another state or country and the car is registered in the person's name in the other state or country.

7. What is "title to a car" and do I need the title if I own a car?

A title is the official document produced by the state describing the serial number, make of car, owner, and other pertinent information. Every car is required to have such a document and the title must reflect the current owner. When you buy a car, the seller must sign the title document and give it to you. You must file the document with the Minnesota Department of Public Safety and pay the appropriate fees. If this is not done, the prior owner of the car continues to hold title and is legally responsible for the vehicle.

8. If I obtain a car loan, what rights does the bank have over my car?

If you purchase your car with a loan, the bank will have what is called a "security interest" in your car. Such an interest makes the car collateral for the loan. If you default on the loan, the bank may repossess and resell the car, and sue for any amount of the unpaid loan they do not collect by the resale. The bank may also require you to carry insurance on the car so that if the car is damaged, the bank's interest in the car will be protected.

9. Does Minnesota require me to carry car insurance?

Yes. Minnesota law requires the owner of every motor vehicle to carry insurance. Proof that the vehicle is insured is also required. Failure to produce proof of insurance when required may result in a criminal charge and a revocation of driving privileges. Failure to have auto insurance is a misdemeanor punishable by 90 days in jail and up to a $700 fine. In addition, such a conviction results in mandatory revocation of driving privileges. You may be charged even if there is no driving accident. Rates for insurance will vary from company to company and person to person, and depend on the automobile you are planning on driving.

10. What other necessary requirements and expenses are involved in owning a car?

Other expenses include the cost of keeping your car in proper operating condition, so that it passes air pollution and emissions standards and safety requirements. In addition, you must pay the costs of registering the vehicle and yearly licensing fees.

11. What must I do if I am involved in a car accident?

Minnesota law requires the driver of any vehicle involved in an accident resulting in death, personal injury, or property damage to stop at or as close as possible to the accident scene and stay at the accident scene until all the required information has been given. Any victims, drivers, occupants of vehicles, or police officers at the scene investigating the accident must be given the driver's name, address, and date of birth; the vehicle's registration number; the name and address of the insurer of the vehicle; and the identity of the local insurance agent. The driver must also render reasonable assistance to any person injured in the accident.

If the driver strikes an unattended vehicle or other private property, the driver must locate and notify the owner. If the accident results in personal injury or death, the driver must also notify the police. If the accident results in personal injury or death, the driver must also notify the police. If the accident results in personal injury or death to any person or total property damage is $500 or more, the driver must also complete an accident report form and send it to the commissioner of public safety.

Failure to comply with any of these requirements can result in charges ranging from a misdemeanor to a felony, depending on the severity of the accident and the specific violation. The maximum possible sentence can range from ninety days in jail and a fine of $700 to ten years in prison and a fine of $20,000. In addition, such a conviction can result in the loss of driving privileges.

12. What is "drunk driving"?

Currently, drunk driving (also called driving while under the influence of alcohol) technically means driving with a blood alcohol concentration of .10 or more. The amount of alcohol that must be consumed to reach this concentration varies from person to person depending upon body size and metabolism rates. Everyone reacts to alcohol differently. It is important to keep in mind that even if your blood-alcohol level is not that high, you may still be stopped and charged with reckless driving if your abilities are in any way impaired as a result of your consumption of alcohol.

13. What are the penalties for drunk driving?

The first offense is a misdemeanor. Accordingly, the maximum criminal sentence would be ninety days in jail and a fine of $700. A second offense committed while a person's license is suspended, revoked, or cancelled is a gross misdemeanor.

A violation committed within five years of a prior "impaired driving conviction" or within ten years of two prior "impaired driving convictions" is a gross misdemeanor. If the violation results in "substantial bodily harm," "great bodily harm," or death to a person or unborn child, drunk driving is deemed to be a felony with a maximum sentence varying from three to ten years in prison and fines up to $20,000.

The criminal charge will also be a gross misdemeanor if you have passengers in the car with you who are under the age of sixteen or at least thirty-six months younger than you. In addition to criminal penalties, there are administrative sanctions where your driving privileges are revoked for varying periods of time. The length of revocation increases with each offense and is affected by other factors such as whether injuries occurred. You may also have the license plates to your car taken away for varying periods of time for repeat offenses. You may also be required to abstain from using alcohol and controlled substances and submit to a random alcohol test or urine analysis.

A drunk-driving conviction remains on your record permanently. Convictions while you were a juvenile are not erased from your record when you turn eighteen and all of your offenses will accumulate over time and make subsequent offenses all the more serious in terms of criminal charges, revocation periods, and fines. Drivers convicted of driving while intoxicated also face increased insurance costs. They may be required to undergo chemical abuse assessment or treatment. They also must pay reinstatement fees to regain their driving privileges.

14. If stopped by the police, must I submit to alcohol testing?

If you refuse to be tested, your license will be revoked and, depending upon your record, you may be subjected to various criminal penalties. The basis of this action is Minnesota's implied consent law. This law provides that by accepting the privilege of driving on Minnesota public roads, the driver agrees to submit to such testing when an officer believes the driver is impaired because of the consumption of alcohol or the use of drugs.

In the ordinary case, officers will not take blood or urine tests by force. Where the incident involves personal injury or death, however, and the officer has probable cause to believe that the person has been driving while impaired by alcohol or controlled substances, a test sample can be obtained without consent.

Drivers under the age of twenty-one who are found to have a blood-alcohol content of .10 or higher will have their drivers licenses suspended for a minimum of six months.

15. What are the consequences if I refuse to submit to such testing?

Refusal to submit to testing can result in criminal as well as administrative sanctions. Regardless of the driver's age, it will result in the revocation of driving privileges for varying periods of time, depending upon your history of drunk driving charges. Such revocation is not a criminal punishment, but rather an administrative sanction carried out by the Department of Public Safety.

Criminal sanctions depend on your prior record of alcohol-related offenses. Effective January 1, 1993, it is a crime for anyone to refuse to submit to implied consent testing. It is also a separate crime to refuse testing if the person has a prior alcohol-related driver's license revocation within five years or two prior convictions within ten years.

16. Are penalties for driving under the influence of drugs the same as for driving under the influence of alcohol?

Yes, the penalties are generally the same. Also, effective August 1993, if you possess or sell drugs while driving a motor vehicle, your driver's license will be revoked for thirty days.

17. Is it legal to hitchhike or pick up hitchhikers in Minnesota?

Minnesota law does not expressly prohibit hitchhiking or giving hitchhikers a ride. The law does, however, provide that no person shall stand in a roadway for the purpose of soliciting a ride from the driver of any private vehicle. The term "roadway" does not include sidewalks or shoulders. Furthermore, when posted, no pedestrians are allowed to walk on a controlled-access highway.

Role Play

1. You were just released from the County Home School and got a job at Taco Bell three miles from your house. You do not have a license, so you cannot drive. You want a bike to ride to work but you cannot afford to buy one. Your cousin approaches you and asks if you want to buy a new bike from him for $20.00. He tells you he stole it. What would you do?

2. It is 3:45 P.M. on Monday afternoon. You are due at aftercare group at the Northwest YMCA at 4:00 P.M. You cannot find a ride and live eight miles away. What do you do?

3. You were recently released from the County Home School. You are driving along in the car you just legally bought. A police officer drives up behind you and appears to be following you. You have not done anything wrong that you are aware of. He continues to follow you and eventually signals for you to pull over. How do you handle the situation?

Job Skills: Finding and Keeping A Job

Exercises and Lessons

- Identifying interests in employment
- Assessing vocational opportunities
- Looking for a job that fits you
- Filling out job applications
- Learning how to follow-up on jobs that you have applied for
- Filling out W-4's
- Writing resumes
- Learning how to interview for a job
- Understanding how to maintain a job

Activities

- Discussion
- Mock interviews
- Role playing

Assignments

- Read and discuss all job skills materials
- Fill out the sample application for a job that you want
- Fill out a W-4 form
- Answer the questions for "You be the interviewer"
- Answer the interviewing questions true/false
- Participate in the job skills role plays and mock interviews
- Write down three job-related goals

Hints for Calling about a Job Opportunity

1. Introduce yourself.

2. Explain why you are calling.

3. Ask to speak to the appropriate person.

4. Re-introduce yourself and explain why you are calling.

5. Ask about picking up an application or dropping off a resume.

6. Ask appropriate questions that would automatically qualify you for the job. Some examples are the following:

   - How many hours a week?

   - How many days a week and which days?

   - Day, evening, night shift?

   - What are the qualifications?

   - Is the job located on a bus line?

SAMPLE APPLICATION

You may wish to take this with you when you go on an interview and fill out an employer's application.

General Information

Name _____ E-mail _____

Present Adress _____

Permanent Adress _____

Phone # _____

How did you hear about this position? _____Referred by_____

Are you authorized to work in the United States? Yes___   No___

Position Desired _____ Date Available _____

Full time_____ (35-40 hrs per week) Part Time _____(0-34 hrs per week)
Seasonal: Summer___   Fall___ Winter___   Spring___

Please indicate the hours you are available to work during both days and evenings

Sunday	Monday	Tuesday	Wendesday	Thursday	Friday	Saturday

Employment History

List below your complete employment history, but do not provide dates of employment for jobs held more than five years ago. Attach additional pages or resume, if necessary or applicable.

Employed Month, Day, Year	Name and Address of Employer Supervisor's Name	Salary	Position	Reason for Leaving
_____ _____ Phone _____ E-mail _____ May we contact? Yes_____ No_____				

SAMPLE APPLICATION, *Continued*

Employed Month, Day, Year	Name and Address of Employer, Supervisor's Name	Salary	Position	Reason for Leaving
_____ _____ Phone _____ E-mail _____ May we contact? Yes_____ No_____				
_____ _____ Phone _____ E-mail _____ May we contact? Yes_____ No_____				

Education

Identify all licenses or certifications that you currently hold

Education	Name & Location of School	Relevant Course Work or Degree Area	Diploma
High School			
College/University			
College/University			
Other Training or Education			

Name of license/certification _____

License/certification number _____ **Issuing state** _____

Have your licenses/certifications ever lapsed? _____

If yes, state reason for lapse, revocation or suspension _____

_____**Date of reinstatement** _____

Foreign language(s) spoken fluently? _____

SAMPLE APPLICATION, *Continued*

In addition to your work history and educational experience, what other experiences, skills or qualifications do you have that would fit for the positions you are applying for?

_____

_____

_____

References

Give the names and contact information of three persons, not related to you, whom you have known for at least one year

Name	Address	Phone and E-mail	Business	Years Known

Have you ever pleaded guilty to, or been convicted of a criminal offense?
Yes_____   No_____

If yes, give dates and circumstances _____

_____

Date _____ Applicant's Signature _____

Interviewing Tips

Pre-Interview Tips

1. Personal appearance should be neat, well-groomed, and appropriate
2. Know where you are going
3. Know the interviewer's name and correct pronunciation of that name
4. Arrive 15 minutes early at the exact place
5. Know the full name of the company
6. Know as much as possible about the company
7. Be able to explain how you can contribute to the company
8. Know what questions you can ask
9. Know the type of work you are applying for and how your talents relate to it
10. Never say, "I'll do anything."
11. Have an idea of salary structure
12. Expect to be nervous. Everybody gets nervous, but do not let it get out of hand. A little nervousness can make you perform better.

Items to Take with You on an Interview

After you have arranged a job interview, you should know the name and the address of the interview place, the room number, and the name of the person you will be seeing. It is also a good idea to take the following items with you.

1. Notebook and pen
2. Questions you would like to ask
3. Two copies of you resume (one to leave with the interviewer and one for you)
4. Personal fact sheet (to help in filling out the application)
5. Social Security card
6. List of personal references; with their names, addresses, telephone numbers, and e-mails
7. Birth certificate
8. Driver's license or I.D. card
9. Graduation diploma or certifications from programs completed
10. Know your typing speed and shorthand speed, if relevant to the job

Interview Tips

1. Be polite
2. Be confident
3. Ask questions
4. Be poised
5. You are selling yourself
6. Give more than one-word answers
7. Do not chew gum or smoke
8. Do not use slang words
9. Do not stare at objects around the room
10. Do not complain about anything
11. Do not ask about sick leave, vacations, holidays, and so forth
12. Other than interest, show no other reaction to things said
13. Do not argue with any viewpoints of the interviewer
14. Avoid interrupting pauses prematurely
15. Ask for a brief job description
16. Ask about job priorities and responsibilities
17. Ask about a typical day on the job
18. Do not daydream
19. Do not tap fingers, crack knuckles, and so forth

What Are They Looking for in Your Answers?

1. Your ability to think logically
2. Your ability to express your ideas precisely and clearly
3. Your ability to anticipate, look ahead, or plan intelligently
4. Your ability to get at the central issue in a problem quickly
5. Your ability to probe and your capacity to learn from previous experience

How to Deal with All Those Questions

1. Be prepared to answer questions. Be able to listen and understand the questions you are being asked before answering

2. Think about the question before speaking

3. Answer questions firmly, honestly, clearly, and positively

4. Give information you are asked for. Let the interviewer lead the interview

5. Ask for clarification if questions are confusing

After The Interview

1. If you are offered the job and are uncertain about accepting it, ask for a day to think it over.

2. If no job is offered during the interview, do not worry. Ask when they will be calling back with the results.

3. Thank the interviewer for his/her time and consideration.

Sample Questions You Might Get

1. What can I do for you?

2. Tell me about yourself.

3. Why are you interested in this position?

4. What are your expectations about this interview?

5. What are your job expectations?

6. What do you want to be doing three years from now?

7. Describe the jobs you have had in your past; your duties and responsibilities.

8. Of these jobs, which stand out in your memory? Why?

9. Which job functions have you performed the best?

10. Which jobs were the most disappointing?

11. If you could, what would you change about your last job?

12. Why did you leave your last job?

Other Questions Interviewers Ask

1. What can I do for you?

2. Are you still in school? What grade? Where?

3. Tell me about yourself.

4. Have you ever worked before?

5. Have you done this kind of work before?

6. Why do you want to work here?

7. How did you get along with your former boss and co-workers?

8. What do you know about our company?

9. How do you get along with people?

10. How long do you plan to stay here if you are hired?

11. When are you available?

12. What do you expect as a starting salary?

13. What do you hope to be doing five or ten years from now?

14. What aspects of your previous jobs or schools did you dislike?

15. What would you say is your strongest point?

16. What would you say is your weakest point?

17. Why should I hire you?

18. Why did your last job end?

Your Questions

At the end of the typical interview, the employer will often ask, "Do you have any questions?" It is very much in your favor to ask about something related to the job. However, be careful not to ask a question that was discussed during the interview. This may give the impression that you were not listening.

If the following subjects were not covered during the interview, you could use them as questions:

1. What are the job duties?

2. Who would my supervisor be?

3. What is the pay, and how is it figured? (straight salary, commission, and so forth)

4. Can I see where I would be working?

5. Are there any special clothes or equipment that I need? (uniform, car, and so forth)

6. Would I be working alone or with other people?

7. What kind of advancement is available? Do you provide training?

8. How often is a promotion considered?

If you do not have any questions, say, "I think you have answered my questions for now."

You Be the Interviewer

Which of the responses below would leave the most positive impression on you? Check the appropriate response and be prepared to discuss the positive and negative aspect of the responses.

1. In what type of position are you interested?

    a) Anything that you have.

    b) Sales position.

    c) Anything that pays a good salary and has a decent schedule.

2. What qualifications do you have to offer?

    a) I have worked successfully for one year in a position with similar responsibilities.

    b) I work hard.

    c) I studied about how to keep a job in school.

3. What are your career plans?

    a) Right now, I don't have any. I just want a job.

    b) My goal is to find any job that pays well and is not too far from my home.

    c) I want to build a career in sales. This job will help me get more experience.

4. Why do you want to work with this company?

    a) It is convenient to get to.

    b) It is a growing company and I want to be a part of it.

    c) The pay and benefits to employees are good.

5. What do you know about the company?

    a) It has been in existence for over 20 years and is considered one of the top companies in this field.

    b) Not too much.

    c) Your offer good salaries and benefits.

6. What salary are you looking for?

    a) Whatever you are offering.

    b) $8.00 to $10.00 per hour.

    c) minimum wage + $1.

7. What do you do in your spare time?

    a) Nothing in particular.

    b) Work out in the gym and play racquetball.

    c) Watch TV and sleep.

8. How did previous employers treat you?

    a) Most employers that I have worked for have been fair and easy to get along with.

    b) Most have been jerks. They were always bossing me around and harassing me.

    c) They were okay.

9. What assets will you bring to the company?

    a) I don't know.

    b) I will do a good job.

    c) I am responsible and I will work well with others.

Interviewing Questionnaire (True and False)
Circle the right answer.

1. It is acceptable to lie in an interview as long as I am lying to make myself appear better suited for the job.
   True   False

2. If I cannot make it to a scheduled interview, I should wait until after the interview time and call and explain why I missed the interview.
   True   False

3. It is appropriate to chew gum during an interview.
   True   False

4. When you show up for an interview you should introduce yourself, tell the person you are there for an interview, and ask to speak to whomever you have the interview with.
   True   False

5. It is not appropriate to ask the interviewer questions about the job during an interview.
   True   False

6. If I show up late to an interview, I should just hurry in and not mention anything. The interviewer may not have even noticed I was late.
   True   False

7. If an interviewer asked me what my weaknesses are, I should tell them that I really don't have any. That way, I appear to be a better candidate for the job.
   True   False

8. I should refrain from bringing a group of friends along to my interview.
   True   False

9. It is acceptable to ask when they will notify me about any decision they make.
   True   False

10. When the interview is over, I should thank the interviewer for his/her time before leaving.
    True   False

Maintaining A Job—Acceptable Work Behaviors

1. Try to arrive at work five minutes early so that you may prepare for the day

2. Work all scheduled shifts regularly

3. Return to your job immediately after a lunch period or break

4. Listen carefully to instructions given by supervisors

5. Ask your supervisor if you are unsure of how to complete work tasks and assignments

6. Be well groomed while at work

7. Maintain good sleep and nutritional habits so that you will be at your best while at work

8. Keep busy while on the job

9. Inform your supervisor of progress made at work

10. Give co-workers and supervisor positive feedback

11. Try to plan your day before beginning work

12. Learn company policies and rules

13. Attempt to do the best job possible

14. Be friendly, courteous, and respectful with co-workers and supervisors

15. Be concerned about the quality of your work

16. Be concerned about the amount of work that you are producing

Sorry, I Cannot Come In: Which Excuses Are Acceptable?

1. "I have no way to get to work."

2. "I just don't feel good."

3. "I stayed over at my friend's last night."

4. "There was a death in my family. I have to go to a funeral."

5. "My mom wants me to baby-sit."

6. "I have a lot of homework. I can't come in today."

7. "I have a cold."

8. "I missed my bus."

9. "I'm sick in bed with the flu."

10. "I didn't call in because we don't have a telephone."

11. "The bus passed me by at the bus stop."

12. "I have a big game on Friday. The coach said I have to practice."

13. "A guy I really like asked me out tonight."

14. "My brother came home last night. I haven't seen him in a year. He's leaving tomorrow."

15. "My parents decided to go out of town today."

16. "I was up late last night. I'm too tired to go to work."

17. "I have to go to the doctor today."

18. "My friend and I had a fight last night."

19. "My parents said I can stay home."

20. "My dad wants me to help him today."

Solving Conflicts—What Works?

1. Take time to think through a problem before answering

2. Talk about the problem directly, do not ignore it or run away

3. Check out if you believe a problem can be solved, that it is a problem that concerns you and that you want to solve it

4. Solve the problem you may have with another person using a third party to mediate

5. Admit your part in the problem

6. Try to have a number of solutions to the problem (options)

7. Before deciding what to do about a problem, think about the problem, think about possible long-term effects

8. Try to listen to the other person and understand his or her thoughts and feelings

9. Express how the problem makes you feel

10. Clear up misunderstandings—ask others to explain what they are saying if you are confused

11. Take enough time to work completely through problems.

12. If you feel someone does not understand you, ask them to clarify.

Reasons People Quit Jobs

1. Promotion

2. New skill

3. New interest

4. More education

5. Conflict with schedule

6. Conflict with supervisor

7. Better paying job

8. Better benefits

9. Not enough hours or money to meet needs

10.   Change in major situation (have baby, crisis in family, and so forth)

11.   Job does not go along with own values

Reasons People Get Fired

1. Continuing tardiness or absence

2. Using drugs

3. Practicing unsafe habits on the job

4. Endangering others

5. Not following rules and policies of the workplace

6. Not performing quality work

Quitting A Job—The Do's and Do Nots

DO

1. Give at least two weeks' notice that you are quitting your job

2. Write a letter of resignation to say you are leaving and why

3. Include in your resignation letter where you will be working

4. Ask your boss for a recommendation or letter of reference, if it is appropriate

5. Thank people (boss) at work for any help he/she gave you

6. Leave work area clean and take your belongings home

DO NOT

1. Wait until the last day to tell your boss you are leaving

2. Tell people you work with that you are leaving before you tell your boss

3. Spend your last days bragging about your new job and new salary

4. Make nasty comments about your boss and/or job because you are leaving

5. Attempt "Get Backs" at your boss or co-workers because you are leaving

Job Skills Role-Play

1. You have been working at Target since your release from the County Home School. You do not like the job because other employees are harassing you. You need the job as part of your furlough contract. Role-play a call to your probation officer to discuss this situation and how you plan to deal with it.

2. After three months at your new job, you have not gotten a raise. When you were hired, you were told that if you were doing a good job you would get a raise at two months. Role-play asking for a raise.

3. You are supposed to be at work at 3:00 P.M. Your dad is planning to pick you up at 2:30 P.M. to get you there, but it is 2:50 P.M. and he has not shown up yet. What would you do? Role-play.

Health and Safety Role Play

1. You are invited to a party at a good friend's house. You are pretty sure people will be smoking weed there, but you decide to go anyway. Once there, some friends try to talk you into getting high. They tell you they know a way to avoid getting a dirty UA. What would you do? Role-play.

2. You have just been released from the County Home School. You run into a girl that you know at McDonald's. You kind of like her, but you do not think you are interested in having a relationship with her. She invites you over to her house, and tells you that she is on birth control. What do you do? Role-play.

3. You have been attending an NA meeting by your house. It is going O.K., but you don't really like your sponsor. What could you do? Role-play.

Housing

Exercises and Lessons

- Looking for an apartment/housing
- Filling out rental applications
- What you need to know about leases/security
- Creating a checklist
- Hooking up your utilities
- Getting along with roommates/family
- Creating a chore list

Activities

Discussing Community Resources

Troubleshooting/ Role Playing

Setting Goals

Rental Housing
I. Locating Rental Housing

1. Name four types of rental housing and describe them.

    a) _____

    b) _____

    c) _____

    d) _____

2. Name four places you could look to find an apartment.

    a) _____

    b) _____

    c) _____

    d) _____

3. Name five important factors to consider when looking for housing.

a) _____

b) _____

c) _____

d) _____

e) _____

4. List ten personal values that would be important to you when considering a roommate.

a) _____

b) _____

c) _____

d) _____

e) _____

f) _____

g) _____

h) _____

i) _____

j) _____

4. Translate the following abbreviations commonly found in rental ads:

Apt._____   Avail._____   Furn._____   Dplx._____

Eff._____   Dep. Req._____   Br._____   Crpted_____

Ht pd._____

5. Use the classifieds and find three rental units that may satisfy your personal values and needs.

II. Viewing Rental Housing

1. What are five questions you would ask a landlord or caretaker when calling about rental housing?

    a. _____

    b. _____

    c. _____

    d. _____

    e. _____

2. When you go to look at a place that you may want to rent, what types of things are you going to look at? (In the kitchen, the bedroom, on grounds, in the building?)

_____

_____

III. Utilities

1. Who would you call to get your phone hooked up? Is there a hook-up fee? How much does monthly service usually cost?

2. Who would you call to get long-distance phone service hooked up?

3. Who would you call to get your electricity hooked up? How much does monthly service usually cost?

4. Who would you call to get your gas service hooked up? How much does monthly service usually cost?

IV. Moving From Rental Housing

1. What is "proper notice?"

2. What is a security deposit or damage deposit?

3. What responsibilities do tenants have if they want their deposit back upon moving out?

4. How long does the landlord have to return a damage deposit?

V. Apartment Inquiry Checklist

Instructions: Fill out as much information as you know from the advertisement, and cross off questions that do not apply to you.

Hello, my name is _____

I am calling about the apartment you have advertised at _____

_____

What is the monthly rent? _____

How much is the damage deposit? _____

Does the rent include:

    Heat   _____Yes _____No

    Water   _____Yes _____No

    Electricity _____Yes _____No

    Phone   _____Yes _____No

How many rooms are there? _____

Is there a bus line nearby? _____Yes _____No

Do you know the bus number? _____

Are there laundry facilities? _____Yes _____No

Do you allow pets? _____Yes _____No

Is the apartment furnished? _____Unfurnished? _____

Is there a lease? _____Yes _____No

How long is the lease? _____month-to-month _____6 months _____1 year _____other

Housing Role Play

1. You have told your landlord that there are cockroaches in your building, but she has not done any thing about it. What should you do? Role-play.

2. Your roommate moves out just before rent is due. You do not have enough money to cover his half, and do not know anyone who could move in right away. What could you do? Role-play.

3. Your roommate has invited a bunch of people over. There are several minors who are drinking and smoking, and things are beginning to get very loud and out of control. What would you do? Role-play.

Money Management

Topics

Cost of living and money management

Creating a budget

Engaging in smart spending/shopping

Addressing restitution needs

Activities

Community Resources Discussion

Troubleshooting/Role Playing

Setting Goals

Cost of Living per Month

Apartment	$450.00 / $550.00
Utilities	$150.00 (gas, electric, phone, cable, water)
Transportation	$50.00 / $200.00
Food	$150.00
Clothing	$50.00
Entertainment	$100.00 (out to eat, movies, cigarettes, pop, arcade, and so forth.)
Miscellaneous	$50.00
TOTAL	$1100.00 / $1200.00

For a full-time job that pays $7.00 per hour, you would earn about $1,120 per month.

A single adult on welfare gets $203.00 a month, plus $12.00 in food stamps and medical assistance. You can only get food stamps for a total of three months.

Wage and Salary Conversion Chart

In 2009 the federal minimum wage was $7.25.

Hourly	Daily	Weekly	Monthly	Yearly
$7.00	$56.00	$280.00	$1213.33	$14,560.00
$7.10	$56.80	$284.00	$1230.66	$14,768.00
$7.20	$57.60	$288.00	$1248.00	$14,976.00
$7.25	$58.00	$290.00	$1256.66	$15,080.00
$7.30	$58.40	$292.00	$1265.33	$15,184.00

Money Management Role Play

1. You have been working at Best Buy for two weeks when you get your first paycheck. It is a lot smaller than you thought it would be. What could you do? Role-play.

2. It is Tuesday and you are broke and will not get paid until Friday. Your friends are going out to a movie later that night. None of them can loan you money, but one guy tells you he has a bag you could sell for extra cash. You think you know someone who would buy it. What would you do? Role-play.

3. For the second time this month, your mom has asked you to loan her money. She says it is to pay the phone bill before it gets shut off. You think she is really going to give it to her boyfriend who has a drug habit. If you loan her this money, you will not be able to afford your car insurance payment. What would you do? Role-play.

Sample Budget

How do you fill out a budget?

What expenses do you have?

Practice: Fill out three sample budgets using the scenarios given.

Item	Amount	Description
Rent		
Utilities		
Insurance		
Transportation		
Food		
Child Care		
Clothing		
Entertainment		
Medical		
Total Per Month		

Find the gross monthly income required. For this example, figure that you will have 20 percent of your salary withheld for taxes and benefits. In short, multiply your net income requirement by 80 percent.

_____/.80=_____

Multiply your total monthly budget by 12 to determine how much income you need to take home each year.

12 x $_____ = $_____ annual income required.

Divide that figure by 2,080 hours to determine how much you would need to earn per hour at a full-time job to support this budget.

_____/ 2,080 hours/year =_____ (hourly wage required at a full-time job)

INDEX

ABOUT THE AUTHORS

Joseph Heinz, L.I.C.S.W.

Joseph Heinz received his bachelor's degree in sociology/psychology from Mount St. Mary's College in Emmitsburg, Maryland and a master of social work degree from the University of Minnesota. His career in corrections spans thirty-nine years. His first job was at the Victor Cullen Reform School, a large juvenile training school, in Hagerstown Maryland. Subsequently, he served as a probation/parole officer in Minneapolis and Rochester, Minnesota.

He began working at the Hennepin County Home School in the late 1970s where he initially served as a family and group therapist. In that capacity, he and his colleagues developed and implemented one of the first effective adolescent sex-offender programs in the country, which is still serving youth from across the United States. His career for the next twenty years was in corrections administration. He was Superintendent of the Hennepin County Home School, Director of Adult Pre-Trial Services and Felony Investigations, Director of Juvenile Probation, Director of Juvenile Corrections (Detention Center, Out-of-Home Placements, Probation and Parole) and Director of Adult Corrections (workhouse and adult probation).

Highlights of his career include pioneering work in the field of residential adolescent sex-offender treatment; consulting/training for both the Office of Juvenile Justice and Delinquency Prevention and the National Juvenile and Family Court Association, and publishing works regarding offender restitution ("Restitution or Parole: A Follow-up Study of Adult Offenders," 1976. *Social Services Review*, Vol. 50, No. 1, March, pp 146-156), sex-offender treatment (*A Model Residential Juvenile Sex Offender Treatment Program*, 1987, Safer Society Press, Syracuse, New York) and correctional administration ("The System's Response to Juvenile Sex Offenders," in *Juvenile Sexual Offending: Causes, Consequences, and Correction*, Gail Ryan and Sandy Lane, eds. D.C. Heath and Company/Lexington, Massachusetts, 1991. pp. 185-198).

Theresa Wise, M.Ed.

Theresa Wise (Terry) has thirty years of experience in corrections. She began her career in juvenile corrections at the Hennepin County Home School as its business manager. While working in corrections, she returned to the University of Minnesota and obtained a bachelor's degree in sociology/education/and youth studies. Terry was promoted to Assistant Superintendent, returned to the University of Minnesota and received a masters' degree in education. In 1992, she became the first female superintendent of the Home School.

Terry's work in the field of corrections and human services was broad; she established the first per diems to sell beds and raise revenue for treating juvenile sex offenders, introduced evidence-based practices in Hennepin's juvenile corrections by working with consultants from the Office of Juvenile Justice and Delinquency Prevention on initiatives such as the Intensive Aftercare Program and the Thinking for a Change curriculum with program evaluation and follow-though. Terry has presented at the National Council of Family and Juvenile Court Judges, and chaired Hennepin County's "200 Families Study" (linking the most costly families in Hennepin County's Human Services–including corrections).

Terry worked on and was an advocate for the recently automated approach to case management in Hennepin County's Juvenile System. She was the Director of Juvenile Probation in Hennepin County in 2007 when asked to become the Superintendent of the Hennepin County Adult Corrections Facility. When she retired in June 2009, she was the Superintendent of the three Adult Corrections Facilities in Hennepin County–Women's, Men's, and Work Release, which included electronic home monitoring. She is currently doing consulting work on corrections.

Clemens Bartollas, Ph.D.

In 1973, Clemens Bartollas received his Ph.D. from the Ohio State University. During the four years, it took him to earn his Ph.D., he worked full-time in various positions at the Training School, Central Ohio, a maximum-security institution reserved for older and aggressive male delinquents. This institution, which closed in 1990, was widely acknowledged as one of the most violent juvenile facilities in the nation. In the 1970s, he coauthored one book and many articles that described victimization in this facility in the 1980s and 1990s. He and other coauthors also reported the research they had done on training schools in North and South Carolina, California, and Iowa.

"After questioning the quality of what takes place in out-of-home placements for juveniles in various publications, it is refreshing in this book to report on what can work and be effective in juvenile institutionalization," Bartollas stated.

For twenty eight years, he has been a professor of sociology at the University of Northern Iowa. He has authored or coauthored more than thirty-five books, many on juveniles. Recently, he has been writing biographies, including *Becoming a Model Warden: Striving for Excellence—The Frank Wood Story,* published by the American Correctional Association and the forth coming book from ACA, *A Modal of Correctional Leadership: The Career of Norman A. Carlson.*

Bartollas acknowledges "I have been blessed with a beautiful wife and responsive children." He is a Presbyterian minister with a small church he has served for the past eighteen years. He also has a garden full of David Austin's roses that he tends when he is not playing basketball, testifying in court on behalf of gang members, or writing books.